A Preface to Shakespeare's Tragedies

Michael Mangan

Longman, London and New York.

LONGMAN GROUP UK LIMITED,
Longman House, Burnt Mill, Harlow,
Essex CM20 2JE, England
and Associated Companies throughout the world.

Published in the United States of America
by Longman Inc., New York

© Longman Group UK Limited 1991

First published 1991
Third impression 1993

British Library Cataloguing in Publication Data

Mangan, Michael
  A preface to Shakespeare's tragedies.
  I. Title
  822.33

  ISBN 0-582-35501-X (csd)
  ISBN 0-582-35503-6 (ppr)

Library of Congress Cataloging-in-Publication Data

Mangan, Michael, 1953–
  A preface to Shakespeare's tragedies/Michael Mangan.
    p.   cm. – (Preface books)
  Includes bibliographical references and index.
  ISBN 0–582–35501–X (cased). – ISBN 0–582–35503–6 (paper)
  1. Shakespeare, William, 1564–1616 – Tragedies. 2. Tragedy.
  I. Title.
  PR2988.M335 1991   90–49518
  822.3'3 – dc20   CIP

Set in 10/11pt Baskerville, Linotron 202

Produced by Longman Singapore Publishers (Pte) Ltd.
Printed in Singapore

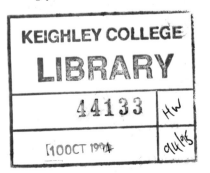

Contents

Contents

List of Illustrations

Acknowledgements

I would like to thank the staff of the Folger Shakespeare Library in Washington DC, who offered invaluable help in the early stages of this book, as did friends and colleagues at the University of Maryland. Maurice Hussey provided patient and expert advice on matters both editorial and academic. Roland Clare and his students in Bristol provided me with a hospitable forum for some of the early ideas on *Hamlet*. Finally, my principal debt is to students and colleagues in the Department of English Literature at the University of Sheffield, and in particular to those involved in the Theatre Workshop there; their contribution to this book is probably far greater than I realize.

We are grateful to the following for permission to reproduce copyright material: National Portrait Gallery, page ii; Trustees of the British Museum, page 7; Methuen Collection, Corsham Court, page 16; Sotheby's, page 21; Shakespeare Centre Library, Stratford-upon-Avon, pages 46, 173; Hofstra University, page 83; Mary Evans Picture Library, page 105; Guildhall Library, London, page 235.

Foreword

The general study of Shakespearean tragedy that I want to consult explores paths through the 1590s that look most promising to us in the 1990s who have been formed by the literature and theatre of our own times. Since Shakespeare is not our contemporary it takes a renaissance scholar such as Michael Mangan to propose the most fruitful areas for discussion in the historical and artistic realms to produce that desirable volume today.

Our theatres, never slackening in the pace of their Shakespearean output, seek a great variety of ways to please the audience. Sometimes we find all-day performances of the English epic plays which remind us of the dawn-to-dusk acting of the York Mysteries, their dramatic ancestors which acted out a larger pattern of history than the tribal rituals of Yorkists and Lancastrians. At other times the greatest individual challenges will be *Hamlet, Othello, King Lear* and *Macbeth*: for directors and actors to deliver the texts without lapsing into fiascos of egocentricity and for audiences to mark and remember the tones of the spoken rhetoric as it projects inward human and moral issues as they take wing in performance. Here, both singly and briefly in inter-relation, Dr Mangan establishes his highly stimulating critique of these four tragedies. He has a fine touch for selecting key moments and major speeches, discussing them undogmatically, showing how they lay down the exposition, development and dénouement of tragedy and how we ourselves should concentrate upon them.

In the earlier half of the book readers find a variety of topics that grow in significance as the studies proceed. Dwelling upon their attitudes to language, for instance, we are prepared for the high level of the dramatic verse in the plays of the period through which we know subtle and life-like characters. Discussing the foundation of the texts as printed books enables us to study the rhetoric at close quarters. *King Lear*, as an example, now seems to us to have been written by the dramatist twice (in versions printed in 1608 and 1623 respectively) and by an earlier, anonymous figure before him in a chronicle play: all these help us to understand the meanings that Shakespeare elicited from a tale that haunted him as he grew older. The whole of Part III below deserves the closest attention, even if the reader has only a primary interest in one of the four plays at the time. Attending to another play will help the student to become more familiar with Shakespeare's technique of developing his imagery and his control of syntax as keys to the intonation, identity and depth of the characters;

the decisiveness of their self-deception, their places in the writer's process of staging human understanding and cognition that take us further than our common notions of sympathy. These parts of Michael Mangan's book deserve study and discussion for the illumination they cast upon plays with which we need to engage because as we read them they seem to read us as well.

MAURICE HUSSEY
General Editor

For Margaret Mangan

Introduction

'Soule of the Age!': The Historical Context of Shakespeare's Plays

When William Shakespeare died in 1616, his great contemporary Ben Jonson wrote a poem entitled 'To the Memory of My Beloved, the Author, Mr William Shakespeare'. In it he included the famous phrase, 'He was not of an age, but for all time!', and by this he meant to offer Shakespeare the compliment of suggesting that his writings would live on beyond his own time, and that Shakespeare would attain a kind of 'immortality' because of the fame and virtue of his works. To an extent, as we know, Jonson's literary instinct was right: we cannot say that Shakespeare has proved himself to be 'for all time', but we can say that he has lasted exceptionally well. Three hundred and seventy years after his death he remains a dominant figure in the two major cultural spheres of theatre and education. He still outsells most other playwrights at the box-office; several English-speaking countries have one or more major professional theatre companies dedicated solely or primarily to staging his plays; most educational establishments, whether universities, colleges or examination boards, still regard it as virtually unthinkable to offer a course in English Literature which does not devote a sizeable percentage of its time to the study of his works. And if his pre-eminence as a cultural force is most noticeable in the English-speaking world, it is not confined to that section of the globe. In France, in Japan, in Russia, in Brazil, his works are known, respected, read, studied and performed. Somehow the works of this particular man, writing at a particular time in history, have become universalized.

Shakespeare's undeniable central importance as a cultural figure has come about, not by magic but because of successive generations of readers and audiences responding to his plays and making sense of them. The sense which has been made of them differs from generation to generation – each age, each culture has its own Shakespeare. Sometimes the differences from one age to another are slight, sometimes they are radical. The process is not at an end. The Victorians had one Shakespeare, the early twentieth century had another: the Shakespeare of the late twentieth century is still in the making.

One of the features of the way in which the late twentieth century is constructing its version of Shakespeare involves a renewed willingness to see the man and his works in their relationship to the culture which produced them. This is not to deny the generosity of Jonson's tribute to Shakespeare: rather it is to see that tribute for what it is,

1

Jonson seems to offer us a choice between Shakespeare's being 'of an age' and his being 'for all time'. It has become far more common in recent years to argue that he is 'for all time' *because* he is 'of an age', and that he continues to interest us today, not because he is somehow 'above' the culture, the society, the ideas and the politics of his own day, but because he is so deeply engaged with them. Ben Jonson, in fact, knew this well: in another, less-frequently quoted line from the same poem, he calls Shakespeare the 'Soule of the Age!'.

But although this view of Shakespeare is becoming more common, it is by no means a universally-accepted one. What is more, those who disagree with it can point to some formidable allies. Compare what Jonson has to say about Shakespeare with an apparently similar tribute from another major poet, Samuel Taylor Coleridge, in his *Table Talk* (1834): 'I believe Shakespeare was not a whit more intelligible in his own day than he is now . . . except for a few local allusions of no consequence. He is of no age – nor of any religion, or party, or profession. The body and substance of his works came out of the unfathomable depths of his own oceanic mind' (T. Hawkes, *Coleridge and Shakespeare*, Penguin, p. 122). If Coleridge's tribute to Shakespeare sounds rather like Jonson's in some ways, in its overall effect and meaning it is quite different. Jonson knew too well from his own professional career that no writer ever operates outside the constraints of his own time. The playwright most of all, who speaks directly to an audience which is present *en masse*, must be continually aware that what he says is received in a particular context, determined by the events and beliefs of the day.

Coleridge argues otherwise. The four major points of his comment are as follows. The first is the highly debatable one that time does not provide any barrier to a comprehension of Shakespeare, that he is as understandable in 1834 – and therefore, presumably, in the 1990s – as he was in his own day. And yet the language which we speak today (and the language which Coleridge spoke in 1834) is only partly the language of Shakespeare. Words have changed their meaning; some of the ones which Shakespeare used are now obsolete and incomprehensible; grammatical conventions have changed, and ways of putting sentences together which seemed natural to Shakespeare and his contemporaries now seem quaint or confusing; theatrical conventions have changed, and some of the techniques used by Shakespeare may now seem artificial and 'stagey' in the hands of any but the very best actors and directors. But most importantly, the world has changed – and this brings us on to Coleridge's second point.

For Coleridge goes on to argue that if we do lose anything, it is only 'a few local allusions of no consequence'. He is wrong on two counts; firstly, we are separated from Shakespeare (and Coleridge was too) not just by a few local allusions, but by the history of our changing culture. The society that Shakespeare writes about is not our society; the customs, habits and ways of feeling that he takes for granted are not those that we take for granted. Take, for example, a single word whose definable meaning has not changed: 'marriage' has the same dictionary definition for us as it would have had for the Elizabethans and Jacobeans. But what about the whole web of social practice that lies behind that dictionary definition? Our experiences of actual marriage, our images of marriage, our expectations about how it should affect our life, our beliefs about when one should marry, why one should marry, whether one should marry, what duties and obligations it should bring with it for one or both partners, our attitudes towards divorce – in all of these, how close is our world to that of Shakespeare? And even those 'local allusions' which Coleridge mentions in passing – that is to say, those points of contemporary reference which a dramatist shares with his or her audience – are they really 'of no consequence'? (I shall argue in a later chapter that some of them may be very significant indeed.) The picture which Coleridge is building up is that of a playwright whose works only have value in so far as they are 'eternal'; in so far as they reflect something of Shakespeare's own age, it is being suggested, they are 'of no consequence'.

Coleridge develops this notion even further in his third point, which contains such a strong echo of Ben Jonson: Shakespeare, he asserts, does not really belong to any single age. But Coleridge is saying much more than Jonson ever said, and for him Shakespeare seems not merely to transcend his own age, but never to have belonged to it in the first place. He is not of 'any religion, or party, or profession'. Coleridge is saying more than just that Shakespeare's plays cannot be reduced to the simplistic formulae of various small factions within a society – although even if that were all that he were saying, it might not necessarily be true. But Coleridge seems to be implying that, unlike ordinary mortals, Shakespeare the writer (if not Shakespeare the man) was somehow 'above' what Coleridge here suggests are the comparatively trivial concerns of an age. He concludes his characterization of Shakespeare by attributing 'the body and substance of his works' to the 'unfathomable depths of Shakespeare's mind' – a mind which, once more, he strives to suggest exists without any attachment to the normal patterns of behaviour of a society.

This book is written in the belief that this view – a view which has proved remarkably pervasive and influential – is wrong, and that to approach a writer as if he or she belonged to no age is at best super-ficial, and at worst totally falsifying. The exact nature of the relation-ship between a literary work and the society to which that work 'belongs' is a much-disputed subject; however, I take it as axiomatic that the reading and writing of literature are practices in society, and that they are not separable from society or subject to special laws. This has two immediate effects on the way a text is approached; firstly, it means that we will treat it as something which was written by somebody who lived at a particular time, in a particular place, while particular events were happening, while particular beliefs were current, and who was initially speaking to an audience living under the same or similar conditions. It is to try and give a sense of what these conditions were that I have begun the book with this chapter on the political, philosophical, social and theatrical contexts of Shakespeare's writing. In my analyses of individual plays, too, I have paid particular attention to some of the meanings which the text generates, if we bear in mind that it originates in the particular historical provenance of late-sixteenth- or early-seventeenth-century London, and that Shakespeare lives in a culture and speaks a language which is, in part at least, foreign to us. Its foreignness is defined not by place but by time, yet it is foreign nonetheless, and if this is in some ways disconcerting, it is to be hoped that it is also a source of pleasure. If, traditionally and understandably, Shakespeare criticism has insisted on the common concerns which unite his culture and ours, there is another kind of pleasure which is made available by a recognition of the differences between the two cultures.

For the second (and perhaps less obvious) effect which my assumptions have on an approach to a text is this: Shakespeare's tragedies may have been written in the early seventeenth century, but they are now being read in the late twentieth century. If, as I have maintained above, the writing *and reading* of literature are prac- tices in society, seen to operate under the rules which govern other social practices, then we cannot exempt from that generalization our own readings of Shakespeare's plays. However much notice we take of the specific cultural conditions of which Shakespeare's plays formed a part, we ourselves cannot 'become' Elizabethans or Jacobeans. The way in which we read is itself inevitably conditioned by assumptions which belong specifically to the culture of the late twentieth century. Any critical work, commentary or piece of scholar- ship which deals with the plays necessarily takes on board the task of attempting to effect a meeting between the conditions in which a text is produced (the age of Shakespeare) and the conditions in which it is received (the age of the present).

Part One
Shakespeare's England

1 Religious and philosophical developments

One of the best-selling, and certainly one of the most influential, books in the reign of Queen Elizabeth was a collection of gruesome descriptions of tortures, mutilations and executions. First published in 1563, it was originally entitled *Acts and Monuments*, and we now know it as Foxe's *Book of Martyrs*. A typical incident from the book is illustrated on p. 7: the execution of William Tyndale, burnt at the stake, is vividly portrayed both in the text and in the accompanying engravings. The author of *Acts and Monuments*, John Foxe, was an English Lutheran who fled abroad during the reign of the Catholic queen, Mary Tudor, and the martyrs whose lives he chronicles and whose deaths he describes so very vividly are not, for the most part, simply Christians who suffered under pagan oppression: they are Protestants, like Tyndale, who died at the hands of Catholic persecutors. It is a book which aimed to keep alive in Protestant hearts the memory of Catholic brutalities, to remind English church-goers of the horrors of the Spanish Inquisition (during a period when there was a continued and justifiable fear of a Spanish invasion), and to confront the young Church of England with a dehumanized image of the Catholic enemy. Queen Elizabeth ordered a copy of the book to be kept in every parish church alongside the Bible and *The Book of Homilies*, and if there was one single book of stories (apart from the Bible itself) which Elizabethan men and women might be expected to have known, that book would have been Foxe's *Book of Martyrs*.

The *Book of Martyrs* was one weapon in the major cultural battle of sixteenth-century England: the battle to redefine the central values of English society. These values had their roots in religious belief and religious practice, and the redefinition of them eventually involved no less than a complete restructuring of men's and women's beliefs about reality itself. Thus, the religious and philosophical developments of the period immediately preceding Shakespeare's own working life were intimately connected with the everyday fabric of social life in sixteenth-century England.

In short, the period from 1534 to 1603 saw the divorce of English religious thinking from that of Rome and the asserting and defending of a religious independence which was also a political independence. The history and cultural effects of the English Reformation are complex and multiple, and what follows is no more than a rough sketch. No historical process is neat, and no changes are ever clean-cut. Yet

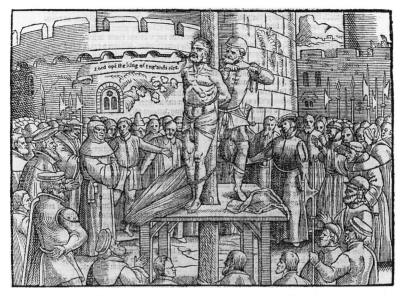

Martyrdom of William Tyndale from Foxe's Acts and Monuments.

changes there are, and the important one for England in 1534 was that the Parliament of Henry VIII passed the Act of Supremacy, which asserted that the 'King's Majesty justly and rightfully is and oweth to be the supreme head of the Church of England'. At the beginning of the reign of Henry VIII, England was a member of a closely-knit community of nations who shared allegiance to the papal authority of Rome. Its religious institution enjoyed a great degree of autonomy from lay controls: it could make its own laws and it enjoyed great wealth, separate from the wealth of the English political institutions it was supposed to serve. Throughout the reigns of Henry's son Edward VI, and of his daughters Mary I and Elizabeth I, England was being pulled this way and that between old allegiances and new independence. By the end of the reign of Henry's daughter Elizabeth, the Church of England had taken root as a national institution. Elizabeth, as head of state, was also head of that Church. And if one result was that the Church of Elizabeth was free from subjection to any external authority, another result was that the Church itself had as much of a vested interest in the kingdom of England as it had an interest in the Kingdom of God.

The establishing of the Elizabethan Church did not take place easily. In what is often referred to as the 'Elizabethan compromise', the institution needed to win grass-roots support from a population,

7

many of whom were indifferent or hostile to the moderate Protestantism which it espoused. Changes occurred slowly. Many of the clergy who officiated at the Anglican mass in the reign of Elizabeth had been Catholic parish priests during the time of Mary Tudor (and some of them had been Protestant ministers before that during the reign of Edward VI). A sign of the Church's weakness at the beginning of Elizabeth's reign was the necessity for the Act of Uniformity of 1559, which made it illegal for men and women to fail to attend Church on Sundays and holy days, and which imposed large fines (never systematically levied) for absenteeism. The measure was never fully successful: one study of church attendance in Kent in the late sixteenth century has estimated that absenteeism was regularly in the region of 20 per cent. Thus, if the growth and establishment of the Protestant Church is the dominant theme in the history of English Renaissance philosophical and religious developments, an essential sub-plot is that of the very real reactions against it. Those reactions sometimes took the form of adherence to older Catholic beliefs; sometimes they broke out into a Puritan denunciation of the incompleteness of Elizabeth's reforms; sometimes they manifested themselves as indifference towards the Elizabethan Church; and occasionally they were expressed in terms of outright atheism and a rejection of Christian belief in Divine Providence. The Elizabethan compromise offered new patterns of belief – but it also offered new possibilities of unbelief.

Resistance to the new Anglicanism tended to intensify the further one travelled from London. The North of England, in particular, remained a stronghold of the Catholic faith. The Northern rebellion of 1569–70 was motivated to a great extent by the Catholicism of its leaders; the Earl of Northumberland proclaimed at his trial that 'Our first aim in assembling was the reformation of religion and preservation of the Queen of Scots, as next heir'. As ever, the question of religion is closely related to the problem of the succession, and articles of religious faith are almost inseparable from issues of political loyalty. The reign of Elizabeth saw only four people executed for heresy, in contrast to the hundreds of Protestants burned during the reign of Mary Tudor. Elizabeth's administration did, however, execute two hundred Catholic priests and laypersons – but the crime they were charged with was treason.

If some of the initial opposition to the new religion was, like Northumberland's, based on positive convictions, a greater part of it probably had more to do with habit – the tendency on the part of many people to cling to the traditional forms of worship with which they had grown up. By the end of Elizabeth's reign, however, this kind of inertia was working in favour of the institutionalized Church of England rather than against it: people had got used to the ways of the Elizabethan Church and had claimed it as their own. If the ways of life, of thought and of belief which it advocated took time before they established themselves as part of the pattern of English life, they did eventually become a part of the national consciousness. Throughout Elizabeth's reign the Church of England fought a slow and unexciting battle for the allegiance of the English nation.

During the early stages of its history, up to the mid-1570s, that battle was waged largely against a traditionalist allegiance to Catholicism. During the 1580s and 1590s it became clear that the Church as a political and religious institution needed to fight on two fronts – both against the Catholic enemy and also against a growing discontent within the radical Protestant ranks at the increasing conservatism of the Elizabethan Church itself. The Puritan attack on the Elizabethan Church sometimes took the form of calls for moderate reform, while at other times it was separatist and revolutionary. Between 1580 and 1640, the relationship between the Anglican Church and the Puritan tendency veered from outright conflict to some degree of co-option. The more radical forms of Puritanism (and most particularly the forms which threatened the intimate alliance of Church and state) were gradually excluded from the Anglican fold, and the resulting growth of Puritan sects was to prove a problem for later ecclesiastical authorities. But the Church of England itself had been influenced from the very start by beliefs, practices and values associated with Puritanism. Even some of the more extreme theological positions, such as a belief in the Calvinist doctrine of election (see below), were shared by mainstream Anglican Protestants and radical Puritans. Indeed, what usually differentiates the Puritan from the Protestant in the sixteenth and early seventeenth centuries is not so much a matter of theological beliefs, as the impact of those beliefs on the everyday organization of social life, and most particularly on the organization of the Church.

The difference between Protestant and Catholic beliefs was more fundamental. To put it crudely, the most important difference between sixteenth-century Catholicism and sixteenth-century Protestantism was this. The Catholic believed that for men and women to understand God, they needed a rigid structure of spiritual authority, whereby God's mysteries could be explained to them. This structure was historically, as well as theologically, validated and depended upon the original nominating of St Peter as 'the rock' upon which Christ built his church. Thus Christ's authority as mediator passed to St Peter, the first pope; Peter's authority was handed down throughout generations of popes to the present day, and the present pope delegates that authority throughout the hierarchy of the Church, through cardinals, bishops, down to the parish priest. The structure of the priesthood was thus a vital channel which connected man to

9

God, and the sacraments, principally The Mass, were the means by which God's grace was communicated.

For the Protestant this was not so. The typical official of the Protestant Church is not a priest with special authority partaking of God's holiness, but a minister, whose wisdom is to be respected, but who is a pastor rather than a mediator between God and man. Men and women approach God and partake of his holiness not by virtue of a mediating priest or hierarchy of authority, but through one's own personal and individual faith. Consequently, a way of thinking grew up in the sixteenth and seventeenth centuries, which has been identified as 'Protestant' (although it was not exclusively the property of those men and women who worshipped in a Protestant Church). Rejecting the authority of ancient traditions, the cornerstones of Lutheran Protestantism were the doctrine of justification by faith alone, and the importance of the Bible as the word of God. There was also a great emphasis on the experience and the conscience of the individual. The answers which Protestantism offers to questions of faith and morality emphasize the primacy of the individual conscience, guided by a careful and honest reading of the Bible. The Bible, being the word of God, will provide advice and instruction. Good Christians, using their intelligence and goodwill, will know when they are in the right, since they will hear God's word telling them what to do.

Central to Calvinism (the brand of Protestantism founded by Jean Calvin) was the doctrine of predestination. This maintains that God has already decided who is to be saved and who is to be damned eternally, and that there is nothing anyone can do to change that. As Jean Calvin asserted in his *Institutes of the Christian Religion*:

> God once established by his eternal and unchangeable plan those whom he long before determined once for all to receive into salvation, and those whom on the other hand he would devote to destruction. We assert that, with respect to the elect, this plan was founded upon his freely given mercy, without regard to human worth; but by his just and irreprehensible but incomprehensible judgement he has barred the door of life to those whom he has given over to damnation.
>
> (Isobel Rivers, *Classical and Christian Ideas*,
> Allen and Unwin, 1979 p. 124)

The 'doctrine of election', as it is sometimes called, maintains that those who are saved will know that they are saved. They have the *certitudo salutis* — the certainty of salvation — and it is, indeed, a sign of salvation that one knows one is already saved! For the Calvinist in moments of confidence, this is a wonderfully reassuring doctrine, of course. But it can be a terrifying doctrine too, since any moments of doubt might then be read as a sign that one is not really one of the elect after all. At its most intense, this leads to a state of extreme psychological insecurity, whereby the individual is constantly seeking for signs of grace in his or her own life so as to be reassured that salvation is, after all, guaranteed.

If the doctrine of election sometimes leads to this sort of interpretative paranoia, it is only an extreme example of something which is common to Protestantism, even in its less neurotic manifestations. For the Protestant frame of mind is by nature one which stresses the need for the individual to be constantly engaged in an act of interpretation whether one is checking oneself for signs of election, or examining the nature of the Faith by which one was to be saved. The traditional sixteenth-century Catholic could safely leave matters of interpretation (whether of the Bible or of social behaviour or of natural phenomena) in the hands of a priest, whose function it was to provide a valid and authoritative explanation for such things. The Protestant, however, was encouraged, or even commanded, by the logic of Protestantism itself to ask about the meanings of things.

Many historians have related the spread of Protestantism to other features of English Renaissance history. Among the developments which have been analysed in the light of the growth of Protestant thought are the increase of literacy in the sixteenth century, the rise of scientific discovery and the rise of capitalism. The first of these, the relationship between Protestant forms of thought and attitudes towards language, will be dealt with in more detail (pp. 32–4). The second and third will bear a little explanation here.

Protestantism and scientific thought

The influence of Protestantism upon the development of scientific thought has been described in two main ways. Firstly, it has been looked at in institutional terms. The sixteenth-century Catholic Church has been seen as an extremely conservative institution, blocking scientific exploration on the grounds that it is not good for man to enquire too deeply into the heart of nature, and perhaps out of a fear that some of its own sacred beliefs might be compromised by the discoveries of scientists.

The second element in the relationship between Protestantism and the rise of science involves the Protestant's enquiring and sceptical cast of mind, in conjunction with the stress laid by Protestant thought on empirical observation and interpretation. These trends, it is argued, laid the foundations for the development of a scientific method. 'Inductive' reasoning, whereby general principles are gradually built up from the available empirical data, has been a central principle of scientific enquiry for so long that it now seems a natural way of progressing. In fact it only dates, as a recognized

11

methodology, from the late sixteenth century. One of the first major theorists of this way of reasoning was Francis Bacon, Lord Chancellor of England in the early seventeenth century and influential philosopher of the new scientific expansion. Bacon wrote and published books about learning and science, partly in an unsuccessful attempt to explain to James I the principles of the new scientific movement, and thereby to persuade him to allocate more money to scientific research. His first attempt, *The Advancement of Learning*, was written in English in 1605; the second, the *Novum Organum* in Latin in 1620. The following quotation comes from the latter.

> There are and can be only two ways of searching into and discovering truth. The one flies from the senses and particulars to the most general axioms, and from these principles, the truth of which it takes as settled and immovable, proceeds to judgement and to the discovery of middle axioms. And this way is now in fashion. The other derives axioms from the senses and particulars, rising by a gradual and unbroken ascent, so that it arrives at the most general axioms last of all. This is the true way, but as yet untried.
>
> (Translated from the Latin by Ellis and Spedding in *Works of F. Bacon*, Vol. IV, 1843, p. 50)

Bacon's two ways of 'searching into and discovering truth', it will be noted, both start out from 'the senses and particulars' and proceed towards general rules in their various ways. Searching into and discovering truth by appeal to traditional authority is not even considered by Bacon.

The story which may be seen as dramatizing the new attitudes towards scientific enquiry is the famous one of Galileo, who, at the end of the sixteenth century, came up with proof that the earth did indeed go round the sun (rather than vice versa) and who was forced by the Church to recant and deny his own findings. Galileo himself was no Protestant, but in the popular version of this story he appears as a kind of Protestant tragic hero, relying on empirical evidence rather than on the authority, bullied by a repressive Church into finally denying his own conscience.

As for the relationship between Protestantism and capitalism, this was first dealt with in detail during the early years of this century in an immensely influential book by Max Weber, *The Protestant Ethic and the Spirit of Capitalism* (written in German, 1904–05). Weber's central thesis, which has been taken up by many other historians (notably R.H. Tawney, in *Religion and the Rise of Capitalism*), is that the Protestant values of thrift, industry and self-reliance paved the way for the growth of capitalism as an economic system, and that the Protestant tendency to look for signs of grace in the everyday incidents of social life encouraged an acquisitive world-view in which a man's wealth was itself seen as a sign of God's favour. Although many details of Weber's arguments have been debated, rejected, modified or qualified, the linking of Protestantism and capitalist enterprise is one which is generally accepted.

Quite how they are linked, though, is a matter for dispute. It is clearly too simple to suggest that the rise of capitalism came about as a direct result of Protestant ways of thought. Moreover, historians have often found that pointing to examples of the Protestant ethic at work is more difficult than it initially seems, and since different analyses locate the rise of capitalism in different historical eras, simple cause-and-effect models are never going to be wholly convincing. And yet Protestant belief did make different demands on people's hearts and minds from those of pre-Reformation Catholicism; capitalism did develop, and Protestant countries eventually proved to be a better soil for its growth than Catholic ones; and in England itself the engineers and ultimate beneficiaries of the emergent capitalist economic and social structures were those groups who had been Protestantism's stronghold: the middle classes.

The history of religious and philosophical developments during the reigns of Elizabeth and James can be brought to bear on a reading of Shakespeare's tragedies in a variety of ways. It is no coincidence that some of the most influential readings of Shakespeare's tragedies in the twentieth century have been ones which insist on a Christian context for them. I do not subscribe to the view which regards Shakespeare as a writer whose plays repeat and elaborate upon Christian dogma — partly because it seems to me that Christian dogma in the early seventeenth century was by no means a stable and settled body of knowledge: rather, it was contentious and problematic, and still an area for debate. But it is nearly impossible to write a tragedy without trespassing on the domain of the moralist, and in a Christian era this means the domain of the theologian as well. More recent criticism has pointed to connections between the religious and political unrest of the time, and the brutal public executions and mutilations with which those who rebelled against established authority were punished. Foxe's *Book of Martyrs* perpetuated the memory of Protestant victims of earlier years, but, as the fate of Guy Fawkes and his co-conspirators reminds us, Catholic bodies could also be broken and burned. These elaborate public executions, it is sometimes claimed, constituted a gruesome kind of 'theatre of punishment', of which the graphically bloody tragedies of Renaissance playhouses are the fictional corollary. Certainly, in Shakespeare's tragedies we see, time and time again, characters for whom the conventional moral and social orders cease to have meaning, and in these plays a debate is conducted concerning the relationship between notions of authority and notions of the primacy of individual conscience – a debate which had been playing itself out on the social and political stage of England from the time of Henry VIII and which was to continue throughout the reigns of Elizabeth and James.

2 Government and authority

Elizabeth I (1558–1603)

Only one of the four great tragedies of Shakespeare's maturity was written and performed during Elizabeth's reign, but it was in Elizabeth's England that Shakespeare spent the first thirty-nine years of his life, and it was in this society that he learnt his craft as a dramatist.

Elizabeth inherited the English throne at a time of political and economic chaos. The English Reformation had forced the country into a comparatively isolated position in Europe, and at home the religious upheavals had taken their toll on the nation's stability. (Elizabeth herself, of course, came to the throne a Protestant. She could hardly have done so otherwise; as daughter to Henry VIII by Ann Boleyn, she was deemed illegitimate by the Catholic Church.) Wars against France, which began in Mary's reign, had devastated the economy and let loose a further round of inflation. The theoretically supreme power of the monarch was continually compromised by the personal interests of the powerful individual noblemen who constituted her aristocracy, and who, at times, presented a very real danger to the crown itself. Throughout Tudor times there were always threats of aristocratic rebellion. The Northern Rebellion of 1569–70 was the last of the great aristocratic rebellions (apart from a lacklustre postscript in the abortive rising of the Earl of Essex in the final years of Elizabeth's reign). There were, however, numerous smaller armed uprisings and riots throughout Elizabeth's reign, often by rural workers in protest against encroachments upon customary rights. For example, enclosure of common land for private profit had been a troublesome issue from the beginning of the century. In 1558, therefore, the year in which she came to the throne, and six years before the birth of Shakespeare, the future of Elizabeth's England looked very uncertain.

By the time of her death in 1603, the picture was very different. By no means all the problems which raised their heads in her reign had been solved: inflation was once more rampant, thanks to a sequence of disastrous harvests; disease and dire poverty were still endemic; religious differences were still a major destabilizing factor; constitutional crises were looming. In many quarters, perhaps in most quarters, Elizabeth in her latter years was a very unpopular ruler. A

Allegorical portrait of Queen Elizabeth I – English School (c. 1600).

posthumous portrait of her, which shows her grey and careworn and menaced by Time and Death, captures succinctly the sense of staleness of the latter end of her reign (above). But in many respects she had done the job she had set out to do, and was the queen of a country which had emerged from a time of crisis with its own identity intact. England had fought off the immediate danger of foreign invasion; it was recognized and it recognized itself as one of the Old World's major economic and military powers; its capital was one of the most important mercantile centres in the known world; and, moreover, England was beginning to look for colonies overseas in the New World.

Elizabeth's own rôle in this, both as a figurehead and as an administrator, was crucial. She played her part well, employing a variety of means: she chose her own inner 'cabinet' judiciously; she had an efficient and ruthless secret service; she encouraged and manipulated a variety of factions within the court; she refused to marry; she was financially tight-fisted; and she encouraged a cult of personality which identified her with the country which she governed and which represented her as the personification of justice, chastity, peace and wisdom. This eulogizing of her started off spontaneously enough, as an expression of the hopes of Protestant enthusiasts, who wanted her to fit the role which they created for her as God's chosen defender of the Protestant faith. By the middle of the 1570s, however, the queen's image was in official hands, and the Tudor propaganda machine was busy authorizing pictures of a magnificent and eternally youthful Elizabeth, or staging pageants in which she figured either as goddess of justice or as virgin shepherdess – and sometimes as both.

A fine example of the overtly political dimension of Elizabethan allegory can be seen in Edmund Spenser's fascinating and multi-layered epic poem *The Faerie Queene*. Spenser, who was a major poet of the Elizabethan era, was also a senior civil servant of Elizabeth's government, spending much of his career as an administrator in Ireland. His poem is addressed to Elizabeth, who is represented by the 'Faerie Queene' of the title, and who plays a central rôle in the poem's narrative structure. On one level the story is an archaic fantasy, dealing with the exploits of knights in armour and damsels in distress (and occasionally damsels in armour and knights in distress), but it also operates allegorically as an analysis and a celebration of the political and religious conditions of Elizabeth's England.

The Faerie Queene was written during the reign of Elizabeth. The most direct reference to the queen in a Shakespearean play, however, comes from something written ten years after her death. *Henry VIII*, probably co-authored by Shakespeare in about 1613, was a play which dealt with some recent historical events and figures. It ends with the birth of Elizabeth herself, whose future reign is hymned in the following terms:

This royal infant – heaven still move about her! –
Though in her cradle, yet now promises
Upon this land a thousand thousand blessings,
Which time shall bring to ripeness....·
In her days every man shall eat in safety
Under his own vine what he plants and sing
The merry songs of peace to all his neighbours.
God shall be truly known; and those about her
From her shall read the perfect ways of honour...

(V, v, ll. 17–20, 33–37)

We do not know whether Shakespeare or his collaborator, John

17

Fletcher, wrote these actual words; traditional scholarship assigns them to Fletcher. Nonetheless, Shakespeare put his name to the play in which they appeared. It should be repeated, though, that they were written in 1613, ten years after Elizabeth's death, by which time her reign was being seen by nostalgic Jacobeans as a kind of Golden Age compared to the reign of her successor, James I. Shakespeare and Fletcher express no treasonable thoughts towards James, however. Indeed, the passage goes on to foretell the passing of these royal virtues from Elizabeth to her successor:

> Nor shall this peace sleep with her; but as when
> The bird of wonder dies, the maiden phoenix,
> Her ashes new create another heir
> As great in admiration as herself,
> So shall she leave her blessedness to one –
> When heaven shall call her from this cloud of darkness –
> Who from the sacred ashes of her honour
> Shall star-like rise, as great in fame as she was,
> And so stand fix'd. Peace, plenty, love, truth, terror,
> That were the servants to this chosen infant,
> Shall then be his, and like a vine grow to him...
>
> (V, v, ll. 39–49)

James I (1603–25)

James, it is insisted, may not be Elizabeth's immediate offspring, but he is her legitimate and inevitable heir, legitimized by a process which is magical (embodied in the phoenix image) and indeed almost holy – for the phoenix as a symbol of rebirth was much used by Christian writers; its reduplication of the image of Christ rising from the grave made it irresistible. James is hymned as the divinely-sanctioned heir, the natural and blessed successor to Elizabeth. The rhetoric, the imagery, even the rhythms, all suggest a smooth transition of English power from Elizabeth to James.

What actually happened, in fact, was that Elizabeth, who had the constitutional power, established by Henry VIII, of choosing her own successor, had been badgered through much of the last part of her reign by James to name him as the next king of England. She had managed to ignore him most of the time, and his succession was stage-managed in secret by Robert Cecil, her principal adviser. (Since Cecil continued in his post after James's accession to the throne, it might be more realistically thought that the continuity of power which is celebrated in the preceding extract, might be seen to refer to the person of Cecil rather than that of James!)

Nonetheless, Shakespeare and Fletcher's hymn to the smooth transition from the Tudors to the Stuarts has a kind of truth about it.

When the King of Scotland entered his new kingdom, he did so unopposed; no voice was raised in protest, and the welcome given to him by his new subjects was warm and – as far as can be told – genuine. The increasing disillusionment which marked English attitudes to James thereafter should not be allowed to obscure the original smoothness of this transition, and the enthusiasm with which James was initially greeted. But disillusionment *did* set in, and it set in comparatively early, so that by 1610 comparisons between the faults of James and the now-remembered virtues of Elizabeth were common, and by 1620 the reign of Elizabeth was looked back to as a wonderful Golden Age – an image which Elizabeth and her ministers had cultivated in the first place. The Tudor propaganda which could be seen working years after the Tudors themselves had died out, operated eventually in terms of nostalgia. And if, in the early days of James's reign, the passage from one monarch to another was seen as a natural progression, it was not long before it was felt to have been a cultural rupture.

The contrast in personality, beliefs and styles of government of the two monarchs was a major political factor of early seventeenth-century life in England. Its importance for a study of Shakespeare's plays should not be underestimated, for not only do Shakespeare's plays (especially his tragedies) repeatedly take courts for their settings and ruling families for their protagonists, but the very conditions under which Shakespeare wrote his tragedies, and under which they were staged, bear witness to the need for a continual awareness of the monarch's presence. The complex – and almost schizophrenic – position of the theatre in late Tudor and early Jacobean society is something which will be looked at in more detail later in this section. One fact, however, must be mentioned here, since it will be referred to so frequently hereafter. This is the fact that the company for whom Shakespeare wrote, and with whom he acted, was, from a few days after James's accession to the throne, known as 'The King's Men'. James, that is, gave to Shakespeare's company his own personal and institutional patronage (they had previously been under the patronage of the Lord Chamberlain). The king became not only their patron, but also one of their main sources of assured revenue: royal patronage brought with it a substantial increase in the number of court performances they were expected to give. The implication is obvious: that when Shakespeare tackled, as he did in his tragedies, thorny political matters, he did so not in privacy, tucked away in some corner of society, but as a very public figure whose words would, in all probability, be heard by the king himself. The fact that Shakespeare apparently flourished under such conditions is itself significant.

The political situation which James inherited on his accession was less volatile than that which had faced the young Queen Elizabeth, but it was by no means an easy one. Many historians now see James

19

as a man who, having with some difficulty established his rule over the Scots, looked forward to his English 'inheritance' as a well-earned rest. The Scottish nobles who surrounded him had often been personally powerful and plain-spoken, and so he was easily misled by the flattery of English courtiers who looked to him for preferment. The Scottish Parliament had had little power, and so he was unprepared for an English Parliament which was increasingly outgrowing its original rôle as a merely administrative body whose essential function was to carry out the sovereign's will. Perhaps most importantly, James had spent all his life in a poverty-stricken and economically backward country, which left him with a comparatively weak grasp of the complexity of England's economic affairs and an exaggerated notion of the wealth of the English crown. This led to one of the first major problems which James both faced and created.

It is difficult for us today to imagine the national economy of a world power being endangered because of the unbridled spending of one man. Yet this was effectively what happened in England in the early seventeenth century, when James's spending amounted to an annual average of half a million pounds – a formidable sum at the time! This included a Wardrobe account which totalled over £36,000 annually, compared to the mere £9,500 per year of Elizabeth. And whereas Elizabeth had been downright niggardly with personal rewards to individual courtiers, the new king was generous to the point of recklessness. Revelling in his new-found 'wealth', James showered it upon an English court which encouraged his generosity, and which became famous for the vicious circle of flattery and favouritism which ensued. Much of his chief minister Cecil's efforts during James's reign were spent in covering up or ameliorating some of the worst effects of royal inefficiency and extravagance, and in simply attempting to get James to realize the value of money. A famous story tells of James casually granting £20,000 as a gift to a favourite. Cecil, appalled, arranged for the coins to be heaped into a massive pile, and left in a prominent place, so that when the king passed it he would see just how great a sum it was. The ploy had the desired effect apparently, for James, on seeing the pile, 'fell into a passion, protesting he was abused, never intending any such gift: And casting himself upon the heap scrabbled out the quantity of two or three hundred pounds, and swore that he should have no more'.

There was thus a developing friction between James and his Parliament as he came to the realization that the resources of the English crown were actually very limited. His ensuing attempts to force Parliament continually to grant him extra funds made the situation worse, especially since the Englishmen who comprised that Parliament were becoming suspicious that the main beneficiaries of James's generosity would be Scots. The centuries-old distrust of

20

Portrait of King James VI of Scotland, I of England.

England's Northern neighbours was fuelled rather than allayed by the item which headed James's own political agenda during the early years of his reign: his overwhelming desire to see the countries of England and Scotland united permanently and constitutionally. It was James who was first responsible for the popularizing of the name 'Great Britain': in 1604 he was 'proclaim'd King of Great Britain . . . that the name of England might be extinct'. A famous portrait, painted soon after his coronation, shows him wearing in his hat a jewel of the Mirror of Great Britain, made in 1604 in order to symbolize the union of the kingdoms (p. 21). His continued attempts to ratify the matter constitutionally by pushing it through Parliament, and the equally determined resistance of the majority of the Parliament to the whole idea, constituted one of the major political arguments of the early seventeenth century. James never succeeded in this, his dearest wish: too many interests were stacked up against him. But this matter of the 'Union' brought into play a series of hotly-debated issues concerning the nature of kingship in many of the plays which Shakespeare wrote during James's reign.

To put it at its simplest, James argued that as king of both Scotland and England, his blood already united the two kingdoms. For five years the House of Commons debated the matter and came to the conclusion that James had misunderstood the nature of kingship. The Tudor concept of monarchy had been spelled out in the law courts of Elizabeth, and it was a concept which tells us a lot about the way in which thinkers of Shakespeare's day envisaged the relationship between a person and the office which he or she held. The theory of the 'king's two bodies' stipulates a definite division between the private individual and the public role:

> For the King has in him two Bodies, viz, a Body natural, and a Body politic. His Body natural (if it be considered in itself) is a Body mortal, subject to all Infirmities that come by Nature or Accident, to the Imbecillity of Infancy or old Age, and to the like Defects that happen to the natural Bodies of other People. But his Body politic is a Body that cannot be seen or handled, consisting of Policy and Government, and constituted for the Direction of the People and the management of the publick-weal and this Body is utterly void of Infancy, and Old Age, and other natural Defects and Imbecilities which the Body natural is subject to, and for this Cause what the King does in his Body politic cannot be invalidated or frustrated by any Disability in his natural Body.
>
> (Plowden, *Reports* 1779 p. 213)

This separation of the king's identity into 'Body natural' and 'Body politic' offers us ways of approaching some of Shakespeare's plays in which the same issue is treated.

As James sensed more and more opposition within his Parliament, he tended to become increasingly assertive about his own view of his status and power as king. If Elizabeth's lawyers had delineated a complex – almost schizophrenic – model of kingship, James, not surprisingly, tended to rely on a simpler notion, and one which still had great emotive power in the minds of his subjects. In a speech to Parliament in 1610, James described his conception of kingship in the following terms:

> Kings are justly called gods for that they exercise a manner or resemblance of divine power upon earth, for if you will consider the attributes to God you shall see how they agree in the person of a king. God hath the power to create or destroy, make or unmake at his pleasure; to give life or send death, to judge all and to be judged not accountable to none; to raise low things and to make high things low at his pleasure; and to God are both soul and body due. And the like power have kings: they make and unmake their subjects; they have power of raising, and casting down; of life, and of death, judges over all their subjects, and in all causes, and yet accountable to none but God only. They have the power to exalt low things, and abase high things, and make of their subjects like men at the chess – a pawn to take a bishop or a knight – and cry up or down any of their subjects, as they do their money. And to the king is due both the affection of the soul and the service of the body of his subjects....
>
> (Ann Hughes (ed.), *Seventeenth Century England*, I, Ward Lock, Open University, 1980, pp. 28–9)

Most important here is the fact that in 1610 the king was having to *assert* the divinity of the kingship. None of the king's Members of Parliament would have stood up and disagreed with what is said here, yet the slight tone of defiance which is audible in the king's speech reminds us that we are less than forty years away from the day when the men of an English Parliament would resolve that 'the office of a king in this nation...is unnecessary, burdensome, and dangerous to the liberty, safety and public interest of the people', and would cut off the head of Charles I.

No such revolution threatened James; indeed the major threat to his life came from a radical Catholic terrorist group. James's accession to the throne had settled one of the major problems of Tudor political life – the question of the Protestant succession. So, when in 1605 the failure of the Gunpowder Plot provided evidence of continued Catholic activism against both crown and Parliament, the inevitable result was that – for a short while at least – king and Parliament stood united against the threat.

3 Elizabethan and Jacobean Society

Lear First let me talk with this philosopher.
What is the cause of thunder?
Kent Good my lord, take his offer; go into th'house.
Lear I'll talk a word with this same learned Theban.
What is your study?
Edgar How to prevent the fiend and kill vermin.

(III, iv, ll. 154–9)

It is a key moment in *King Lear*: the former king, once the highest in the land, sits and talks on a heath with a character who appears to be one of the very lowest in the land. In fact, 'Poor Tom', the mad beggar, is really the nobleman Edgar in disguise, but Lear does not know that.

This image, of a crucial meeting of the very low and the very high, is one to which Shakespeare returns astonishingly frequently. Again and again in his plays we see him stage an encounter between those in authority, and those outside it: the rogues, the poor, the marginalized, the mad. Some of the plays are more or less plotted around this encounter: *Measure for Measure*, *Henry IV Part I* and *The Winter's Tale*, for example, *King Lear* itself plays an astounding series of variations on the theme of power and powerlessness. In a comedy such as *As You Like it*, where disguise and displacement from social position provide the main storyline, a similar encounter between the nobility and the rural poor is dramatized throughout. *Julius Caesar* and *Coriolanus* focus on noblemen, but their drama is staged against the ever-present backdrop of the Roman plebeians – often dismissively referred to as 'the mob'. In other plays, the encounter is limited to a few scenes, or even to a single scene – though that scene is often a vital one: Henry V talking to his soldiers before the battle of Agincourt; Hamlet and the gravedigger; Macbeth and the witches.

Hierarchy and 'degree'

It is difficult to get a sense of the force – sometimes the shocking force – of these encounters without an awareness of how strongly hierarchical Elizabethan and Jacobean society was. English society in the age of Shakespeare was based on a system of institutionalized social inequality which pervaded all aspects of social life. It was not only food, housing, type of work and clothing which differed from one degree of society to another, but also education, marriage and

24

kinship patterns, the likelihood of being executed for a serious crime (and the method of execution), modes of address and the use of language itself, and one's right to a seat in a church. For nearly everybody such things were determined by the degree of society one was born into. Moreover, the differences were so ingrained in the life and patterns of social behaviour that the hierarchical structures which existed seemed natural, even divinely ordained. Elizabethan and Jacobean writers describe their society almost unthinkingly in terms of stratification, hierarchy, degree and order: it is the natural starting point for them, the obvious way of doing things.

Thomas Wilson's *The State of England 1600* (published in 1601) divides the country into nobility, citizenry, yeomen, artisans and rural labourers. The divisions are based on adult male occupations (women were assumed, like children, to take their definition from the male head of the household), and Wilson tends to ignore the very lowest reaches of the social scale. What he calls 'rural labourers', for example, ranged from the reasonably comfortably-off to the nearly-destitute. Seasonal fluctuations, variations in harvests, inflation, plagues, enclosures and population growth all affected the poorest most severely, and many a man who was a rural labourer in September might, by December, have drifted into that area of society which Wilson hardly acknowledges: the chronically poor, the homeless, the unemployed, vagabonds and beggars. These are the criminal or near-criminal underbelly of Elizabethan and Jacobean society, to which 'Poor Tom' so clearly belongs. While Wilson rather complacently talks about the wealth of the common people of England, the problem of chronic poverty and vagrancy was actually a massive one for the Elizabethan authorities, and much attention was paid to trying either to alleviate it by a system of poor relief, or to control its potential threat to the well-to-do by a series of laws decreeing harsh penalties for begging and vagrancy.

Having distinguished what he sees as the main sectors of society, Wilson then goes on to distinguish sub-groups in each of these sectors. The nobility, for example, included far more than our present-day use of the term suggests. Wilson divides the category into the *nobilitas maior* (greater nobility) which included earls, barons, viscounts, bishops and deans, and the *nobilitas minor* (lesser nobility) comprising knights, esquires, gentlemen, lawyers, professors, ministers, archdeacons, prebends and vicars. The title of 'gentleman', in particular seems to have been a vital transitional point for socially ambitious mercantile families, since it marked a promotion from the ranks of citizenry to those of nobility. Needless to say, only those citizens who were of 'some competent quantity of revenue fit to be called into office and authority' qualified for such promotion.

The structure of inequality of Elizabethan and Jacobean England was thus based partly on wealth, partly on more nebulous concepts of 'status' or 'degree'. For the most part, the two went hand in hand, and while sixteenth-century conservatives deplored the fact, it became more and more common throughout the period for men to be able to buy status with new-found wealth. In 1611 James I institutionalized the practice by creating a new hereditary title, the order of baronets, and then selling off these baronetcies for £1,095 each. Long before that, however, the seemingly static and immutable social hierarchy of England had been undergoing changes. For while the hierarchical structure was not very flexible, neither was it absolutely rigid: it was not impossible for people to move up (or down) the social scale. Indeed, Shakespeare himself is a good example of a young, upwardly mobile playwright. His father, John Shakespeare, was still described as a yeoman in a property deed of 1597, but William ended his days a gentleman, a large property-owner, and the bearer of a coat of arms. Stories such as this were not uncommon by the turn of the century.

One of the main things which made movement possible, despite the restrictions of the ingrained faith in hierarchies, was the changing economic pattern of the culture. The sixteenth and seventeenth centuries saw a transition from an economy which was predominantly feudal in 1500 to one which was predominantly capitalist in 1700. The economy of feudal England based itself around the manor, or village, which consumed the food it produced and which had little left over for sale. However, during the sixteenth century, a new and more aggressive economic system grew up alongside and in competition with the old one. The discovery of gold and silver in the New World made money available for investment – and the profitability of financing voyages of discovery made investment attractive. The Protestant emphasis on the primacy of the individual conscience went hand in hand with a new economic individualism which replaced disapproval of lending and borrowing at interest by approval of 'prudent investment'. As it became easier and more respectable to accumulate individual wealth, so it became possible to make that wealth generate more wealth. The growth of towns, and especially of London, was both cause and effect of the new capitalist economic patterns, as the centre of economic activity shifted away from the manor and became located in urban life, where mercantile activity flourished in the form of great trading companies and of individual entrepreneurs.

The new acquisitive spirit is continually attacked in the drama of the period, including many of Shakespeare's own plays. *The Merchant of Venice*, for example, deals in detail with the processes of mercantile capitalism — although Shakespeare is more ambiguous in his attitude towards it than some of his more conservative contemporaries. Time after time playwrights make the point that the expansiveness of the new mercantile capitalism tends to shatter the old order of human relationships, breaking old ties of duty and tradition, destroying communities and leading to personal excess and self-aggrandisement. A stock figure in the satire of the late sixteenth century is the landowner who sells off his land, disinheriting his heirs, and ignoring his traditional obligations towards his tenants in order to make a quick financial profit on a short-term investment. Even the seemingly-idyllic Forest of Arden is not immune from such depredations: Corin, the old shepherd explains to Rosalind that

> ...I am shepherd to another man
> And do not shear the fleeces that I graze,
> My master is of a churlish disposition,
> And little recks to find the way to heaven
> By doing deeds of hospitality,
> Besides, his cot, his flocks, and bounds of feed
> Are now on sale...

> (*As You Like It*, II, iv, ll. 73–9)

And if Shakespeare's own family history tells of the possibilities for social advancement, there were plenty of families whose story was more like that of Orlando in *As You Like It*: the story of men and women of noble birth who are reduced to destitution.

'The Elizabethan world picture'

It is against this background that we should view what we call the 'Elizabethan world picture'. The phrase was made famous as the title of a book by E.M.W. Tillyard which was published in 1943. Tillyard's intention was to establish the ways in which Elizabethan culture repeatedly makes use of images of 'The Great Chain of Being', images of hierarchy, order and degree. These images, he goes on to argue, represent a basic structure of belief for the Elizabethans – a belief that has both social and cosmic dimensions. Tillyard's work paved the way for later scholars, and the description which he provides of Elizabethan culture has been vastly influential. Tillyard and others often quote Shakespeare as an example of a writer whose thought is governed by these images, and the most famous expression of the idea is to be found in his play *Troilus and Cressida*, where Ulysses addresses the military commanders on the necessity of order and degree.

> The heavens themselves, the planets and this centre,
> Observe degree, priority and place,
> Insisture, course, proportion, season, form,
> Office, and custom, in all line of order;

27

... [But] when degree is shak'd,
Which is the ladder of all high designs,
The enterprise is sick! How could communities,
Degrees in schools, and brotherhoods in cities
Peaceful commerce from dividable shores,
The primogenity and due of birth,
Prerogative of age, crowns, sceptres, laurels,
But by degree stand in authentic place?
Take but degree away, untune that string,
And hark what discord follows! Each thing melts
In mere oppugnancy: the bounded waters
Should lift their bosoms higher than the shores,
And make a sop of all this solid globe;
Strength should be lord of imbecility,
And the rude son should strike his father dead;
Force should be right; or, rather, right and wrong –
Between whose endless jar justice resides –
Should lose their names, and so should justice too.
Then everything includes itself in power,
Power into will, will into appetite;
And appetite, an universal wolf,
So doubly seconded with will and power,
Must make perforce an universal prey,
And last eat up himself.

(I, iii, ll. 85–8, 101–24)

This speech sums up a certain conception of the Elizabethan world picture. It is suggested that, above all, the Elizabethans valued order and degree. At its most magnificent, this love of order and degree has a cosmic and metaphysical dimension (suggested here by Shakespeare when he talks about 'the heavens themselves'): the 'Great Chain of Being' places every natural and supernatural phenomenon in one massive and complex hierarchy in which God reigns supreme at the top, and in which stones and earth have their place at the bottom. Vegetable life is higher in the chain than inanimate matter, but within both of these categories there are hierarchies too (the oak is nobler than the nettle; the ruby is nobler than clay). Animals come next, and they too have their hierarchical divisions (the eagle is the king of the birds; the lion the king of beasts). Man exists somewhere in the middle of the hierarchy – lower than the angels, but in dominion over the beasts of the field – and the hierarchical order of Elizabethan society itself is thus given a metaphysical justification.

The concept of the Elizabethan world picture has come in for much criticism, especially in the last few years, and there are obvious objections. First of all, evidence such as that of Ulysses' speech is very dubious: Ulysses is a character in a play, and his speech in context turns out to be more like a clever piece of political manoeuvring than an objective speech about the value of order. Secondly, the very idea of an Elizabethan world picture may seem a little reductive – suggesting as it does that everybody in the period thought in the same way, or that Shakespeare's thought may be reduced to a rather simple political or metaphysical scheme.

And yet, as I have tried to suggest in the earlier part of this section, we find an insistence on notions of degree nearly everywhere in writings about society. For example, in the book of *Certain Sermons or Homilies appointed to be read in Churches*, which was mandatory reading in the Elizabethan Church, we find the following in 'An Homilie against disobedience and wilfull rebellion':

> Thus became rebellion, as you see, both the first and the greatest and the very root of all other sins, and the first and principal cause both of all worldly and bodily miseries, sorrows, diseases, sicknesses and deaths, and, which is infinitely worse than all these... the very cause of death and damnation eternal also... GOD forthwith, by laws given unto mankind repaired again the rule and order of obedience thus by rebellion overthrown, and besides the obedience due to his majesty, He not only ordained that, in families and households, the wife should be obedient unto her husband, the children unto their parents, the servants unto their masters, but also, when mankind increased and spread itself more largely over the world, He by his holy word did constitute and ordain in cities and countries several and special governors and rulers, unto whom the residue of his people should be obedient.

Tillyard himself is not so simple-minded as to rely only on speeches from plays, but draws his evidence from political writings, sermons, pamphlets and proclamations as well. It is very difficult to get away from the conclusion that the Elizabethans were obsessed with the idea of order. And if that is the case, then it has a bearing on a study of Shakespeare; for, as I said at the very beginning, I do not believe that Coleridge was right in suggesting that Shakespeare somehow operates outside the constraints of his own age. If this concern with order *were* an Elizabethan obsession, then we should consider ways in which it can be seen to operate in Shakespeare's plays.

The point is that the concern with ideas of order must be seen as part of the larger social issues. I have described Elizabethan society as one in which traditional, hierarchical structures were coming under stress from new and changing economic patterns. Rather than see Tillyard's Elizabethan world picture as a settled doctrine of Elizabethan faith to which everyone gave placid assent, and which everybody believed represented life as it actually was, we can regard it as an intervention in the social processes which were taking place. To put it simply: when Elizabethan authorities insisted on ideas of order and degree, they did so because they were aware that the order and degree of their own society were under threat. The above homily against rebellion, for example, was first included in *The Book of Homilies* in 1571, and was a direct response to the Earl of Northumberland's Catholic rebellion of 1569–70. The homily goes on to insist on the divine sanction of the anointed ruler and the absolute duty of subjects to obey that ruler. But it was written precisely because there were subjects who were *not* doing that.

Thus the Elizabethan world picture which is painted by such writings is a picture of the world as certain men and women thought it *should* be, rather than as it actually was. The image of a settled hierarchy was attractive to them precisely because they felt the need to defend the status quo. For it seems to be the case that most of the writers quoted by Tillyard (and others) had a vested interest in maintaining the political and social structures of authority; and one effective way of doing this is to argue that this structure has a grounding in the very nature of reality itself, and to affirm that the hierarchies of English social and political life, from the throne to the hearth, are but one small part of a cosmic hierarchy which reaches from the height of heaven down to the very lowest forms of nature.

This need not be taken to imply that such writers were cynical hypocrites, attempting to trick their readers into the acceptance of a fraudulent form of authority. On the contrary, they were often people who were writing out of a real sense of commitment to a particular way of looking at the world, at the universe and at social organization. At times they seem not to be trying to convince an audience at all, but to be merely voicing assumptions which to them (as Tillyard says) seem totally natural and self-evident. Nonetheless, it must be recognized that their commitment and their assumptions have social, economic and political dimensions which are intimately bound up with the changing structures of Elizabethan life.

Does this mean, then, that Shakespeare himself is merely a propagandist (consciously or unconsciously) for a certain kind of political theory – essentially a rather conservative one? I do not think so. For while he cannot have been unaffected by the obsession with order and degree, there is no need for us to assume that therefore he shared it wholeheartedly, or that he always accepted it unthinkingly. After all, it has traditionally been supposed that one of the artist's functions is to examine critically the shared beliefs of his or her time. (It is, perhaps, harder for an artist to do this than we sometimes think; the process by which it happens is anything but clear-cut.) At times Shakespeare does seem to me to be making the same assumptions about order and degree which are made by so many of his contemporaries. At other times he seems to be bringing those assumptions out into the light in order to subject them to questioning. At different times in his career as a playwright he comes up with different answers to his questions; sometimes these answers tend in one direction, sometimes in another; sometimes they are ambiguous or even self-contradictory, and sometimes he comes up with no answers at all. In the tragedies, and especially in *King Lear* and *Macbeth*, we see some of this questioning process in action.

In essence, then, the shape of Elizabethan and Jacobean society can be described in terms of two opposed and contrasting elements. On the one hand there is a conservative, traditionalist and hier-archical structure, static in tendency and based around a local, rural economy; on the other hand there is a force for change, expressing it-self through the institutions of the new capitalism, urban in character, dependent on a national and even an international economy, en-couraging social mobility and thereby threatening previous patterns of social life. The interplay between these two elements is complex and far-reaching; sometimes they appear as opposites, and their relationship is antagonistic. At other times, however, one can see the old hierarchical structures coming to terms with the new capitalism – accepting it, internalizing it and eventually using it for its own ends. It would be a mistake to imagine that men and women in sixteenth- and seventeenth-century England were ever offered a conscious choice between two opposing value-systems. Rather, they were caught amidst turning tides, and the waters which swirled around them were (whether they recognized the fact or not) the waters of the changing economic practices of England. The feudal hierarchies are embedded most deeply in the history of the Tudor period, and the new capitalist practices came to predominate during the Stuart era. And it was precisely then that Shakespeare's great tragedies were written: during the years of that very turning-point, of the transition of power from Elizabeth to James, from Tudors to Stuarts. It was a period in which a sense of permanence and stability was constantly jostling with a sense of rapid change – societal, political, economic and ideological – which affected all aspects of people's lives. Not least among the changes were those which concerned the very language which people spoke.

4 'Words, words, words': Shakespeare's English

Society and language: from script to print

The late sixteenth century was the period when England began to define itself as a nation state of international importance. It was also the period when the English language finally won the long struggle to establish itself as a respectable medium of intellectual thought. These two events are not unconnected.

In the first place, it is only to be expected that a nation, during a period when national pride is particularly strong, should manifest an interest in its own language. Most especially, an emergent nation, concerned with establishing its own identity, but whose demotic language has for centuries been considered second-rate, might well be expected to turn its attention to establishing the validity of that language. Language, after all, comprises the essential structures of thought whereby we relate to the world around us: it will be a matter of necessity for a people bent on self-definition to demand that they be allowed to operate within their own structures rather than somebody else's.

But in the England of the late sixteenth century and early seventeenth century, the matter takes a specific turn which links it firmly with the religious issues of the period. As was suggested in the previous section, the growing sense of English national identity during this period was intimately bound up with the Protestantism which was England's national religion. It was stressed, too, that the Protestant turn of mind was one which emphasized a personal relationship with God, unmediated by any hierarchical structures of papacy or priesthood.

The relationship between these religious changes and the development of the English language is as follows. The answer is simple. If one's immortal soul depends upon one's personal knowledge of and relationship with the Creator, and if there is no longer a hierarchy of authority to help one to know that Creator, what is left to help one? God's word itself, of course – the Bible. It is a central tenet of Protestant belief that salvation is to be found by reading and understanding the Bible. In order to liberate the text of God's word from the control of established authority and linguistic obscurity the first, and vital stage, is that the Bible itself be translated into the vernacular – into English.

This means two things: first of all, the Protestant, if he or she can read, will have direct access to the word of God, and thus to guidance in the struggle for salvation. This, in part at least, explains the sudden rise in the literacy rate in mid- and late-sixteenth-century England. Petty schools and village schools sprang up, often taught by the local vicar or curate; merchants, gentlemen and nobles endowed grammar schools in order to produce good members of the Church and commonwealth, and to instruct young boys in the principles of religion, as well as preparing some of them for the universities. The founding of a school was seen not only as socially beneficial but as spiritually desirable – providing others with the means whereby to cure their own souls. A close reciprocal relationship existed between forms of Protestant belief and an intensified interest in the word.

This intensified interest, however, put an immense burden on the users of words – on the translator to get the translation right (for how many souls might be lost if a phrase of God's word is wrongly translated into English?), and on the reader to read it correctly (for a misunderstanding of the word, or a misreading of it, might lead to perdition.) What is more, these questions of interpretation were not merely a matter for the individual; they had a political dimension as well. The history of sixteenth- and seventeenth-century Europe shows the extent to which issues of interpretation could involve physical risk. Throughout this period men and women went to the gallows, the stake and the torture chamber not only over major issues of individual conscience, such as the right to interpretation, but also over seemingly small issues – such as how certain words, phrases or sentences should be translated from Latin or Greek into English. Nor did this happen only in Continental Europe: England had its own history of persecution of heretical interpreters. William Tyndale's translation of the New Testament appeared in 1525, during the reign of Henry VIII, but before Henry's break with Rome. Tyndale himself was eventually burnt at the stake, and men and women put themselves in mortal danger merely by reading his, or any other vernacular translation. A proclamation of Henry VIII in 1530 asserts that those who 'buy, receive, keep or have' a translation of the Old or New Testament into English, French or Dutch 'will answer to the King's highness at their uttermost perils'.

The harshness of Henry's response should alert us to the power of the vernacular Bible. One of the reasons for this power was that by the sixteenth century, the notion of a Bible translation was no longer a matter of a few isolated manuscripts: it was potentially a mass movement. In earlier years, for example, during the fifteenth-century, a Catholic priest had privileged access to the Bible in more than one sense. Firstly, it was written in Latin – a language which he could understand, but which many of his parishioners would not. Secondly, since all books had to be copied by hand, he would in all probability have the only physical copy of the Bible for many miles around. The invention of printing changed all this. William Caxton introduced printing into England in 1476, less than a century before Shakespeare's birth, and from that date on knowledge becomes, suddenly and astonishingly, both secularized and democractic. By 1564, the year of Shakespeare's birth, the printed book had completely taken over from the manuscript book. And if the spread of Protestantism in sixteenth-century Europe posed a challenge to the hierarchical authority of the Catholic Church, the challenge already posed by the invention of the printing press had been equally serious. From the very beginning, the access to ideas and information which the printed word made possible was recognized by at least some of those in authority as potentially dangerous.

Literacy

This new availability of printed books, together with an increased interest in the necessity of literacy and education, made for an important shift in English culture during the sixteenth century: the movement away from an oral culture towards one in which the written – or rather, the printed – word was paramount. It must be stressed, however, that in Shakespeare's lifetime this change was under way, but by no means fully completed. The sheer availability of the printed word makes it tempting to think of Europe as having a totally book-centred culture by 1600. In England in particular, where the benefits of education, learning and literacy were constantly and enthusi-astically extolled, and where the founding of schools underwent a startling increase, it often seems that the shift was total. But the surge of interest in education which the sixteenth century saw was not for everybody. For those seeking an apprenticeship in the expanding world of business and trading, literacy was now of great importance, as it always had been for the aspiring clergyman or lawyer. To the aristocracy and upper gentry literacy and education were assuming a more central rôle in the attributes of a gentleman. But while the literacy rate underwent a dramatic increase during the period before 1600, and while the provision of educational facilities blossomed, these developments were uneven, and access to them was limited. Not everyone could afford tuition fees, nor the loss of their children's labour, especially in the fields at crucial times of the year. The grammar schools were for boys alone: girls whose families could not afford a private tutor would receive nothing beyond the level of the most elementary education – and many of them not even that. For the yeoman, the husbandman, the unskilled labourer, the servant and the urban artisan, literacy was often unattainable or irrelevant. On the whole, the main beneficiaries of the educational expansion were men from the middling and upper ranks of the social scale. For example, in rural Leicestershire (which was particularly well-documented) we find that in the 1590s, 23 per cent of comparatively prosperous yeomen had achieved a basic level of literacy, and that this then rose to 45 per cent by the 1640s. The poorer husbandmen of the county, on the other hand, had a literacy rate of only 13 per cent in the 1590s, rising to 19 per cent in the 1640s; still further down the scale, Leicestershire labourers appear to have been totally illiterate in the 1590s: by the 1640s only 4 per cent of them had attained basic literacy. London, the nation's capital, richest city in the country and centre for trade, industry and arts, had a substantially higher literacy rate than the rest of the kingdom; yet recent scholarship estimates that only about a third of adult males in Shakespeare's London could read or write.

Even so, this represents a substantial increase in the literacy rate over previous years. And as literacy increased, and as a book-buying public developed, — based largely, but not exclusively, in London — so at the same time, the language was changing. England's growing importance as a trading nation brought with it both new opportunities, and a greater necessity, for linguistic growth. Exchange of commodities involved increasingly sophisticated communications systems, spreading over greater areas, bringing Englishmen into contact with new countries and new parts of their own country, and opening the way to exchange of ideas. In particular, London's position as an expanding international trading port involved not only a new cosmopolitanism because of its links with Europe and other parts of the globe; it also brought an influx of people from all over the country into the capital. These contacts brought into currency both foreign words and phrases, borrowed from French, Italian and Spanish, and also English local dialect vocabulary. London became a linguistic melting-pot, for in London, more than anywhere, the English language had to change with the times. There was a new need for a richer and more precise vocabulary to cope with the rapid changes taking place in crafts and sciences, in the world of technical skills and intellectual pursuits, and also in everyday life. The development of a sufficiently complex vocabulary to meet the needs of a changing world was one of the major obstacles which the English language had to overcome in its struggle for recognition. It succeeded, not only by absorbing and naturalizing influences from contemporary Europe, but also by raiding the classics and coining new English words based on Latin roots. It has been estimated that between 1500 and 1650, over ten thousand new words entered the language.

Vocabulary and grammar

This expansion of the vocabulary did not meet with universal approval. The development of the English language which took place in the sixteenth century was the product of two opposing tendencies – a radical tendency which promoted change, and a conservative one which sought to preserve the status quo. In particular, the borrowing of words from other languages caused concern to many traditionalists and purists. Just as in the twentieth century, the expansion of vocabulary which has taken place to meet the changing needs of the technological age has encountered opposition, so the strangeness of many of the new words in the sixteenth century incurred hostility. Today we call words which seem over-specialized and obscure 'jargon'; in Shakespeare's day they called them 'inkhorn terms'.

A typical condemnation of inkhorn terms can be seen in the following passage from Thomas Wilson, whose book *The Arte of Rhetorique* (first published in 1553 and going through eight editions in the next thirty years) was one of the most popular and important books on language and writing of the period. (In the following quotations the original spelling is retained.)

> Among all other lessons this should first be learned, that wee never affect any straunge ynkehorne termes, but to speake as is commonly received: neither seeking to be over fine, nor yet living over-carelesse, using our speeche as most men doe, and ordering our wittes as the fewest have done. Some seeke so far for outlandish English, that they forget altogether their mothers language. And I dare sweare this, if some of their mothers were alive, thei were not able to tell what they say.
>
> (A. Baugh and T. Cable, *A History of the English Language*,
> Prentice-Hall, 1957, pp. 217–18)

He goes on to illustrate these inkhorn terms in a parody of a letter, supposedly written by a Lincolnshire man in search of a clerical living, and stuffed full of words new in Wilson's day:

> Pondering, expending, and revoluting with my selfe your ingent affabilitie and ingenious capacity for mundaine affaires: I cannot but celebrate, & extol your magnifical dexteritie above all other. For how can you have adepted such illustrate prerogative and dominicall superioritie, if the fecunditie of your ingenie had not been so fertile and wonderfull pregnant.
>
> (Ibid., p. 218)

Wilson makes his point. However, it is instructive to note that while many of the terms he condemned as inkhorn – such as 'expending' (meaning 'considering'), 'dominicall' (meaning 'pertaining to an absolute lord') and 'adepted' (meaning 'acquired') – have sunk into oblivion, nevertheless many others – such as 'celebrate' 'ingenious' and 'superiority' – have become part of everyday vocabulary.

Shakespeare's own vocabulary, of course, was extensive – one of the largest of any writer in the English language. But he could also, like Wilson, poke fun at the verbal eccentricities of the age. The young courtier Osric is introduced into Act V of *Hamlet* specifically to serve as the butt of Hamlet's parody of over-refined speech:

> Sir, his definement suffers no perdition in you; though I know to divide him inventorially would dozy th' arithmetic of memory, and yet but yaw neither in respect of his quick sail. But in the verity of extolment I take him to be a soul of great article, and his infusion of such dearth and rareness as, to make true diction of him, his semblable is his mirror, and who else would trace him, his umbrage, nothing more.
>
> (Act V, ii, ll. 112–20)

Shakespeare himself was a great innovator in language, but his linguistic innovations were not confined to his ready acceptance of new words; his unconventional and resourceful use of everyday language, his puns and his wordplay, had the effect of extending the meanings of individual words, and of generating suggestions which go far beyond the paraphrasable meanings of his sentences. And although it is easy to mock the jargon of inkhorn terminology, it should be remembered that the influx of new words into the language during the period was a response to a serious problem: the widely held doubt as to whether the vernacular language was resourceful, sophisticated and flexible enough to act as a serious instrument of thought, and the anxiety that in the modern world there were, as one writer put it 'more things than there are words to express them by'.

The changing language needed more than just extra words, however. If the fertile expansion of vocabulary showed a tendency to diversity, the changes in grammar show a more conservative force at work, one which led to greater standardization of the structures of language. For example, the printing press made books available and introduced people to new words, but it also encouraged the acceptance of standard grammatical structures which would allow the new words, the new meanings to be understood. The new educational foundations helped to promote a new interest in the written English language, and simultaneously they helped to solidify the rules and structures of that language. Upward social mobility demanded a sophisticated vocabulary, but it also tended to standardize the language, as the upwardly mobile emulated the manners and discourses of their superiors. As a result, rules began to be formalized, prescribing the ways in which different elements of a sentence are related to each other. It is possible to discern in the sixteenth century the beginnings of the standardization of modern English grammar.

Only the beginnings, however. The grammar of Shakespeare and his contemporaries was still an unsettled thing, with many alternative forms and a great variety of usages. Standards of correctness in English grammar, as we understand them, had not been established, and the Elizabethans were, for the most part, not particularly interested in them.The first moves towards standardization happened, not as any kind of conscious educational programme, but in reaction to the increased richness and complexity of the overall linguistic environment. It was not until the middle of the seventeenth century that rhetoricians began to develop a programme of grammatical reform. When they did, they started a grammatical revolution, which defined standards of correctness in the organization of sentences, and produced a grammar recognizably like our own. But Shakespeare was writing before that happened, and the structures of Elizabethan English are based on a grammar which is different from our own, which has its own rules and conventions, but which is also less insistent on the following of rules. If one of Shakespeare's great strengths as a poetic writer is the flexibility with which he moulds his language to his own use, it is precisely because the language which he and his contemporaries used was itself more flexible, without some of the logical rigidity imposed by later grammatical developments.

By the time the seventeenth-century rhetoricians turned their attention to grammar, the English language had more or less won its battle for recognition. This battle, however, was fought throughout the sixteenth century. We should remember that even as Shakespeare was about to begin his career as a playwright there was a strong body of opinion which held that the English language was unworthy of serious consideration. George Pettie in his book *Civil Conversation* (1586) complained that 'There are some others yet who wyll set light by my labours, because I write in Englysh: and . . . the woorst is, they thinke that impossible to be doone in our Tongue: for they count it barbarous, they count it unworthy to be accounted of' (quoted in Baugh and Cable, *A History of the English Language* p. 206). For even with its expanded vocabulary, English in the sixteenth century had to struggle for its status. While an established tradition of popular literature was growing up in English, it was not easy to dislodge the ancient languages, and especially Latin, from their positions as the languages of power. Access to the discourses of philosophy, medicine and the law was limited to those privileged enough to have a thorough grounding in the classics; it is hardly surprising that a strong body of opinion amongst philosophers, lawyers and medical practitioners insisted that English was not a proper language for these disciplines. The educated, academic and professional classes of Elizabeth's reign understood very well the extent to which their knowledge of Latin and Greek confirmed them in their positions of influence. Thus, many of the arguments which were advanced against the recognition of English had a firm basis in the self-interest and territorial possessiveness of the Elizabethan élites. Apart from the poverty and the immaturity of English, it was urged that Latin was a common European tongue which enabled scholars of different nations to converse with each other, that the study of classical languages would decay if English became too important, and (finally) that it was necessary to prevent the uncultivated from dabbling in matters of philosophy, law and medicine.

In the end, however, the pressure towards the recognition of English as a proper language for intellectual disciplines was irresistible. Richard Mulcaster, the headmaster of the Merchant Taylors' School was one of the influential spokesman for the language; in his defence of English he combines pragmatic reason about the effort involved in learning classical languages with a fervently nationalistic rhetoric about English being the language of liberty:

> For is it not in dede a mervelous bondage, to becom servants to one tung for learning sake, the most of our time, with losse of most time, whereas we maie have the verie same treasur in our own tung, with the gain of most time? our own bearing the joyfull title of our libertie and fredom, the Latin tung remembring us of our thraldom and bondage? I love Rome, but London better, I favor Italie, but England more, I honor the Latin, but I worship the English.
>
> (Ibid., pp. 203–4)

National self-assertiveness, theological and political considerations, and a popular demand for access to knowledge, all added impetus to the growth in importance of the English language. So did the commercial spirit. Books in English sold better than books in Latin. Booksellers and printers were not likely to object to the popular market which now existed for books of all kinds in English. For by the end of the sixteenth century, language had become a prime item in the commodities market.

The limits of language

Shakespeare, then, was born into and flourished in a culture which was intensely interested in questions of language. It is not just that he was fortunate in living at a time when the language was fertile in vocabulary and flexible in its structures – though this is important. But equally important is the extent to which his culture presented him with a consciousness about language which he shared with his generation. Language for Shakespeare and his contemporaries was an issue – even a problem. In his plays, we find his characters continually talking about words and language. A debate which surfaces time and again in his plays and in his poems is the debate about the limits of language – the extent to which words are adequate to 'capture reality', and the way in which meaning continually slips away. In his sonnets he swings from a triumphant faith in the power of language to encapsulate and immortalize the object of his love, to an abject despair at the ability of words even to approximate to the reality. One moment he proclaims

> Yet, do thy worst, old Time. Despite thy wrong,
> My love shall in my verse ever live young.
>
> (Sonnet 19)

while at another he laments

> Who will believe my verse in time to come
> If it were fill'd with your most high deserts?
> Though yet, heaven knows, it is but as a tomb
> Which hides your life and shows not half your parts.
>
> (Sonnet 17)

The problem is not just that his own language is inadequate to the task; it is that even if he succeeded in doing it to his own satisfaction, future generations would not believe him. In fact, the more accurate he is, the less likely he is to be believed. This sonnet is partly a conventional gesture of flattery to the loved one, of course (although the whole point of the poem is to say that it is not, and that the loved one really is more beautiful than words can say!) but it dramatizes effectively the sense in which linguistic communication is at best an approximation.

The theme runs through his plays, too. In *King Lear* it is the main-spring of the action. When Goneril says to Lear, 'Sir, I love you more than word can wield the matter', she is saying much the same thing as the speaker in the sonnet, but she is lying. For Cordelia, who in this same scene must 'love and be silent', these words are the literal truth – which is precisely why she cannot say them to Lear. Other characters confront the problem in different ways. Hamlet lives in a court where, he believes, language has been debased and 'marriage vows [made] As false as dicer's oaths'. At the beginning of his play he finds the burden of silence intolerable ('Break, my heart', he says, 'for I must hold my tongue'); later he takes refuge in 'wild and whirling words', only to feel self-disgust as he attempts to 'unpack [his] heart with words'. And if the heroes and heroines ponder upon the disparity they perceive between language and the reality it is supposed to denote, the villains and the figures of evil exploit that disparity. 'I am not what I am', says Iago, before he weaves his web of words which will ensnare both Othello and Desdemona. This motif of the relationship between appearance and reality surfaces repeatedly in the tragedies, and more often than not it has a linguistic foundation. In *Macbeth*, for example, the signal is given very early that we are in a world in which 'fair is foul and foul is fair' and 'nothing is but what is not' – a world, in other words, in which common-sense notions of language and reality no longer apply. The witches chant spells and enchantments, and words are spoken in incantation which may have power to change reality or which may completely misrepresent reality. And here, as in *King Lear*, language is a prime mover in the plot of the play: the ambiguous words of the witches govern Macbeth's actions from the first moment that he hears them.

More will be said in Part Three of this book concerning the way in which language frequently becomes a theme in Shakespeare's tragedies. Consequently I shall at this point refer to an incident from one of the comedies in order to illustrate one of the most important elements of this theme. In both the comedies and the tragedies there are moments when a character is faced with the breakdown of language and a kind of semantic chaos looms before them. In the following incident from *A Midsummer Night's Dream*, Bottom the Weaver has just been released from a spell which gave him an ass's head and forced the Queen of the Fairies to fall in love with him. Not unnaturally, he believes the whole thing to have been a dream.

> I have had a most rare vision. I have had a dream, past the wit of man to say what dream it was. Man is but an ass if he go about to expound this dream. Methought I was – there is no man can tell what. Methought I was, and methought I had, but man is but a patch'd fool, if he will offer to say what methought I had. The eye of man hath not heard, the ear of man hath not seen, man's hand is not able to taste, his tongue to conceive, nor his heart to report, what my dream was. I will get Peter Quince to write a ballad of this dream. It shall be called 'Bottom's Dream', because it hath no bottom; and I will sing it in the latter end of the play, before the Duke.
>
> (IV, i, ll. 202–20)

Bottom's language repeatedly breaks down as he tries to explain his experience. It is, he concludes, 'past the wit of man to say what the dream was'. Significantly, his response to this is to 'get Peter Quince to write a ballad of this dream'. He looks to art for a form which will begin to deal with the difficulty of saying exactly what he means. For Shakespeare too, art, story-telling, playwriting represented

41

a possible way of coming to terms with, and perhaps overcoming, some of the limitations of language.

A play like *A Midsummer Night's Dream* shows a breakdown of language – and indeed of meaning, for the fairies' wood is a place of some kind of madness – but in a comic and ultimately harmless context. In the tragedies, though, when language and meaning break down, people are destroyed. The last words of the dying Hamlet are 'the rest is silence'; Lear makes his final entrance wailing, simply 'Howl, howl, howl, howl!'; when Othello is eventually convinced of Desdemona's faithlessness his linguistic collapse prefigures a physical collapse as he falls into an epileptic fit; Macbeth reduces life to 'a tale Told by an idiot, full of sound and fury, Signifying nothing'. One of the central issues which Shakespeare's tragedies dramatize is the way in which the meanings which men construct for themselves through their words, their language and their social conventions are subject to collapse.

5 Plays into print

Printing Shakespeare

Popular as Shakespeare was in his own time in the theatre, his plays would have vanished into obscurity if they had not, in their own time been printed. How, then, did he plays find their way into print?

The first point to bear in mind when considering the printing of Shakespeare's plays is that the theatre company for whom he worked, and of which he was a major shareholder, would not have considered it to be wholly in their own interest to have his plays in print. For while the 'book of the play' might have provided some useful publicity to push up the audience figures at the next performance, it would also have made the text available to rival theatre companies. Since the notion of copyright which existed at the time did not extend beyond the rather basic idea that whoever first printed a book was deemed to have the right to print it again, this meant that rival companies would be able, without paying any compensation, to buy a copy of the play, stage it, and effectively steal the Globe's audience. No wonder, then, that the sharers of the Globe would feel at best lukewarm about the idea of making their plays more generally available.

Printers, on the other hand, were very happy to publish plays. They might be regarded by intellectuals as a rather vulgar and ephemeral literary form, but the plays of the more famous dramatists seem to have sold fairly briskly (we can tell this from the number of reprints which many of the plays went through). Moreover, printed copies of playtexts were cheap to produce, since they nearly always came out in flimsy paperback rather than in beautifully-bound hardback editions. The paperback editions, which were always of a single play, not of a collection, were called 'quartos' – a name which refers to their physical size. If you take a standard printer's size sheet of paper, and fold it in half, that is called 'folio' size. Fold it again, so that it is in quarters, and this is called 'quarto' (4°) size. Thus, obviously, a folio covers twice as much area as a quarto. Other sizes were 'octavo' (8°), which was half the size of a quarto; 'duodecimo' (12°), which was a third of the size of quarto; and a tiny format called 'sixteenmo' (16°) – half the size of an octavo! (We use a similar convention today when we buy writing or typing paper; the commonest kind of paper is A4 format – which refers to the fact that paper of a particular size has been folded and cut four times.)

Almost inevitably, the result of this friction between a desire on the part of the printers and booksellers to get hold of the plays and sell them, and the desire of the playhouses to keep the texts to themselves for as long as possible, was that very often plays first found their way into print by way of a kind of literary black market. A printer or bookseller would find that he was being offered a manuscript text of a new play for sale for a few shillings. Beyond checking, as far as he could, that it was not a total fake, there was little for him to do besides accept it or reject it. It did not matter who was selling the text – as noted above, there were no copyright laws as we understand them, so nobody actually owned the words. If it were the author himself selling the manuscript, so much the better, since then the bookseller could be reasonably sure that he was buying the genuine article, and that none of his rivals would be bringing out an alternative or authorized version within a few months. But if it was not the author, but someone else claiming to be acting for him, or even simply offering the text for sale with no questions asked – then in all probability no questions *would* be asked, and the work would be printed and put on sale anyway.

Who brought these unauthorized manuscripts along to the bookseller or printer? While it is possible that some audiences included 'bootleggers', professional scribes who wrote down as much as they could of the dialogue while the play was in progress so that they could then offer the text either to booksellers and printers or to rival theatrical companies, or to both, it is likely that many of the 'pirated' or 'reported' texts of Shakespeare's plays were provided by the actors themselves, sometimes working singly, sometimes in a group. Certainly, some of the existing quartos of Shakespeare's plays are believed to have been provided by actors, who wrote nearly everything down from memory. Actors' memorial reconstructions have their disadvantages, but they have their advantages too. On the debit side, the actors seem to have remembered some parts (presumably their own) better than others, and when memory failed them, they seem to have filled in with paraphrase, or with lines half-remembered from other plays. (In his *Art of Coarse Acting* the writer Michael Green defined a Coarse Actor as one who could remember the lines, but not the order in which they come: it sometimes appears that Shakespeare's plays were pirated by the coarsest actors in his company.) Often, too, the reported text is much shorter than the original, with whole scenes, as well as lines and speeches, missed out. On the credit side, however, some of the reported texts offer far more in the way of stage directions than do texts which have been authorially prepared for the printer. This suggests the mind of the professional actor at work, and it also offers valuable information about how the plays might originally have been staged.

Not all the early versions of Shakespeare's plays were pirated, however. For various reasons – such as the need to respond to the circulation of an unauthorized version of a play – some of them were printed from authentic manuscripts during Shakespeare's own lifetime. Other plays of which 'good' quartos (i.e. quartos which are believed to have descended, via written documents, directly from an authorial manuscript) exist, include *Titus Andronicus, Richard II, Hamlet, Love's Labour's Lost, Henry IV Parts I and II, A Midsummer Night's Dream, The Merchant of Venice,* and *Much Ado About Nothing.* More contentious candidates are *King Lear, Othello* and *Troilus and Cressida.*

In 1616 two events occurred which had important repercussions on the printing of Shakespeare's plays. Firstly, Shakespeare himself died. Secondly, in an unprecedented display of artistic bravado, Ben Jonson included a collection of his own plays to date in his collected *Workes.* This decision to publish his dramatic works alongside his poems was a brave gesture on Jonson's part, and one which attracted to him much scorn from writers of more conventionally 'respectable' literary forms; for no English playwright had ever before had his plays collected together and published as if they were literary *works,* and thus to be taken as seriously as poems or romances, or the great Latin classical writers like Seneca. Much less had any dramatists done the job themselves in their own lifetime. To many of his contemporaries, Jonson must have seemed to be showing an appalling arrogance. In effect, what he was doing was announcing that the playwright had arrived as a literary and cultural force to be reckoned with.

The First Folio (1623)

The initial effect of this conjunction of events was that two stationers, William Jaggard and Thomas Pavier, soon attempted to cash in on the idea of a *Collected Works,* and to take advantage of the fact that a major best-selling playwright had recently died. In 1619 they started to bring out an unauthorized *Complete Works of Shakespeare* in single volumes, play by play. Only five had appeared, however, when the Lord Chamberlain issued an order prohibiting them from producing any further volumes. Almost certainly, the Lord Chamberlain was acting on behalf of the King's Men, two of whose members were themselves preparing a new, revised edition of all his known plays 'cured and perfect'. This was the famous First Folio (p. 46).

John Heminges and Henry Condell had been friends and colleagues of Shakespeare. Both had been actors with the King's Men, and Heminges had also been its business manager. In his will,

A CATALOGVE

of the feuerall Comedies, Hiſtories, and Tragedies contained in this Volume.

Contents page of Shakespeare's first folio.

46

Shakespeare remembered them, along with Richard Burbage, and left each of them 26s 8d to buy a mourning ring by which to remember him. But the method they chose of honouring his memory was far more impressive. With care, intelligence and patience, they prepared Shakespeare's *Complete Works*. They sorted out, as far as was possible, which were the 'good' quartos and which were the bad, avoiding making use of the latter; and they had access to the records of the King's Men – including what remained of the prompt books and other theatrical documents, which allowed them to go further than we have any right to expect in their reconstruction of Shakespeare's texts. Here is what they themselves have to say about their edition:

> It had been a thing, we confess, worthy to have been wished, that the Author himself had lived to have set forth and overseen his own writings. But since it hath been ordained otherwise, and he by death departed from that right, we pray you do not envy his friends the office of their care and pain to have collected and published them, as where before you were abused with diverse stolen and surreptitious copies, maimed and deformed by the frauds and stealths of injurious impostors that exposed them, even those are now offered to your view cured, and perfect of their limbs; and all the rest, absolute in their numbers, as he conceived them.
>
> (Shakespeare, *Complete Works*, ed. Alexander, Collins, p. xxvii)

It was the First Folio which assured Shakespeare his unique place in literary history. It contained eighteen plays which had never before appeared in print, along with eighteen which had appeared in a variety of quartos of varying reliability: of the dramatic canon only *Pericles* was omitted – possibly because of its having been written in collaboration.

The story of the printing of Shakespeare's plays, told this way, seems to be a bit of a fairy-tale plot in itself. The plays were written, some unscrupulous pirates attempted to hijack them, but friends of the author loyally restored them to their true state. Moreover, the tale seems to delineate clearly its own heroes and villains: the actors who first pirated the quartos and Jaggard and Pavier who tried to cash in on Shakespeare's memory are the villains, of course, while the King's Men are the heroes, valiantly trying to ensure that posterity inherited nothing but the true and authorized versions of Shakespeare's plays. Initially, it is true, they seemed reluctant heroes, but with the labours of Heminges and Condell they proved themselves true heroes after all. Inevitably, though, there is the reminder at the end; 'things are not quite as simple as that'. The opportunist Jaggard, who tried to bring out the unauthorized *Complete Works*, was also the main printer of the First Folio. And if it was actors who first kidnapped the plays and sold them down the river, it was actors, too, who restored them.

Editing Shakespeare

There is another warning that should be entered here concerning the story as I have told it. My narrative seems to suggest that although the plays were butchered early on by reported and pirated texts, we can easily identify which ones are 'bad' quartos and which are 'good', and that the bad can safely be ignored. Moreover, it might be thought to imply that the First Folio provides us with a foolproof, authorized version, of which Shakespeare himself would have approved. Unfortunately, once more, things are not as simple as that.

First of all, few books are free of misprints, and the First Folio is no exception – so even if Heminges and Condell were copying direct from one of Shakespeare's own manuscripts, mistakes would have crept in. And in fact the folios abound with mistakes. Moreover, since printing was fairly costly, printers tended not to throw away faulty offprints and start again, but would correct the mistake, and then keep on printing, adding the new 'correct pages' to the pile of faulty ones which had already been run off. As a result, no two extant *copies* of the First Folio are exactly alike: all of them have some variations which are unique to that particular copy. These are comparatively small problems, of course, since careful study (and over the years the First Folios have been very carefully studied indeed) can reveal most of what are misprints and what are not. Much more problematic is the whole matter of the choice of one version of a line or word rather than another.

For we have no manuscript of any of the plays in Shakespeare's own handwriting (except, just possibly, a small fragment of *Sir Thomas More*, to which he may have contributed some passages). Nor is there any sign that he saw his own plays through the presses, or even proof-read them – even in the good quartos. Thus, when there is any discrepancy between one quarto and another, or between a quarto and the First Folio, we cannot turn to Shakespeare himself for any help in deciding which is the correct version. And sometimes these discrepancies are glaring. Take, for example, Hamlet's famous soliloquy, beginning 'To be or not to be'. It is one of the best-known of Shakespeare's soliloquies, and this is how we usually read its opening lines in modern editions, which are based on the First Folio:

To be, or not to be, that is the question:
Whether 'tis nobler in the mind to suffer

The slings and arrows of outrageous fortune,
Or to take arms against a sea of troubles
And by opposing end them. To die – to sleep,
No more; and by a sleep to say we end
The heart-ache and the thousand natural shocks
That flesh is heir to: 'tis a consummation
Devoutly to be wish'd. To die, to sleep;
To sleep, perchance to dream – ay, there's the rub ...

(III, i, ll. 56–65, Arden edn)

However, any Shakespeare enthusiast who sought a text of the play in 1603, a couple of years after its first appearance on the London stage, might have gone to a bookseller and bought a quarto copy of *Hamlet* in which the Prince's soliloquy begins:

To be, or not to be, I there's the point,
To Die, to sleepe, is that all? I all:
No, to sleepe, to dreame, I mary there it goes,
For in that dreame of death, when wee awake,
And borne before an euerlasting Iudge,
From whence no passenger euer return'd,
The undiscouered country, at whose sight
The happy smile and the accursed damn'd.

(1603 quarto, ll. 815–22)

The Hamlet that we know takes ten lines to reach the thought that death may amount to more than a dreamless sleep. The Hamlet of the 1603 quarto leaps there by the beginning of line three, missing out rather a lot of the poetry in the process. And while this does at least have the virtue of brevity, the effect is quite spoilt by the terrible mess he makes of the rest of the sentence, which rambles through to its full stop without ever finding its own main clause.

It is now generally agreed that the 1603 quarto is a corrupt and unreliable reconstruction of the play, undertaken by some unauthorized person. Some of the discrepancies between the texts suggest how it came into being. The unstructured sentence about and 'euerlasting Iudge' and 'the undiscouered country' is a muddled version of what, in the First Folio, appears towards the end of the speech, where Hamlet speaks of 'something after death. The undiscover'd country, from whose bourn No traveller returns'. It is noticeable that the noun 'bourn' from the First Folio, meaning 'boundary', appears in the 1603 quarto as the verb participle 'borne', meaning 'carried'. This use of words which have such similar sounds but different meanings suggests that whoever prepared the manuscript on which the 1603 Folio was based, was working from a memory of how certain words sounded, together with a general sense of the passage. It is widely accepted that the culprit may well have been the actor who played the part of Marcellus.

It is not, however, the demonstrably corrupt texts, like the 1603 quarto of *Hamlet*, which provide the worst headaches for a modern editor of Shakespeare. The seemingly reliable texts, such as the folios and the 'good' quartos, often pose much more intractable problems, since their apparent reliability immediately opens up a series of questions: 'Why is this text reliable?'; 'What were the editors, or the printers, working from?'; 'Was it a manuscript in Shakespeare's handwriting, or a manuscript in somebody else's handwriting which had been copied from one in Shakespeare's?'; 'Could it have been a prompt-book or a previously-published quarto, or perhaps a combination of two or more of these?'; 'Assuming it was a combination, then what guided them when there was any contradiction between one source and another?'; 'Did they always follow the manuscript, if they had one, or did they simply trust their own memories and their own tastes?' Thus the unnerving possibility opens up that we may be reading, studying and performing the *Complete Works of Heminges, Condell and others, Based on an Original by William Shakespeare.*

The 'others' include modern editors of Shakespeare. The fact that the earliest printed texts of Shakespeare's plays do differ from each other, coupled with the need of modern editors to produce a single readable text, has led to a situation today in which, if we go out and buy six different editions of a Shakespeare play we will find that no two of them are exactly alike. Modern editors will already have made a series of choices which will determine the exact nature of the text that we read.

To illustrate some of the ways in which these choices have traditionally been made, let us look at a brief moment from one of Othello's longer speeches. It is early in the play, and he is recounting before the duke how he used to be invited to the house of Desdemona and her father, where he would tell stories of his travels and adventures:

> Wherein I spake of most disastrous chances,
> Of moving accidents by flood and field;
> Of hairbreadth scapes i' th' imminent deadly breach;
> Of being taken by the insolent foe
> And sold to slavery; of my redemption thence,
> And portance in my travel's history;
>
> (*Othello*, I, ii, ll. 133–8)

The passage is given here as I found it in my old *Complete Works of Shakespeare* (edited by Peter Alexander, and published by Collins): for many years, therefore, I have been reading this speech as I print it above. I want to focus only on the last line of the passage, where Othello talks about his 'portance in my travel's history'.

Othello was not printed at all until six years after Shakespeare's death, and nearly twenty years after it was first performed. In 1622 it was brought out in quarto, and then a year later it appeared in the 1623 folio. In neither of these versions does the line appear as quoted above. In the 1622 quarto the line comes out as 'With it all my travel's history'. In the folio, it reads 'And portance in my travellour's history'. Not until the publishing of a second quarto of *Othello* in 1630 do we get the line as I have quoted it. This second quarto, however, is believed to have been a compilation of the two existing printed editions. It has no authority based on any manuscripts: it is simply an attempt to get the best of both worlds.

These, then, are the possibilities:

'And with it all my travel's history' (First quarto, 1622)
'And portance in my travellour's history' (Folio, 1623)
'And portance in my travel's history' (Second quarto, 1630)

Which is the right version? We simply do not know. Editors choose one reading over another by virtue of a range of criteria. They have to take into account the ways in which words change their meanings and their spellings over the years, and the fact that handwriting on original manuscripts can be difficult for printers to read when they are setting up their typeface. They have to estimate the probabilities of corruption in early printed texts, from the likelihood of the original manuscript being pirated through to the possibility that a compositor has misread an individual word or made a careless error such as putting an 'n' upside down into the printing press form so that it comes out as a 'u'. They have to bear in mind the appropriateness of a word to its grammatical context and to its dramatic context, and weigh up the different meanings and implications generated by their decision. The process is a complex one.

In many cases, moreover, there may not be a 'right' answer. For plays, unlike most poems or most novels, do not freeze into their final form when first they are made public. A play may change between the first day of a rehearsal and the last, or between the first performance of the run and the last, or between its original production and a revival, as the playwright or the company decide that certain scenes do not work, or are too long, or need lengthening. While it is very rare for a poet to rewrite a poem that has been published, and even rarer for a novelist to rewrite a novel that has been published, it is very common indeed for playwrights to make changes to a play, either after performance or after publication. This is especially true in a context where, as in Elizabethan London, the published play is seen as ephemeral anyway; there is then no pressure to say 'Well, it's in print now, let's let well alone.' It is even more likely to be changed if the publication is a pirated one in the first place.

What this amounts to is this: that some of the discrepancies between various editions might be due, not to early errors of transmission or transcription, but to the fact that the text has been revised by the author. This throws the whole game into disarray, for now, even if we could prove that such-and-such a quarto was based on a manuscript in Shakespeare's own hand, we would still have to prove that changes in any later editions of the play were not the result of authorial revision. We will have to decide what we mean by 'authentic', and whether we are more interested in recovering the plays as they were first performed, or in the state they might be in after the author has had second thoughts about them and revised or rewritten them. What is more, we will have to entertain the possibility that some of the bad quartos which we have might – just 'might' – be bad, not because they were badly-reported by actors who were unable to remember very precisely the brilliance of Shakespeare's language, but because Shakespeare himself wrote a less-than-perfect first draft, which he did not revise until *after* the first performances. At its most subversive, this line of thought leads to this: that some of the improvements between a bad quarto and a later good quarto, or the folio, might be the result of Shakespeare having written a bad line which was later changed (either deliberately or unintentionally) by someone else into something better. The notion of somebody writing even a single line better than Shakespeare is so alien to us that it is probably better not to dwell on it too long, lest we find it too disturbing. But the scenario which I have just sketched out is distinctly possible.

I do not wish to paint too extreme a picture. It is true that Shakespeare, more than any other great author of the last four hundred years, 'absents' himself from his own texts, leaving little or no manuscript trace, not preparing the text for the printer, seeming, in fact, hardly to care whether they get printed or not and leaving us to guess whether or not he is responsible for any of the later changes in versions. (Compare him to Ben Jonson, meticulously preparing his own texts and seeing them through the press.) But if it is true that we can never be absolutely sure that what we are reading or hearing is precisely what Shakespeare wrote, and that there is in all of this an element of the party game of 'Chinese Whispers', which might detract from the pleasant illusion of being allowed direct and unmediated insight into a writer's mind, then we can take comfort in the fact that nobody has deliberately attempted to distort the message, that the worst that anyone can be accused of is carelessness (or improvisation!), and that from the time of Heminges and Condell, many intelligent, patient and knowledgeable people have put in a tremendous amount of work to offer us as honest an account as possible of what Shakespeare *did* write.

The plays on which this study concentrates, the four major tragedies, appeared originally in the following ways. *Macbeth* was not printed at all until 1623, when Heminges and Condell included it in the First Folio. We know comparatively little about the history of *Macbeth*'s composition, although over the years many scholars have claimed that various scenes and passages in the play are interpolations by other writers, such as Thomas Middleton. In particular, the scenes or parts of scenes in which Hecate appears (III, v and IV, i, 11, 39–43) are held to be suspect. The exact extent of the interpolations is something about which we can only guess, as is the possibility that other Shakespearean scenes might have been removed to make way for them. Stanley Wells, in his capacity as general editor of *The Oxford Complete Shakespeare*, is pessimistic, saying that 'the surviving text gives every sign of being an adaptation: if so there is no means of recovering what Shakespeare originally wrote'.

Othello, as mentioned above, was never published in Shakespeare's own lifetime, and first appeared in print in 1622 in a quarto. The version which Heminges and Condell printed in the 1623 folio is a little longer, and has more than a thousand differences in wording; modern editorial scholarship tends towards the opinion that the folio represents some of Shakespeare's revisions of the original text of the play, although many editors also believe that it contains some non-Shakespearean distortions. There is also a later quarto of 1630, which seems to have been printed from a collation of the 1623 folio and the earlier quarto.

Hamlet is a more problematic case. The 'bad quarto' of 1603, which we have looked at briefly already, is almost certainly a text constructed from the memories of one or more actors; it is very short and not at all reliable. In 1604 a much more carefully printed second quarto edition came out. This was nearly twice as long as its predecessor, and was probably printed from Shakespeare's own manuscripts. It is generally supposed, and there is no reason to doubt this, that this 1604 quarto was authorized by Shakespeare and his colleagues at the Globe in an attempt to undo some of the damage which had been done to the play's reputation by the scrappiness of the unauthorized 1603 version. The folio version is different again: about 300 of the second quarto's lines are missing, and seventy new lines have been added.

There is debate as to the nature of the relationship between these three texts of *Hamlet*. It was once thought that the 1603 quarto represented Shakespeare's earliest version of the play, which he later rewrote. However, modern scholarship now suggests that although the play may indeed have passed through various stages of growth, the earliest stage is represented not by the earliest printed text but by the 'authorized text', the second quarto of 1604. Some of the revisions had already been incorporated by the actor or actors into their memorial reconstruction in the 'bad quarto' of 1603 – which is therefore not to be discounted entirely. The folio, it is now believed, represents a more reliable text of that revised version.

The most difficult case of all, though, is that of *King Lear*. It originally appeared in quarto in 1608, and the version which appears in the 1623 folio is very different from that earlier text. On the one hand, 300 lines from the 1608 quarto are omitted from the folio; on the other hand the folio text contains approximately 100 lines which do not appear in the quarto. These changes alter the balance of the play in ways that are subtle but not insignificant. For example, in the quarto, the Duke of Albany puts up a much more spirited resistance to Goneril's evil than he does in the later folio text, which omits his most vigorous condemnations of his wife. Goneril in the quarto is roundly condemned: in the folio she is virtually unopposed by any force for humanity. In the quarto, too, the shocking scene in which Gloucester is blinded by Cornwall is followed by a moment in which some trace of humanity is reinstated. Appalled by what they have just witnessed – and been involved in – two of Cornwall's servants say:

> *Second Servant* I'll never care what wickedness I do
> If this man come to good.
> *Third Servant* If she live long,
> And in the end meet the old course of death
> Women will all turn monsters
> *Second Servant* Let's follow the old earl, and get the bedlam
> To lead him where he would; his roguish madness
> Allows itself to anything.
> *Third Servant* Go thou; I'll fetch some flax and whites of eggs
> To apply to his bleeding face. Now heaven help him!
> (*King Lear*, III, vii, ll. 98–106)

This exchange offers some slight amelioration of the horror which has preceded them. When the great modern theatre director Peter Brook omitted it from his 1962 production of the play, it caused a great controversy, and Brook was accused of tampering with the text in the pursuit of his bleak vision. But it was not Brook who first made the cut: the folio version of the play also omits the conversation between the servants.

The *King Lear* which we usually read is neither the quarto nor the folio version, but a conflation or mix of the two. Over the years, editors have agreed to amalgamate the two texts, which, it was assumed are both imperfect versions of a single Shakespearean text, the *King Lear* which Shakespeare really wrote. Recent scholarship has challenged this view, however, suggesting that the two texts, with all their differences, represent a play which Shakespeare wrote in the form published in 1608, and which he then revised. The 1623 folio text, it is now claimed, largely represents Shakespeare's own rewriting of the play. This more recent and radical view of the text has led the editors of the *Oxford Shakespeare* to publish *King Lear* as two separate texts, and to argue that attempts to conflate the quarto and the folio into a single play obscure Shakespeare's own intentions. It has also led scholars to ask serious questions about the way in which we have traditionally gone about editing Shakespeare: the traditional search for the single, fixed, authoritative text has been replaced by the more fluid notion of plays which underwent a series of revisions. A more radical interpretation of the implications of this argues that the instability of the text means that it is impossible to locate authorial intention at all.

The recent important research which has been carried out on the texts of *King Lear* (and other plays) by the editors of the *Oxford Shakespeare* and other like-minded scholars may well change the way in which future generations read these plays. We should be grateful for this work, and for the work of the unconventional textual scholar who occasionally defies conventions, rethinks some of the editorial problems of the plays, and thereby offers us new ways of thinking about them. Above all they have stimulated an awareness that the text of any Shakespeare play has been produced by generations of scholars, critics and editors, most of whom have seen it as their task to recover what their author originally wrote. We should be grateful too, therefore, for the broad level of general agreement about textual issues which still exists among conventional modern editions of the plays. For those who wish to follow the intricate paths by which many of the texts were established, the Arden Shakespeare Series is still, as it has been for many years, the essential starting point and a standard work of reference. In this book quotations from the four major tragedies are taken from the Arden texts, while for other plays the Alexander edition of *Complete Works* (Collins) has seen used.

Part Two
Shakespeare and the Theatre of His Time

6 Elizabethan and Jacobean tragedy

The great age of English tragedy

Not every age has produced tragedies – or at least, not tragedies that are still read today. Broadly speaking, when we look back over the history of English literature, certain ages seem to have put their best energies into particular literary forms: for the Victorians it was the large-scale realist novel that demanded their greatest effort; for the early eighteenth century it was the urbane satire in verse or prose; for the Romantics it was the contemplative poem. This is not to imply that there were no novels written during the Romantic period, or that the Victorians did not write poetry: we are talking here only about some basic trends and the way in which particular art forms capture the imagination of a culture at particular times. The late sixteenth and early seventeenth century in England was a period when there was a variety of literary activity going on: lyrics, epics, satires, jest-books, sermons, sonnets, essays all abounded. But it is usual to see this age as the great age of the English drama, and in particular as the great age of English tragedy. It is worth asking why this was so.

A relationship may be posited, for example, between the writing of great tragedies in the early years of the seventeenth century and the social and economic conditions which were prevalent in England at the time. This relationship, it should be warned, is not a simple and direct one. Perhaps it would be reassuringly straightforward if it were: if, for example, one could say that the predominance of tragedies in this period were a direct result or expression of a social and economic crisis. Things are rarely that neat in literary history, however. The years we are talking about, from about 1590 through to about 1615 were not devoid of social, political and economic problems, as earlier sections have shown, but the crises of the period were no greater than those of the years immediately before and after this period. The constitutional and ideological upheavals of the mid-sixteenth century and the revolutionary years of the mid-seventeenth were more traumatic than anything that was happening between 1590 and 1615. If anything, it is more realistic to see this period as a comparative lull between the various storms which preceded and followed it.

Moreover, for the Jacobeans themselves it probably did not seem to be an 'age of tragedy' at all. What records we have of plays in performance at the time show that comedies, romances and heroic tales of adventure were every bit as popular amongst Elizabethan and Jacobean audiences. It may well be that the apparent pre-eminence of tragic art in the period is actually a trick of the light, visible only from the vantage point of the twentieth century. To this end the question could almost be rephrased as, 'What is it about our own reading habits, about our own cultural biases and value-systems that makes the tragedies of the period loom so large in our conscious-ness?' Nor is it just in the twentieth century that tragedy has been ranked high in the spectrum of the arts: other ages have also felt its importance. There are a variety of reasons for this: tragedy is one of the oldest forms of literature we have, dating back to the Ancient Greek writers, Aeschylus, Sophocles and Euripides. Not only do many of their plays survive, but so too does a seminal work of criticism which deals centrally with tragedy – Aristotle's *Poetics*, one of the foundations of Western literary criticism and theory. More recent theories of tragedy have concentrated on its ritual element and origins, and stressed the links between tragedy and the varieties of religious experience by means of which men and women have long tried to make sense of their world. And even without this religious dimension, of course, the subject-matter of tragedy demands to be taken seriously: stories of men and women in extreme situations, facing death and destruction.

What we are dealing with is not a question of quantity but one of quality – even if that notion of 'quality' can be seen to be culturally conditioned. It is not the case that suddenly every playwright in the early seventeenth century was writing tragedies; rather it is that so many of the tragedies which *were* written were so good, and have lasted so long, and are still read, performed, studied and enjoyed today. There seems to have been a sudden advance in tragedy-writing in the late sixteenth and early seventeenth centuries, as if writers now had at their disposal new techniques or new subject-matter. The result was that not only Shakespeare but many of his contem-poraries – Tourneur, Webster, Middleton and others – began writing plays which gave access to a new range of tragic experience.

The 'lull between . . . storms' (which is how I earlier characterized this period) is itself an intensely interesting time. The shock waves of old upheavals were dying away, but their influence might still be felt. More importantly, men and women were finding methods of inter-nalizing the great ideological and social changes of the Reformation and its aftermath, of incorporating them into their ways of life, into the structures of their thoughts, beliefs and feelings. Simultaneously, the distant rumblings of future conflicts were to be heard in the land. The Earl of Essex's abortive uprising marked for good and all the last twitches of old-fashioned aristocratic power; no single nobleman was able any longer to pose an effective challenge to the monarchy. What was emerging as a force in the land, however, was Parliament, with its base among the higher gentry and bourgeoisie. The shift from a feudal economy to a capitalist one had implications in terms of power politics, as it did in terms of ideology. The different patterns of thought which had been set into conflict by the Reformation were still a dormant element of political life, and the seeds of future Puritan political strength were germinating in the soil of Jacobean England. The 'new philosophy calls all in doubt', said John Donne:'...' Tis all in pieces, all coherence gone' – and one of the legacies of the sixteenth century's intellectual upheavals was an increasing spirit of sceptical enquiry, not only into the natural and theological foundations of the universe but also into the social and political institutions which had always been promoted as their natural corollaries. Attitudes to James himself and to the court over which he presided were complex and contradictory. To some he was a breath of fresh air coming after the stifling last few years of Elizabeth's long-drawn-out reign: the bad harvests and subsequent inflation of the 1590s had left the country feeling the strain. To others, however, James's self-promotion and his favouritism provided dreadful evidence of what the world was coming to: certainly his wanton profligacy helped neither the economy nor his subjects – save for the lucky few who were the beneficiaries of his misplaced generosity. For many people he was both a blessing and a curse. Certainly, his accession was felt to mark some sort of new age, and it generated a strange blend of enthusiasm and cynicism.

The picture I am painting is of a time when things were felt to be changing, for better or for worse. Every age is an age of change, of course, but there are some ages which are more preoccupied with their own changeableness than others, and the period 1590–1615 was one of these. Literary forms frequently emerge and evolve in response to such societal pressures; however it would seem that the literary form most likely to be generated in such a time would be one which would concern itself with current social trends, and which would look with a sceptical eye at what was happening in the world around. The form which the age demanded seems to have been not tragedy but *satire*.

And this is what seemed about to happen: the 1590s was the first great decade of English satire. Writers such as Marston, Middleton, Hall, Donne, Lodge, Nashe, and many others produced a torrent of works whose roughness of metre was matched by a roughness of tone. Pessimism, assertiveness and anger were the keynotes of these satires, in which the shortcomings of the age were catalogued and castigated in ways which sometimes resembled the religious homily, sometimes the personal libel. A generation of writers took it upon themselves to become the correctors of morals for society – and society responded predictably. On 1 June 1599 the Archbishop of Canterbury and the Bishop of London ordered the burning of a great list of satirical writings, and issued an edict prohibiting the future publication of formal satires.

The actual efficacy of that edict is open to question: not all the books listed were burned, nor did publication of satire immediately cease. But it was a warning shot across the bows of certain writers, and what happened next was influenced by the Bishops' Edict to some extent. Robbed of one form of expression, writers of satires turned sharply to another. The satirist's voice was heard increasingly on the stage from 1599 onwards, and while 'pure' formal satire never took comfortably to the stage, it was soon found that satire blended with either comedy or tragedy could be used to powerful effect. John Marston's *The Malcontent* featured a character-type which reappears throughout the drama of the period: the cynical commentator on a corrupt society. This is the new element which, incorporated into the tragedies of the early 1600s, allows for the increased range and relevance of the best tragedy. When Hamlet snarls that 'Denmark's a prison' or makes fun of the foppish Osric; when Lear discourses on the 'image of authority' or Edmund upon 'the excellent foppery of the world'; when Iago complains that 'preferment goes by letter and affection, not by the old gradation', the authentic voice of the Elizabethan satirist is heard. Tragedy, a dramatic form which traditionally focuses sympathetically upon the misfortunes of a single central protagonist assimilates into itself a literary form which takes a cynical panoramic look at the ills of a whole society. The result is a broadening of perspective, a greater variety and inter-relationship of tones, and a significantly enriched kind of drama.

Definitions of tragedy

One thing which many writers on tragedy now tend to agree upon is that it is almost impossible to reach a satisfactory definition of the term 'tragedy' itself. The scheme which Aristotle articulated in his *Poetics* concerning the noble hero with the fatal flaw (*hamartia*), whose reversal of fortunes (*peripeteia*) is brought about by some moment of recognition (*anagnorisis*) and whose fate arouses pity and fear, and suggests some kind of spiritual cleansing (*catharsis*) has long been found unhelpful. When it is borne in mind that Aristotle was not laying down prescriptive rules for all time, but attempting a description of the plays written by his contemporaries and near-contemporaries, this is not surprising. What *is* surprising is that there are still people, even today, who assume that Aristotle's two-thousand-year-old description was actually a timeless set of rules to which all tragedies must adhere. It is inappropriate to apply the criteria of Greek tragedy of the pre-Christian era to the plays of the Jacobean age. Indeed, the very term 'tragedy' is one which was used in a variety of ways by Shakespeare and his contemporaries, and the instability of generic boundaries which allowed for a free merging of tragedy and satire is a basic feature of the drama of the time.

When John Heminges and Henry Condell published the First Folio of Shakespeare's plays, they divided those plays into different genres. They decided that Shakespeare had written, basically, three types of play, which they called histories, tragedies and comedies. The plays which they designated 'tragedies' were as follows:

Coriolanus
Titus Andronicus
Romeo and Juliet
Timon of Athens
Julius Caesar
Macbeth
Hamlet
King Lear
Othello
Antony and Cleopatra
Cymbeline

It seems, perhaps, a fairly obvious list. Most of the plays that we would expect to be in it are in it. There are one or two, like *Cymbeline*, which today would be more likely to be classed elsewhere. *Troilus and Cressida*, which was printed with the tragedies but omitted from the title-page because of the lateness of its inclusion, is another case in point. But on the whole it seems unexceptionable. The point is, however, that it was Heminges and Condell who made the decision to group the plays in this way, and it was they who first decided that certain plays should be seen in a certain light. For example, we would not think twice about classing *King Lear* as a tragedy: for many people it is *the* tragedy above all others. It may therefore seem perverse to suggest that since it is a play which deals with British history and a British king (albeit in a misty past), and since it uses the same Elizabethan history book for its source material as do the various history plays, then it should be classed along with those history plays rather than with the tragedies. But when *King Lear* was first published in quarto form in 1608 it was indeed entitled *The History of King Lear*. And while it may have been Shakespeare who was responsible for some of the textual changes which took place between the 1608 quarto and the 1623 folio editions, there is no sign that he himself had anything to do with the assigning of various plays to various genres. It seems to have been Heminges and Condell who decided that

King Lear was a tragedy when they compiled the Folio in 1623. When Shakespeare wrote it, he may well (if he thought about these things at all) have thought of it as a history play. On the other hand, both *Richard II* and *Richard III*, which we, along with Heminges and Condell, customarily think of as history plays, were originally entitled *The Tragedy of King Richard II* and *The Tragedy of King Richard III*. In all probability Shakespeare's own contemporaries would not necessarily have thought of history and tragedy as being mutually exclusive.

We need, therefore, a certain flexibility in the way we think about the relationships between the genres. We should be very wary of supposing that when Shakespeare wrote *Hamlet, Macbeth, Othello*, or *King Lear*, he was working according to any overall model of what constitutes a tragedy. It may be that for most Elizabethans, including Shakespeare himself, a tragedy simply meant a story which ended unhappily. This is certainly how Shakespeare's contemporary, the playwright Thomas Heywood, saw it. In 1612 he wrote, in his *Apology for Actors*, that 'Tragedies and comedies ... differ thus: in comedies, *turbulenta prima, tranquilla ultima*; in tragedies, *tranquilla prima, turbulenta ultima*: comedies begin in trouble and end in peace; tragedies begin in calms and end in tempest.' Perhaps we create problems for ourselves if we approach the tragedies of the English Renaissance with anything more rigid in mind than this.

Yet it is hard not to bring certain assumptions to bear on Shakespeare's tragedies – assumptions about the way in which we will respond to the hero of a tragedy as opposed to the hero of a history or a comedy, for example, or about how we expect the plot to develop. These assumptions are always with us, whether consciously or unconsciously, and they usually comprise a mixture of ideas inherited from a variety of sources. Some of these assumptions might be ones which we would share with an Elizabethan or Jacobean audience; others are the result of more recent events in the history of ideas. For example, we have inherited, from writers and thinkers of the nineteenth and early twentieth centuries, additional senses of the word 'tragedy' which would not have been available to Shakespeare's generation. Debates have taken place concerning the 'tragic spirit' and the 'tragic view of life'; about whether tragedy is possible in a Christian or post-Christian culture; about whether words like 'tragedy' and 'tragic' should be reserved for dramatic purposes, or whether they can be appropriately used to refer to events in real life. Many of these debates would have seemed incomprehensible or irrelevant even to a well-educated man or woman in early seventeenth-century England. This is not to say, however, that Shakespeare and his contemporaries were not themselves interested in attempting to define the nature and function of tragedy in their own time.

The function of tragedy: a Renaissance debate – Sidney and Greville

Elizabethan rhetoricians were particularly fond of constructing rules and definitions about language and literature and although many of these were arbitrary and contradictory, we can occasionally catch a glimpse of how people of Shakespeare's England might have thought of the purpose of tragedy. One note that is sounded repeatedly is the note of moralizing. In *The Art of English Poesy* (published 1589), George Puttenham proclaims that the function of tragedy is to show the 'mutability of fortune, and the just punishment of God in revenge of a vicious and evil life', Ben Jonson, in his collection of observations entitled *Timber* (published 1641), saw tragedy as having the function, which Sir Philip Sidney ascribed to poetry in general, to 'both delight and teach'. Sidney himself, in fact, was a little more specific concerning tragedy as a moral and political force. In *An Apology for Poetry* he talked of

> ...the high and excellent Tragedy, that openeth the greatest wounds, and showeth forth the ulcers that are covered with tissue; that maketh kings fear to be tyrants, and tyrants manifest their tyrannical humours; that, with stirring the affects of admiration and commiseration, teacheth the uncertainty of this world, and upon how weak foundations gilden roofs are builded.
>
> (*An Apology for Poetry* (1595), reprinted in
> *English Critical Texts*, ed. Enright and Chickera,
> Oxford University Press, 1962, p. 25)

Sidney's *Apology for Poetry* is in general a rather mild document, which spends most of its time attempting to prove by a series of ingenious stratagems that poetry (meaning any kind of creative fiction) is not harmful either to the state or to the mind of the individual because it does not engage directly with real life. The poet, says Sidney famously, 'nothing affirmeth, and therefore never lieth'. The *Apology* is, consequently, a surprising place to find the kind of definition of tragedy which Sidney offers here. For this definition has three main elements, and all of them work by means of images which suggest a vision of tragedy which is both radical and political. The image of tragedy displaying the ulcers covered with tissue suggests tragedy as a stripping away of a protective covering; the medical imagery is reminiscent of many Renaissance definitions of satire, and implies something which shows the truth beneath the surface. Certainly, in many Renaissance tragedies – including Shakespeare's own – the spirit of satire is often present.

The central image – that tragedy 'maketh kings fear to be tyrants, and tyrants manifest their tyrannical humours' – is tantalizingly ambiguous: it could just be referring to the subject-matter of tragedies as being kings and tyrants, but it is more likely to be expressing a more specific idea — that tragedies may be aimed at a royal audience, and that the moral lesson they have to offer is aimed in particular at tyrannical, or would-be tyrannical, rulers.

The final part of the definition, where Sidney talks about tragedy teaching the uncertainty of this world, sounds conventional enough, and could be describing any simple Christian commonplace. But the political context has already been established with the references to kings and tyrants, and so when Sidney comes to the image of 'gilden roofs' built upon weak foundations, the implied picture is that of a palace tumbling to the ground. Sidney himself was hardly a revolutionary figure: indeed he was in many respects the very model of an aspiring and conformist young Elizabethan courtier. Yet when he talks about tragedy, his language takes on an apocalyptic tone, redolent of that streak of European Puritanism which believed that heavenly justice would eventually bring about the reversal of earthly social structures. At any rate, his fluid definition seems to suggest a conception of tragedy which is both transcendent and topical, and whose effect is to be sought both in the abstract realms of metaphysics and in the pragmatic world of *realpolitik*.

Sidney's close friend and biographer, Fulke Greville, in his *Life of Sidney* (*c.* 1610–12), also stresses that element in tragedy which infers the working out of a divine scheme. He, however, puts a rather different stress on it. He contrasts the tragic drama of his own day with that of the ancient world, and asserts that classical tragedy had been essentially concerned 'to exemplify the disastrous miseries of man's life ... and so out of that melancholic vision, stir horror, or murmur against Divine Providence'. In contrast, he sees modern tragedy as being an illustration of the working-out of 'God's revenging aspect upon every particular sin, to the despair, or confusion of mortality'. To put it another way, ancient tragedy was rebellious and contentious, showing man raging and striving against the authority and the power of the gods. Elizabethan and Jacobean tragedy, says Greville, is conformist and submissive; it does not offer resistance to God's will, but on the contrary it functions to confirm the workings of Divine Providence.

It may be, incidentally, that Greville had a rather personal reason for taking the line that he does. A few years earlier he had himself written a tragedy based on the story of Antony and Cleopatra, a play which he then immediately suppressed in the light of suggestions that it might prove politically dangerous. He feared that it would be read as a topical satire, criticizing 'vices in the present Governors, and government'; the specific danger was that it might be read as a reference to the relationship between Elizabeth and Essex. If Sidney sees it as one of the great strengths of tragedy that it can 'catch the conscience of the King', Greville, at one stage in his life at least, seems to have seen it as one of the great dangers of the form. By the time he writes his *Life of Sidney* he simply wants to insist that tragedy is essentially conformist and non-contentious.

The points of view of Greville and Sidney, resembling each other as they do in outline but differing in points of emphasis, set the parameters for debates about the nature of Elizabethan and Jacobean tragedy which are still going on. Sidney's phrase about kings fearing to be tyrants finds sympathy with those critics and scholars who tend to see the drama of the period as being intensively engaged with contemporary political issues. Greville's account of tragedy as a demonstration of providential theology has been used by some twentieth-century critics in support of a reading of Renaissance tragedy which insists on its Christian spirit. It might be more useful for students of Shakespeare's tragedies to rephrase Greville's assertions in the form of questions: *is* a play like *Othello* essentially about the workings out of a divine and providential scheme? Is there no sense of 'horror or murmur against Divine Providence' at the end of *King Lear*? In recent years, Greville's argument has been turned inside out by some critics, who have argued that in the tragedies of the period can be charted a disintegration of that very belief in the workings of Divine Providence which Greville says they illustrate.

Varieties of tragedy

Two main points have been made so far. First, that tragedy in the early seventeenth century was not a single clearly-defined entity with rigid boundaries but a loose 'umbrella' term which referred to a variety of plays. Secondly, that Sidney and Greville have different, even contradictory, ideas as to what tragedy does or should do. These two points should be seen in the light of one another: the very variety of the plays which could be called tragedies ensures that both Sidney and Greville are right. Both of them could point to individual texts which would exemplify their own ideal of tragedy. Playwrights in Elizabethan and Jacobean England did not have a single unanimous 'message' to deliver about the human condition. Rather they were engaged in explorations of various situations in which men and women find themselves: and if these explorations led some writers towards an affirmation that Heaven will put all to rights, it led others towards an increasingly sceptical view of the workings of the universe.

To insist on the variety of Elizabethan and Jacobean tragedy is not to say that it was so varied as to be undefinable. With the benefit of hindsight, we can discern in some plays of the late sixteenth and early seventeenth centuries certain common features. These were not rules that authors of the time were bound by, but tendencies that began to appear in their works for a variety of reasons. It is these tendencies which make it possible to risk some general statements about the tragedy of the period. Even so, it is probably better to think in terms of varieties of tragedy rather than a single monolithic form called 'Tragedy' and to bear in mind continually the way in which these varieties are related to other dramatic forms. The four plays of Shakespeare with which this book primarily deals all have things in common with each other; they also all have their roots in the drama of the time and each of them – though to varying extents – has drawn on the available traditions of tragedy of the time.

Tragedy and revenge

One of the most popular stories of the Renaissance theatre is the story of the revenger. In this, an initial crime is committed, either early on in the play itself or before the play begins; for various reasons the usual processes of law and justice are unavailable to avenge that crime, and so an individual, working outside the law, sees it as his duty to exact a private revenge upon the criminal, who is often politically very powerful. The play charts the protagonist's attempts to do this: this may involve a period of doubt, in which the protagonist decides whether or not to go ahead with the revenge, and it may also involve some complex plotting (in both senses of the word) as the protagonist decides to take revenge in an apt or fitting way. The revenger, by deciding to take revenge, places himself outside the normal moral order of things, and often becomes more and more isolated as the play progresses – an isolation which at its most extreme becomes madness. Usually, but not always, the revenger dies in the act of committing the revenge or is sentenced to death immediately afterwards. Other typical features of this story are: the setting, which is usually in a European Catholic court; the appearance of a ghost, often in order to charge the hero with the duty of revenge; the revenger is often a malcontent-figure –an alienated commentator on the society of the play, sceptical and satirical and having an especially close relationship with the audience by means of asides and soliloquies; the original crime which is to be avenged is nearly always sexual or violent and very often both; nearly always the crime has been perpetrated against a member of the revenger's family.

There is an inherent tension in the revenge story – the tension between the demands of the narrative and the demands of conventional morality. On the one hand the revenger's point of view usually dominates the play. It is not just that we are made to feel he has a valid motive for revenge – although usually we are made to feel that. But on a more basic and obvious level, the very nature of the story encourages the audience to *want* the revenge plot to go ahead. The pleasure of the story demands that it should. But it should not be supposed, therefore, that revenge plays merely dramatize a current Elizabethan assumption that private revenge was morally justifiable. On the contrary, Church, State and conventional morality were unanimous in their insistence that private revenge was not to be tolerated. Authorities, both English and European, were clear on this point. It is repugnant on theological grounds, since Christian orthodoxy posits a world ordered by Divine Providence, in which revenge is a sin and a blasphemy, endangering the soul of the revenger. The following extract from a sermon by Edwin Sandys, published in 1585, is typical:

> For so doth Ecclesiasticus well teach us: 'He that seeketh vengeance shall find vengeance of the Lord; and he will surely keep his sins.' Forgive thy neighbour the hurt that he hath done to thee: so shall thy sins be forgiven thee also, when thou prayest. Should a man bear hatred against a man, and desire forgiveness of the Lord? He will shew no mercy to a man that is like himself; and will he ask forgiveness of his own sins? If he that is but flesh nourish hatred, and ask pardon of God, who will entreat for his sins?

The key biblical text was Romans 12:19: 'Dearly beloved, avenge not yourselves, but rather give place unto wrath: for it is written, Vengeance is mine; I will repay, saith the Lord.' We hear condemnation of private revenge everywhere we turn in the literature of the time. Not only was it seen as theologically repellent, but also as unnatural – as the 1602 English translation of Innocent Gentillet's *Discourse . . . Against Nicholas Machiavelli The Florentine* makes clear.

> Surely [revenge] is not onely farre from all Christian pietie, but also from all humanitie and common sence; yea, brute beasts, which have no reason, are not so unreasonable: for a dog which we have offended, will be appeased with a piece of bread . . . and for such as say, that vengeance is lawfull by right of nature, are greatly deceived, as the beasts named before doe shew.

On a more pragmatic level, the potential psychological dangers to the revenger were stressed by John Eliot in his translation of de Loque's *Discourse of Warre and Single Combat* (1591):

> [Revenge] maketh thee take no quiet rest in thine house, and thou hast no assurance to bee in the fieldes: shee tosseth thee with continuall cares, she tormenteth thee with ten thousand feares, shee carrieth thy judgement and reason cleane out of their proper seats, and playeth the tyrant over them. When thou thinkest thy selfe safest, then shee threatneth thee most: shee is importunate with thee, shee gnaweth thee to the hart, she devoureth thee.

Even Francis Bacon's famous definition, which has so often been quoted as proof of Elizabethan approval of private revenge, is actually a condemnation of it. In his *Essays* (1597–1625) Bacon says that 'Revenge is a kind of wild justice', seeming thereby to condone the practice. But he goes on, 'which the more man's nature runs to, the more ought law to weed it out. For as for the first wrong, it doth but offend the law; but the revenge of that wrong putteth the law out of office' (*Essays*, ed. Michael Hawkins, J.M. Dent, 1972, p.13).

Bacon, the lawyer, pinpoints the key legal issue: that private revenge 'putteth the law out of office'. If the Church condemned revenge because it was contrary to the law of God, the state condemned it because it usurped the function of the law of the land. The revenger, by taking the law into his or her own hands, was implicitly challenging the political authority of the state.

We should not, then, assume that common opinion in the Elizabethan age sanctioned private revenge. On the contrary, revenge was vociferously and unanimously condemned. When the revenger in a play decides, eventually, to take arms against the sea of troubles, he might claim to be the instrument of providence, and thus seek some sort of theological justification. But few revenge-heroes of the period have much confidence in this argument. And in any case, the revenger has lost faith in the 'proper mechanisms' of justice, those legal institutions which have been ordained for the working out of God's justice. Rather than patiently waiting for Divine Providence to make things turn out right, the revenger takes the task upon himself. In doing so, he effectively rejects the official wisdom of a culture, a wisdom which portrays the universe as ordered and controlled according to Divine Providence, working through earthly authority. In its place, the revenger substitutes a more secular vision of the universe, one which sees it as disordered, violent and individualistic. It is the conflict between these two visions of the world which the revenge play dramatizes.

The basic revenge story may be subject to any number of variations. The outcome may turn out to be comic rather than tragic; the tone may end up as being ironic rather than serious. The story itself does not always surface in its entirety. In some plays it may be relegated to a sub-plot, or only faint shadows of it may appear; in others, it may be displaced and varied in any number of ways. In Shakespeare's tragedies traces of the revenge story can be seen in *Macbeth* (a version of the corrupt ruler who is so often the avenger's main target) and in *Othello*, where Iago plays the part of an avenging malcontent in response to Othello's imagined cuckolding of him. Even in *King Lear* a variation of the story crops up in the sub-plot. The wronged Edgar has no recourse to any figure of authority either in his father's house nor in the court; accordingly he goes into hiding, disguises himself, feigns madness and finally returns to avenge himself upon his half-brother in a climactic fight. However, the most obvious use that Shakespeare makes of the revenge story is, of course, in *Hamlet*, where it comprises the very core of the play.

Tragedy and usurpation

The story of the usurper is another favourite narrative of English Renaissance drama. It might also be described as the story of 'killing the king' and it is told not only in plays like *Richard II* and *Richard III*, but also in *Julius Caesar*, and *Macbeth*. The usurper is, of course, the man who challenges established authority on a grand scale. Unlike the revenger, whose motive is usually the righting of a perceived personal wrong, the usurper does not stop at revenge, but wants to displace the original authority completely and replace it by himself. The usurper may indeed be motivated by the desire to avenge personal injustice; or he may have the wider interests of the kingdom at heart; or he may be driven by pure ambition and self-interest; or by any combination of the above. His usurpation might be carried out by stealth and guile, like Claudius's, or he may wage war to achieve his ends. (Thus Henry Bolingbroke, wronged by Richard II, raises an army against him, defeats him and eventually replaces him, becoming Henry IV.) The story of the usurper typically involves more than just matters of individual personalities: the story is about the state of the nation as much as about the individual, and the damage done to the whole country by the actions of a few men is a recurrent theme. The issues raised by the story of the usurper involve, inevitably, questions of the relationship between the individual and the office he holds, and also the claims of an ideal order (a king, for example, who can appeal to divine sanction in support of his rule) compared to the demands of *realpolitik*.

The story of the usurper is a repeated motif in Shakespeare's history plays. In the earlier part of his career, Shakespeare had made his name as a dramatist whose interests were widespread; but the single most impressive project upon which he had embarked was the systematic dramatizing of fifteenth-century British history. Shakespeare was not the only writer of his generation to write history plays, of course. Of his contemporaries, Christopher Marlowe's name stands out: his *Edward II* (1592) is a dark and brilliant play about power and corruption – and also one which deals with a story of usurpation. But what differentiates Shakespeare's approach to history-writing from that of his colleagues is the sheer scale of what he achieves; his is a far more ambitious project than anything ever conceived of by his contemporaries. By 1600 he had written nine plays which had translated into theatrical terms more than a century of British history. The reigns of Henry VI, Edward IV, Edward V and Richard III, and then (going back in time) of Richard II, Henry IV and Henry V, had been dramatized in two sequences of four plays each which effectively present a survey of fifteenth-century English history, up to the time of Henry VII, the first of the Tudors. Also dating from the same period is a much-neglected play about the thirteenth-century King John. In addition to these plays from the 1590s, Shakespeare at the very end of his career even felt able to deal with comparatively recent history. In collaboration with John Fletcher he wrote a play about the reign of Henry VIII, father of Queen Elizabeth I.

Like the revenger, the usurper is someone who, for one reason or another, is going against the orthodox teachings of the time. That orthodoxy, perpetuated by successive Tudor and Stuart monarchies and their spokesmen, insisted on the duty of the subject to obey the monarch, however unjust. Bishop Latimer, in the early years of the century, stated that

> If the king should require of thee an unjust request, yet art thou bound to pay it and not to resist and rebel ... the king indeed is in peril of his soul for asking of an unjust request; and God will in His due time reckon with him for it: but thou must not take upon thee to judge him ... And know this, that whensoever there is any unjust exaction laid upon thee it is a plague and punishment for thy sin.
> (Anthony Fletcher, *Tudor Rebellions*, Longman 1968, p. 2)

The argument that a ruler's tyranny was a divine punishment for a subject's sinfulness was probably one which gave more comfort to the monarch than to the commoner: the Great Chain of Being looks more attractive from the top of the chain than from the bottom. It may not be surprising, therefore that we hear a very precise echo of Bishop Latimer's words in the voice of James VI of Scotland, writing about 'The True Law of Free Monarchies' in 1598, five years before he became James I of England:

> A king at his coronation, or at the entry to his kingdom, willingly promiseth to his people to discharge honourably and truly the office given him by God over them. But presuming that thereafter he breaks his promise unto them never so inexcusab[ly]; the question is, who should be the judge of the break ... Now in this contract, I say, betwixt the king and his people, God is doubtless the only judge ... and revenger of the breakers. For in his presence, as only judge of oaths, all oaths ought to be made. Then since God is the only judge betwixt the two parties contractors, the cognition and revenge must only appertain to him.
> (Ann Hughes, *Seventeenth-Century England*, I, Ward Lock Open University, 1980, p. 28)

According to James, only God may judge a king. The usurper story, however, is one which dramatizes a challenge to that orthodoxy. The plays concerned with fifteenth-century history cover not only Bolingbroke's rebellion against Richard II, but also a period which includes the Wars of the Roses, a period of history in which claims and counter-claims to the throne abounded. James I was fond of invoking the theory of the Divine Right of Kings, but what Shakespeare's historical sequences had shown above all was the arbitrary foundation of such apparently divinely-sanctioned power.

Thus, while the usurper story seems at first to suggest, in its most basic form, a fairly cut-and-dried ethical structure, in actuality it could be varied in a number of ways. Sometimes the king is the hero-victim and the usurper is the villain of the piece; sometimes the usurpation is presented as a justified rebellion and the ethical claim of an individual's right to justice is shown to be in conflict with the rigid demands of a contradictory constitutional theory. Macbeth, for example, is a usurper and a regicide, but so, according to the legal implications of Latimer's and James's declarations, is Malcolm. As in the history plays, the contradictions inherent in the myth of a monarch's divine sanction are ironically exploited. *King Lear*, too, contains elements of the usurper story. Lear, it is true, abdicates of his own free will, but thereafter the familiar theme of usurpation surfaces in the play. On the one hand, there is the ambitious 'usurper' figure of Edmund, the bastard, who first displaces his brother in their father's affections, and eventually aspires to the crown of Britain itself. On the other hand Lear's enmity against the tyrannical Goneril and Regan turns them into kinds of usurpers. As they begin to quarrel with each other, they threaten to plunge the country into civil war – a war only postponed by their need to combine against the third sister, the dispossessed Cordelia, whose moral right to the throne is balanced against their legal one. Thus Cordelia in this respect, resembles Bolingbroke in *Richard II*, the 'justified' usurper. The crucial difference between them is that whereas Bolingbroke's invasion succeeds, Cordelia's fails.

Tragedy and the morality play

In many respects Bolingbroke in *Richard II* is a typical Shakespearean hero. His stand against Richard is portrayed as a justified one, but that does not prevent the guilt of his situation as a usurper from eating into his soul when he has become king in *Henry IV*. Figures like Bolingbroke and Brutus, men who make bloody choices for honourable reasons, seem to be of particular interest to Shakespeare. Such reluctant usurpers have much in common with the protagonists of our third major type of story – the Everyman story.

Of the various narrative archetypes which figure prominently in the make-up of Shakespeare's tragedies this is the one with the longest pedigree in the English drama: the morality plays of the fifteenth and early sixteenth centuries, plays such as *Everyman* (*c.* 1500) and *Mankind* (*c.* 1465), told a story which plotted a man's progression through a series of situations designed to test his moral fibre. The story, roughly, is that of an ordinary man who starts out in comparative innocence, and is then confronted by the representatives of various virtues and vices: he is tempted by the vices and admonished by the virtues, but ends up falling into sin, only to be redeemed in the end by heavenly grace. The everyday ethical choices which an individual faces are dramatized in the context of a cosmic struggle between the powers of heaven and hell, in which the prize is the soul of man. The two essential features of the story are the idea of temptation, and the idea of a metaphorical journey towards self-knowledge. The protagonist moves from innocence to experience, and the story, in its emphasis on eventual redemption, celebrates the optimism of the Christian message. The morality play is also, of course, a didactic kind of theatre. At the end of *Everyman*, for example, a character called the Doctor warns the audience:

This moral men may have in mind.
Ye hearers, take it of worth, old and young.
And forsake Pride, for he deceiveth you in the end.
And remember Beauty, Five Wits, Strength and Discretion –
They all at the last do every man forsake,
Save his Good Deeds there doth he take.
But beware! And they be small
Before God he hath no help at all;
None excuse may be there for every man.
Alas, how shall he do then?
 (*Everyman*, ed. G.A. Lester, Benn. 1981 p. 102, ll. 902–11)

Like the other stories mentioned, however, the morality structure may be subject to a series of variations. One of the greatest plays of Elizabeth's reign was Marlowe's *Doctor Faustus*, which took the format of the morality play and turned it on its head, telling the story of a man whose journey into sin leads him eventually to the point of no return: like Macbeth, Faustus ends up 'Stepp'd in so far, that, should I wade no more, Returning were as tedious as go o'er' (*Macbeth*, III, iv, ll. 136–7). Moreover, although the central energy of the morality tradition derives from an allegorical account of the salvation of the individual soul, writers long before Shakespeare had found that the structure was infinitely adaptable. Thus the morality play became integrated with political allegory and satire in works such as John Skelton's *Magnyfycence* (*c.* 1516) and John Bale's *King Johan* (1538–39).

73

For example, in the following exchange from *King Johan*, the abstract allegory suddenly breaks into historical specificity. Four characters 'Private Wealth', 'Usurped Power', 'Dissimulation' and 'Sedition' are forming an alliance to undermine King John's authority.

> *Usurped Power* I made this fellow here [Sedition] the Archbishop
>   of Canterbury
> And he [John] will agree thereto in no condition.
> *Private Wealth* Then hath he knowledge that his name is Sedition?
> *Dissimulation* Doubtless he hath so, and that drowneth his
>   opinion.
> *Usurped Power* Why do ye not say his name is Stephen Langton?
> *Dissimulation* Tush, we have done so but that helpeth not the
>   matter.
> (*Four Morality Plays*, ed. P. Happé, Penguin, 1979, ll. 937–42)

As 'Sedition' is identified with Stephen Langton, (Archbishop of Canterbury during John's reign), 'Usurped Power' with the Pope, and 'Private Wealth' with a Cardinal, the allegorical abstractions turn into historical figures, which then conspire, as morality-play Vice-figures, to undo the innocent King John.

The debts which Shakespeare owed to the morality tradition have been well documented by modern scholars. Some argue that the relationship was a very close one and that many of Shakespeare's plays were direct descendants of the late morality plays which were still being written in his own time. Others maintain that Shakespeare's debt to the morality tradition was a more indirect one, which had more to do with the way in which the popular morality tradition had shaped Elizabethan playgoers' expectations than it did with Shakespeare's own dramatic skill. But while most commentators agree that the Shakespearean stage was enriched by the late medieval traditions which it inherited, we should be aware of the differences, as well as the similarities, between Shakespeare's dramas and the dramas of the past. In Shakespeare's versions of the Everyman story, Macbeth and Hamlet are led into temptation by (among other things) supernatural forces; Othello is deftly manipulated by Iago. In all these cases, however, the interest lies not in any redemptive scheme of Christian consolation, but in the process which leads men towards acts which their whole ethical apparatus tells them to be wrong – and in the aftermath of their actions.

These archetypal stories play across not only Shakespeare's tragedies but across the whole spectrum of Elizabethan and Jacobean drama. Without doubt there are other important stories, too, which could be shown to operate repeatedly in the work of Shakespeare and his contemporaries. Those that I have singled out are particularly relevant to the great tragedies of Shakespeare's maturity. As can be seen, they are stories which generate questions of how an individual relates to the structures of authority – earthly and heavenly, theological and political – of Elizabethan and Jacobean England. Such problems were explored relentlessly by the drama of the period, a drama springing from a theatre which itself existed in an ambiguous relationship with the power structures of its time.

7 Shakespeare's theatre

'Common players in interludes'

Shakespeare's career led him from boyhood in Stratford-upon-Avon to acting, writing and finally investing in the London theatre, and thence back to Stratford again, where he ended his days a well-to-do gentleman, owner of the best house in town and a fair bit of land besides. But in many ways it is the career of Ben Jonson, Shakespeare's greatest rival in the theatre of his day, which is the more revealing about the social position of the theatre in the late sixteenth and early seventeenth century. In 1597 Jonson was imprisoned for his part in a play called *The Isle of Dogs*, in which he collaborated with Thomas Nashe. The play, according to the Privy Council, contained 'very seditious and slanderous matter', meaning that it was critical of the government. The following year, he killed an actor named Gabriel Spencer, was convicted of murder, and only escaped hanging by pleading benefit of the clergy. In 1605, he was back in jail for his collaboration in another 'seditious' play, *Eastward Ho!* , which satirized James I's policy of liberally handing out titles to his Scottish followers. That same year, however, he also began his collaboration with Inigo Jones on a series of brilliant court masques, and in 1616 (the same year in which he brought out a folio edition of his *Works*) he received from James I a life pension, which rewarded his achievements as a writer of court entertainments, and gave him an official status akin to that of poet laureate.

At one point Jonson is in and out of prison for both political and criminal offences; at another he is a court favourite with royal patronage. His erratic career is in many ways a microcosm of the position of the theatre in Elizabethan and Jacobean England. The actor, in particular, occupied an extraordinarily insecure position. Since the Act for the Punishment of Vagabonds in 1572 actors, the 'common players in interludes', had been classed with rogues, vagabonds and other 'masterless men'. This meant that unless an actor was affiliated to a company which enjoyed the patronage of one 'Baron of this realm or . . . honorable personage of greater degree' he was deemed to be a potential criminal. Up until the end of the 1590s there was an escape clause which allowed a company of players to be licensed by two high-ranking Justices of the Peace 'at the least, whereof one to be of the Quorum', but in 1598 this loophole was closed. On the one hand this legislation limited the number of, and encouraged the professionalization of, acting companies in the kingdom – a kind of Elizabethan version of Equity! On the other hand it underlined the essential insecurity of the theatre, and the extent to which its survival depended upon the tolerance of the nobility. Sometimes this tolerance spilled over into enthusiasm. Although Elizabeth I has the reputation of having been very fond of the theatre, it was in fact James who supported it most actively. Always more liberal with public funds, he took the patronage of three major London theatre companies into his own and his family's hands only a few weeks after his accession. James's court became a major and regular venue for the best players of his day – including, of course, Shakespeare's own company, which had been renamed The King's Men. The players did not make a huge financial profit from court appearances (the fee for the company was £10 – about the same as a good day's takings in the playhouse), but they gained in prestige. It is unlikely that the players themselves came to consider their public performances mere rehearsals for the royal command performances, but this is how some of their enemies saw things, and this almost certainly afforded them some measure of protection from their more virulent opponents. Theatre in the Jacobean age became a particularly royal pastime.

Yet if royalty and nobility were prepared to support the theatre, they also kept a watchful eye on its political affiliations. Elizabeth's patent to James Burbage's company in 1574 made express provision that 'the said comedies, tragedies, interludes and stage plays be by the Master of our Revels for the time being before seen & allowed': the Master of the Revels was effectively in charge of stage censorship during the period. And if anything should by chance escape the censor's eye, there was always the law to deal with it. Under both Elizabeth and James, Ben Jonson ended up in prison for collaborating in plays which overstepped the invisible mark of acceptability as regards political criticism. Theatre practitioners had a strong vested interest in ensuring their work did not offend their patrons.

They also had to tread warily with another important and powerful group, whose interests and opinions were by no means identical with those of the aristocracy. This comprised the City Fathers in the Guildhall, the seat of local government in Elizabethan and Jacobean London. London, of course, is where all the major theatres were based. Traditionally, a theatre appropriately named 'The Theatre', which was opened by James Burbage in 1576, has been regarded as the first of these permanent professional theatre buildings. Recent research, however, has suggested that the short-lived 'Red Lion' playhouse, built in 1567, should properly be thought of as the first purpose-built permanent theatre in London. But these, like the other famous public playhouses of Shakespeare's day – the Swan, the Rose, the Curtain, the Fortune, the Boar's Head and, pre-eminently Shakespeare's own Globe – were built just outside London, beyond the City walls and outside the legal jurisdiction of the Puritan-influenced Guildhall.

Strict Puritans had always been unambiguously opposed to the players. Their complaints included the charges that playhouses were places where thieves, prostitutes and other unruly elements would congregate; that they were often the scenes of disturbances; that they were unhygienic and increased the chances of an epidemic in time of plague; and that they distracted citizens from work during the week and from worship on the Sabbath. All this was undoubtedly true. They also claimed, in terms with which we are all too familiar today, that the stage portrayal of tales of lewdness, violence and immorality would inevitably encourage lewdness, violence and immorality among the good citizens of London. The more extreme Puritans were scandalized by the fact that the rôles of women were taken by boys, thus offending against the scriptural injunction against men dressing in the clothes of women. This became a favourite theme among Puritan preachers of the day.

The theatre of Shakespeare's day often ended up as a pawn in the power game which was continually being played between the crown and the City. The legislation of 1598 which deprived players of the protection of licensing magistrates was passed by Elizabeth's Parliament as a concession to the Guildhall. It could have been a lot worse: the previous year she had nearly been pressurized into a 'final suppressing of stage plays' in an unlikely agreement with Puritan City authorities stemming from the fuss about *The Isle of Dogs*, the play for which Jonson was first imprisoned, and which seems to have criticized the government both of the country as a whole and of the City of London. If so, Jonson and his collaborators had been excep-tionally tactless. The tension between the Privy Council and the Guildhall served for the most part to protect the players from the attacks by the City Fathers; to offend both these bodies simultaneously must have been a tactical error of the highest magnitude.

The City authorities should not be seen simply as autocratic authoritarian killjoys. To a great extent they were reflecting the desires and the attitudes of their class, the wealthier sector of London bourgeois society. In 1596 James Burbage attempted to establish Shakespeare's company. The Lord Chamberlain's Men, in a new theatre in well-to-do Blackfriars. He had bought a site which was within the City walls, but free from the jurisdiction of the City since it stood on old monastic ground. The local residents, however, did not want their neighbourhood ruined by a public playhouse.

They presented a petition to the Privy Council, asking that Burbage be prevented, since the playhouse

> ... will grow to be a very great annoyance and trouble, not only to all the noblemen and gentlemen thereabout inhabiting but also a general inconvenience to all the inhabitants of the same precinct, both by reason of the great resort and gathering together of all manner of vagrant and lewd persons that, under colour of resorting to the players, will come thither and worke all manner of mischief, and also to the great pestering and filling up of the same precinct ... and besides, that the same playhouse is so near the Church that the noise of the drums and trumpets will greatly disturb and hinder both the ministers and parishioners in time of divine service and sermons.

(A. Gurr, *Playgoing in Shakespeare's London*, C.U.P. 1987, pp. 210–11)

But if some Londoners were hostile to the theatre, many others clearly were not. The playhouses lived not just by noble patronage: their main income came from paying customers at public perform-ances. There is a good deal of debate as to what sort of people these play-goers were. The old model proposed by the scholar Alfred Harbage was that the characteristic audience at a Shakespeare play would be made up of City workers, a middle- and working-class crowd representative of a unified nation. More recently, Ann Jennalie Cook has taken this view to task, arguing that the play-goers of Shakespeare's London were taken mainly from the ranks of the élite, the privileged, the gentlefolk and the idle rich. More recently still, Andrew Gurr's book *Playgoing in Shakespeare's London* explores the variety which existed between various playhouses and the changing patterns of play-going during the late sixteenth and early seventeenth centuries. His analysis is detailed and persuasive, suggesting that different playhouses developed in different ways, eventually defining their various audiences.

'The house with the thatched roof': the Globe Theatre c. 1599

Some of the best first-hand descriptions we have of play-going in Elizabethan and Jacobean London come, as it happens, from the pens of foreign visitors to London. The Swiss traveller, Thomas Platter, was in London in 1599, and this is how he describes a visit to the Globe to see *Julius Caesar*:

> On September 21st after lunch, about two o'clock, I and my party crossed the water, and there in the house with the thatched roof witnessed an excellent performance of the tragedy of the first

Emperor Julius Caesar with a cast of some fifteen people; when the play was over, they danced very marvellously and gracefully together as is their wont, two dressed as men and two as women . . . Thus daily at two in the afternoon, London has two, sometimes three plays running in different places, competing with each other, and those which play best obtain most spectators. The playhouses are so constructed that they play on a raised platform, so that everyone has a good view. There are different galleries and places, however, where the seating is better and more comfortable, and therefore more expensive. For whoever cares to stand below only pays one English penny, but if he wishes to sit he enters by another door, and pays another penny, while if he desires to sit in the most comfortable seats which are cushioned, where he not only sees everything well but can also be seen, then he pays yet another English penny at another door. And during the performance food and drink are carried round the audience, so that for what one cares to pay one may also have refreshment. The actors are most expensively and elaborately costumed; for it is the English usage for eminent lords or knights at their decease to bequeath and leave almost the best of their clothes to their serving men, which it is unseemly for the latter to wear, so that they offer them for sale for a small sum to the actors.

(Gurr, *Playgoing in Shakespeare's London*, Cambridge UP, 1987
pp. 213–14)

From Platter's account, which matches many others, several key details emerge. The time of performance, two o'clock: after the midday meal, but early enough for the last act not to be played in total darkness – for plays were performed mainly in the darker months of the year. The theatrical season began in September, playing through to the beginning of Lent, then after Easter until early summer. During the main summer months a company might take on a provincial tour: playing in the capital was severely circumscribed because of the risk of outbreaks of plague, which was highest in the summer. During actual times of plague, of course, the theatres were closed.

'Julius Caesar with a cast of some fifteen people', says Platter. Unless his counting was much awry, this tells us something significant about Elizabethan staging, *Julius Caesar* has thirty-two named parts in it, excluding the soothsayer; in addition, there are all the 'Senators, Citizens, Guards, Attendants etc.', some of whom have lines to say. Assuming that the play that Platter saw was Shakespeare's (and the probability is overwhelming that it was), then it points to a massive use of doubling and trebling of parts. This is not surprising, of course. If the first rule of theatre economics has always been the one about bums on seats, the second rule has always been that the fewer actors you need to pay, the healthier your profit at the end of the day.

Platter makes much of the dancing which followed the performance. This was a favourite feature of play-going in Elizabethan times, and was one of the specific targets of the enemies of the stage. The jigs at the end of plays were repeatedly censured for their bawdiness and ribaldry, and even some of the dramatists seem to have found them tiresome – perhaps because they recognized that too many people, like Platter, took more notice of the dancing than of the plays them-selves. Ben Jonson, no friend of the Puritans, complained several times about the custom. So did the authorities, and in 1612 an order was issued 'for suppressing of jigs at the end of plays'.

Platter also points to the element of competition between the theatres, and the fact that on any day there was a choice of two or three theatres to go to. Throughout our period the exact number of theatres and companies operating fluctuates, as does the regularity of their playing. On the whole, though, it is likely that any one theatre would be playing most days of the week. In 1617 the English traveller, Fynes Morison, reported that 'The city of London alone hath four or five companies of players with their peculiar theatres capable of many thousands, wherein they all play every day of the week except Sunday' (Andrew Gurr, *The Shakespearean Stage, 1574–1642*, Cambridge University Press, 1980, p. 10). Sunday playing was prohibited – but the prohibition was not always observed.

The physical description Platter gives of the stage, the 'raised platform', tallies with contemporary drawings of Elizabethan theatres. It is one of the few contemporary documents which tell us anything about the theatre at which *Hamlet*, *Othello*, *King Lear* and *Macbeth* would have first been presented to a public audience. Numerous attempts have been made to reconstruct the auditorium of the typical Elizabethan playhouse (see pp. 82–3). The most ambitious and scholarly of these is the current Bankside Globe project, organized under the auspices of the Globe Playhouse Trust, which aims to reconstruct, as accurately as possible, the Globe as a working theatre on Bankside. This project has generated a renewed interest in the details of Elizabethan theatre architecture – as have the archaeological discoveries made in 1988 and 1989 concerning the remains of the Rose Theatre nearby the Globe site.

The 'typical' Elizabethan playhouse has generally been thought of as a large building comprising a three-tier polygonal or circular auditorium, with a raised performance platform thrusting a long way out into a flat yard where the 'groundlings' in the audience would stand on three sides of the stage. Actors' entrances and exits would be made by way of doors in the upstage walls. One of the

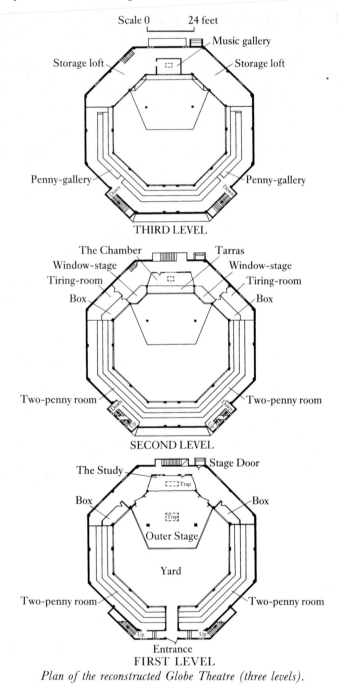

Plan of the reconstructed Globe Theatre (three levels).

John Cranford Adams' reconstruction of the Globe Theatre.

most contentious issues has been the debate as to whether there was an inner stage or discovery space located behind the main thrust stage: scholarly opinion now tends to discredit this notion. The use of trapdoors may have allowed for one or two special effects, but scenery was minimal and necessarily portable. A company's scenic stock would probably have been composed of various pieces of stage furniture, to be carried on and off between scenes, or occasionally lowered from a flying-space above the stage. The theatre manager, Philip Henslowe, made inventories of the properties of his company, who were based at the Rose theatre. The inventory for 1598 lists some special costumes, such as a pope's mitre, a ghost's crown and a pair of wrought gloves; and some hand-props, such as spears, mattocks and shields, but also some sizeable pieces of scenic furniture: a rock, a cage, a tomb, two moss banks, a bay tree, a cauldron big enough for a man to fit in and 'the city of Rome'. The audience would have been alerted to what was playing at the theatre by means of hand-written playbills posted around the town. For those among them who could afford something more comfortable than standing space in the yard there were galleries of raised seats around the sides and the back of the auditorium. These offered the attraction of additional shelter from the elements, since they were covered by the thatched roof which Platter mentions.

However, the archaeological discoveries of the Rose have reopened scholarly debate on some of these issues. Excavations have uncovered the foundations of a theatre with a shallow stage, which was thirty-seven feet wide at its widest point at the back, and it narrowed to twenty-five feet at the front. It did thrust out into the audience – but only a little way, and the performance would have been much more of an 'end-on' affair than was formerly supposed. Perhaps because of this, the yard was not flat, but raked to give a better view to those at the back. What is most striking about the Rose, however, is its intimacy. Assumptions that Elizabethan acting styles needed to be exaggerated and bombastic in order to fill a large arena may have to be revised, for the overall diameter of the Rose was only approximately seventy feet, and the front of the stage was only thirty-six feet from the gallery at the back of the auditorium. And even so, this small theatre was designed to hold over two thousand spectators: on a good night for a popular play the audience (even if Elizabethans were, on average, smaller than we are) must have been quite tightly packed in!

The Rose is where some of Shakespeare's early plays may have first been staged; he may even have acted there himself. But the Globe is the theatre with which he was most closely associated, and many of the discoveries concerning the Rose may or may not be applicable to the Globe. (It seems certain, for example, that the

Globe was a larger playhouse than the Rose.) What is clear is that there is still much to learn about theatre architecture and staging practices in the theatres of Shakespeare's day.

'One English penny': theatres and prices in Shakespeare's London

The cost of admission was not exorbitant, although it is unlikely that many apprentices could afford to while away every working day (as they were accused of doing) at the theatre. The penny which remained the basic admission price to most outdoor theatres between 1567 and 1642 fluctuated in real value during this time, especially after the bad harvests of the 1590s. However, an average weekly wage of six shillings (seventy-two pence) was not uncommon for a hard-working skilled artisan in London, and artisans' wages did not change much throughout this period. What did change was what could be bought for the same amount of money. Translations from earlier currencies into modern terms are always misleading, but in Elizabethan times a penny would buy a pound of beef whereas by the middle of the seventeenth century the same amount of beef would cost fivepence. Thus, set against the weekly wage the basic theatre admission price might be thought of as the equivalent, in modern currency, of £2.50–£3.00. Set against food prices they dropped from about £4.00 in early Elizabethan times to under £1.00 by the closure of the theatres in 1642 – by which time, however, the average weekly food bill was taking up most of the average weekly wage packet. Even so, this minimum admission cost compares well with modern prices for entertainment in London: at the time of writing West End cinema seats cost from £3.00 to £7.00, and seats for a popular show at a major West End theatre cost between £7.00 and £25.00.

That basic penny admission price, however, was limited to the 'public' or 'outdoor' theatres. These were one of the two basic types of theatre which were operating in Elizabethan and Jacobean London; the other type were the 'private' or 'indoor' theatres. These indoor theatres were actually no more 'private' than the outdoor ones: both kinds were privately owned and managed, and both kinds played to whatever audience could afford the admission fee. This fee, however, was significantly more expensive in the indoor theatres, where seats (there was no standing area) cost a minimum of sixpence, rising later to a shilling, and the very best seats could cost two shillings and sixpence. As a result, the indoor theatres inevitably played to a more privileged audience. The increased prices bought the play-goer complete protection from the vicissitudes of the weather; it also gave access to a kind of drama more appropriate to the smaller enclosed space, one in which the stage was illuminated by artificial lighting, in which stage effects became more ambitious, and in which the use of music before, during and after the play became increasingly elaborate.

Until 1609, however, these indoor theatres were used for perform-ances by companies of boy actors. These are what Rosencrantz refers to when he tells Hamlet about the 'aery of children, little eyases, that cry out on the top of question and are most tyranically clapp'd for it' (*Hamlet* II, ii ll. 342–4). There may have been a particular bitterness to Shakespeare's jibe, since one of the major children's companies was playing in the indoor theatre at Blackfriars, which James Burbage had bought a few years earlier for the Chamberlain's Men, but had been unable to use as a professional theatre because of the success of the residents' petition. The extent to which these children's companies were a genuine rival to the adult professional theatre is signalled by the fact that in *Hamlet* they are shown as threatening to put the adult tragedians out of business. In the first few years of the seventeenth century, audiences seem to have taken particular pleasure in watching dramas of incest, murder, rape and vengeance played out by children. But by 1609 their vogue was more or less over. In that year, Richard Burbage, William Shakespeare and the (by now) King's Men finally moved into the Blackfriars premises. The King's Men ran their indoor theatre in tandem with their outdoor one until 1613, when the Globe was destroyed by fire during a performance of Shakespeare and Fletcher's *Henry VIII*.

The organization of the Globe theatre

All of Shakespeare's major tragedies were written for the Globe. The Lord Chamberlain's Men/King's Men played there from 1599 to 1613, and the second Globe, (rebuilt in 1614), continued to be used until 1642. We have a fair amount of information about several of the London theatres of the early seventeenth century: there are the manager's accounts and inventory of props from the Rose (*c.* 1587–1605); there is an eyewitness sketch of a performance at the Swan (1595–*c.* 1637); and there is a detailed contract, dating from about 1599, with instructions to the builder for the building of the Fortune. About the Globe itself, however, our documentary infor-mation is disappointingly scanty. We have Platter's report, quoted above, of course – although the majority of that is about theatres in general rather than about the Globe in particular. We know that it stood on Maiden Lane (now Park Street) in Bankside. We have some drawings of London and Bankside which show it to be a round or polygonal, thatched building. Most of the rest of what we 'know' about the Globe is the result of comparisons drawn from other theatres, especially the Swan, and of extrapolations from stage directions from plays known to have been staged there. We also know that it was built with the timbers of the old Theatre in Holywell Lane and believe it could accommodate an audience of 3,000.

James Burbage owned the building of the Theatre itself but not the land it stood on; the lease for that had run out in 1597 and since then the company had been without a secure and permanent theatre in which to perform. The legality of Burbage's response was dubious, but his action was effective. He took out a thirty-one year lease on some land on the South bank of the river; he hired some labourers; and on the night of 28 December 1598 he began to dismantle the Theatre and to cart the timbers across the river to the site on Bankside. Attempts were made to stop him, but they were unsuccessful. The Globe opened in 1599.

The company of actors who played at the Globe had more than an artistic interest in their theatre; they had a commercial one as well. The financial organization of the Lord Chamberlain's/King's Men was a rather unusual one for the theatre of the time. Instead of the theatre being owned by a single person, it was held in joint-tenancy by a group of shareholders – also known as 'the housekeepers'. This was largely composed of a small group of the actors themselves. Richard Burbage and his brother Cuthbert (who was a theatre manager rather than an actor) after their father's death became the principal shareholders: between them they owned 50 per cent of the company, bore 50 per cent of the expenses and took 50 per cent of the profits. The other half of the company was split between a number of sharers which seems to have varied between five and eleven in the period that concerns us. To trace in detail the actual development of who owned how much of the company and when would take us into the realms of higher accountancy. Sufficient to say, therefore, that the main actors were also the main sharers, among them Augustine Philips, Thomas Pope, John Heminges, Henry Condell and Robert Armin – and of course, William Shakespeare. Shakespeare was an early shareholder in the Chamberlain's Men, buying his share in 1594. He owned about an eighth of the company, and it was an investment that set him on the road to becoming a gentleman.

Shakespeare and his fellow sharers and housekeepers thus had a direct financial interest in the company and in the theatre. In contrast to these, the élite of the company, there were the hired men, who were paid on a daily or weekly basis – and sometimes not paid at all. Thomas Killigrew, the seventeenth-century dramatist who grew up in Jacobean London, used to go as a boy to the Red Bull theatre and wait around outside before the performance for one of the actors or stage crew to come and shout for volunteers to act as extras, with the reward that they would get to see the play for nothing! The regular hired men did a little better: in good times their daily pay might be as high as one to two shillings. Back-stage staff were hired at similar rates, but musicians were paid more and had to be licensed separately by the Revels Office.

A key member of the Elizabethan or Jacobean stage crew was the book-keeper. At the Globe he might have been a well-paid hired man, or he might have been one of the sharers. Most likely there were variations from time to time. The book-keeper was an amalgamation of a prompter, a stage-manager, a director and a producer. He had to get the script licensed by the Master of the Revels and then prepare it for production, ensuring that what went on on stage bore some resemblance to the words which the author wrote and the order in which he wrote them. It has to be remembered that, unlike a modern theatre company, Elizabethan and Jacobean players would not be working from a printed text. Nor, of course would there be photocopying or stencilling machines to reproduce the author's manuscript. The only way was to write the play out by hand. Clearly, to produce a full text of each new play for each actor would be unacceptably labour-intensive. And so a single copy of the play would be written out, then cut up and pasted into parts – one for each actor, with only brief stage directions and two- or three-word cues from other actors written into it. Each actor would then be given his part of the play to learn, pasted onto one long piece of paper and rolled up: Edward Alleyn's part from Greene's *Orlando Furiosos*, which has survived to the present day, is seventeen feet in length. When we talk about an actor playing a character in a drama, we use the word 'part' or 'rôle': to the actors of Shakespeare's day these words would have been quite literally accurate.

To prevent the kind of disaster to which this sort of system must have been dangerously prone (such as actors forgetting where they are in the play), part of the book-keeper's job would involve writing out a synopsis of the play's episodes and hanging it somewhere prominent – such as in the tiring-house, the Elizabethan equivalent of a dressing-room behind the scenes. This running-order would list the stage properties or special effects needed in each scene. It would also list both the names of the characters and the actors playing them. This last may well have been particularly important. It may sound a ludicrous notion that an actor could forget the name of the character he is playing. But then, in a modern provincial theatre a well-employed actor will spend several weeks rehearsing a part in a play. (Sometimes, if doubling is called for, it may be more than one part.) The actor will then perform that part in that play for a run lasting perhaps a few weeks. During the run of this play he or she might be working on rehearsals of another play – or two at the most. Even so, this is a fair call on an actor's concentration. In a theatre in

Shakespeare's London a well-employed actor would be in a different play every day of the week (excluding Sundays, in theory). The next week there may be a repeat performance of one or two of those plays, together with three or four new ones. And so on. The implications are clear. The demands made on an actor's memory were colossal. So were the demands on his time, energy and versatility. Rehearsal time was limited and there was no director as such – although it has been suggested that the book-keeper, or the author if available, might have been involved in some rudimentary directing.

The business of putting on a play in the Elizabethan and Jacobean theatre was thus very different from modern professional theatre practice. It sounds, perhaps, a little makeshift and a little haphazard. In some ways it was. In all likelihood the players relied largely on an ability to improvise their moves on stage within a series of traditional guidelines, and on their rapport with each other and with the audience. To use a slightly tendentious analogy, if a production of Shakespeare in the professional theatre today is comparable to a well-conducted symphony orchestra playing in a concert hall, in Shakespeare's own day a theatre must have been more like a jazz club. We can guess how audiences in the public theatres were likely to behave from an order issued by the authorities of Cambridge University, which instructs an undergraduate audience how *not* to behave. It concerns a performance, presented in a Cambridge College, of Peter Hausted's *The Rival Friends* which had been commissioned to entertain King Charles I in 1634. The undergraduate audience was instructed that it was forbidden that

> ... any humming, hawking, whistling, hissing, or laughing be used, or any stamping or knocking, nor any other uncivil or un-scholarlike or boyish demeanour, upon any occasion; nor that any clapping of hands be had until the *Plaudite* at the end of the Comedy, except his Majesty, the Queen, or others of the best quality here, do apparently begin the same.

> (Gurr, *Playgoing*, p. 46)

This document serves to illustrate more than just the expected norm of audience behaviour. It also reminds us that the playwrights of the sixteenth and seventeenth centuries had more than one kind of audience to write for. Professional companies would perform at Oxford and Cambridge, just as they would put on performances in the more prestigious Inns-of-Court, or mount provincial tours during the summer, or play command performances for special occasions at great lords' houses. As well as playing to the mixed bourgeoisie of London, they had to be prepared to perform before more specialized audiences. But in particular, plays were royal entertainments, from the time of Elizabeth to Charles I. And, especially after 1603, the title page of many of Shakespeare's plays bears some kind of inscription boasting that this particular play had been presented at court, or 'played before the King's Majesty at Whitehall'. Shakespeare was writing for the citizens of London; but he was also writing for the King of England, who had claimed Shakespeare's company of actors as His Majesty's Servants, and who had made Shakespeare and his fellow-sharers Grooms of the Royal Household.

8 Plays and audiences

In order to complete the meaning of a play it is necessary to have an audience. Each audience brings to a performance a series of assumptions and preconceptions, its own concerns and its own ways of making meanings. A skilful playwright understands this, and understands too that a play's meaning is created in the interaction between what an audience already knows (or thinks it knows) and what it is offered by the play it sees. Nor is any single audience completely homogeneous: it is possible to aim different parts of a play at different parts of an audience, or different levels of meaning at different levels of understanding. This is what Hamlet does, of course, when he stages his version of *The Murder of Gonzago*. If his suspicions are correct, that play will 'catch the conscience of the King' because Claudius has particular kinds of knowledge which he will bring to the performance, and he will read that performance in a particular way; it will have meanings for him that it cannot have for any 'innocent' member of the audience.

In this section I want to explore the way in which the different audiences for whom Shakespeare was writing may have conditioned what he wrote. I shall pay particular attention to the idea of performance of plays at the court of King James, since these seem to me to have an important bearing on at least two of the tragedies, but I want to make clear at this stage that I am not arguing that we 'must' think about these plays in the context of their early performances. On the contrary, my whole point is that each audience experiences a play differently and that there is no single 'right' way to interpret these tragedies. I suspect that one of the reasons that Shakespeare seems to be 'not for an age but for all time' is that he learned comparatively early in his development as a dramatist the skill of constructing a play so that it would offer different things to different audiences – to the audience at court, to the audience at the Globe, and to the audience in the provinces.

'Hamlet' in London and the universities

THE / Tragicall Historie of HAMLET / Prince of Denmarke / By William Shake-speare. / As it hath beene diuerse times acted by his Highnesse ser- / uants in the Cittie of London: as also in the two V- / niuersities of Cambridge and Oxford, and elsewhere / At London printed for N.L. and Iohn Trundell.

This is how *Hamlet* was described when it first appeared in print in 1603. The description comes from the title-page of the first quarto, which as far as the text itself goes is an unauthorized and unreliable document – one of the 'Bad Quartos', those pirated editions of plays. The title-page, however, gives us a brief glimpse into the early stage-history of the play, and by focusing upon what we can gather of early performances and playing conditions we may find things which affect the way in which we read the play.

By 1603, it seems, *Hamlet* had been 'diverse times acted . . . in the Cittie of London: as also in the two Universities of Cambridge and Oxford, and elsewhere'. 'His Highnesse servants' (who would have still been playing as the Lord Chamberlain's Men when they performed *Hamlet* for the first time) apparently took the play on tour as well as playing it in their London theatre. That they played it at the Universities of Oxford and Cambridge seems particularly fitting. Tragedies had always been at home in the universities, of course. College Halls had long been used for the staging of plays, both by undergraduate actors and by travelling professional companies. University drama itself was an important element in the growth of the Elizabethan theatre: it was through the universities that classical influences such as that of Seneca found their way onto the popular stage, and many of the playwrights of the Elizabethan and Jacobean eras were themselves university-educated. The Elizabethan stage had even produced a major tragedy whose protagonist was an intellectual, for Marlowe's Doctor Faustus was a fellow of Hamlet's own University of Wittenburg. *Hamlet*, however, is the only major tragedy of the period to have an undergraduate as a hero.

In some ways Hamlet is a caricature of the young scholar. His language is erudite, his range of reference wide; his quick-witted replies, his continual play of intellect all attest his status as a man of education. When he first learns of Claudius's crime, he calls for his 'tables' in order to set down his discovery that 'one may smile, and smile, and be a villain'. At times he plays the role of absent-minded scholar quite deliberately, incorporating it into his mask of madness as he wanders the corridors of Elsinore immersed in a book, reading 'Words, words, words'. And early on in the play, of course, Claudius's remark about Hamlet's desire to return 'to school in Wittenberg' establishes Hamlet's position and status.

There is, it is true, one detail which throws Hamlet's undergraduate status into a more ambiguous light: the indeterminacy about his age. The computations of Hamlet's age within the play put him, according to the Gravedigger, as a thirty-year-old undergraduate: a mature student by today's standards and even more so by the norms of Shakespeare's day, when a more usual age for a young man to go up to university would have been sixteen. Yet, paradoxically, his youth is emphasized several times in the play: 'young Hamlet' he is called by his friend Horatio; Polonius agrees that 'he is young'; Claudius and Gertrude, of course, treat 'this mad young man' as if he were a boy – but so does his apparent contemporary Laertes, who talks of Hamlet's love for Ophelia as 'A violet in the youth of primy nature'.

The matter hardly seems to be a crucial one, although it has bothered many readers, and perhaps was at the root of some of those approaches to the play which show such immense distaste for this 'immature' thirty-year-old who behaves like a fifteen-year-old. And it is difficult to ignore the overall impression that *Hamlet* is a tragedy which has to do with youth, just as *King Lear* is one which has to do with old age. More precisely, perhaps, *Hamlet* focuses on a young man in a society which is ruled by old men; *King Lear* concentrates on an old man in a society which is being taken over by the next generation.

There are two main possibilities concerning the contradictory information we are given about Hamlet's age: one is quite simply that Shakespeare was being a little careless, and did not realize that he was effectively contradicting himself. This is perfectly possible – there are many instances of similar carelessness in the plays – but it is not entirely likely in this instance. Shakespeare seems very insistent on the thirty-year period, and the Gravedigger establishes it by two separate calculations: the first involves his own period of service as gravedigger, which dates from the day of Hamlet's birth and comes to thirty years; the second concerns the skull of Yorick, which 'hath lien you i'th'earth three and twenty years' – Yorick the jester with whom Hamlet played as a boy. The notion of a thirty-year-old Hamlet seems firmly established here. And so it is worth considering the other possibility – that the play's contradictions concerning Hamlet's age might have some significance.

We are led to see Hamlet as young in the early stages of the play. It is there that so much emphasis is put upon his youth, as if the writer were trying to establish it as an essential fact about his protagonist. We do not get the contradictory detail about Hamlet being thirty years old until towards the end of the play. Now it may well be that Shakespeare is playing around with time-scales (as he does elsewhere in his plays) in order to make some sort of point – to suggest perhaps that although only a few weeks seem to have gone by in stage time, somehow Hamlet has grown up during that time. This, again, is a possibility, although not one that I like very much. Another interpretative manoeuvre might be to see the contradictions about Hamlet's age as being typical of his character in general: this reading would argue that the difficulty that audiences and other

93

characters in the play have in interpreting his character, are mirrored in this detail, that nobody can even say whether he is young or middle-aged.

There is another way of dealing with the contradiction, however – one which does not resolve it but which leaves it intact. In 1601, when *Hamlet* was most probably written and first performed, Richard Burbage, for whom the part of Hamlet was written, was thirty-four years old. The 'Hamlet' whom the original Elizabethan audiences would have seen on the stage, would not have been an adolescent by any means. This may well explain why the audience is told so frequently, early in the play, that Hamlet is young: a playwright sometimes needs to compensate for the visual effect of his actors. By the end of the play, in a comic scene, Shakespeare is confident enough to be able to acknowledge this fact and admit to his audience that this adolescent prince that they have been watching is actually a grown man of thirty-four – or at any rate, allowing for a small sop to Burbage's vanity, thirty....

At first glance this may seem like a disappointingly prosaic way of explaining the paradox of Hamlet's age, but its importance lies in its acceptance of the constraints of the theatre upon the meaning of the text. It is a truism to say that plays differ from other forms of literature because they are written to be performed rather than read. However, the logic of this entails that the original conditions of performance then dictate (to a certain extent) how the writer fashions the story. In *Hamlet* this is a particularly important element, since in this play more than any other Shakespeare makes the whole business of play-writing and performance central to his plot. The paradox of Hamlet's age hinges on the crucial relationship between events within the fiction itself (the age of the fictional Prince) and events in the 'real world' – the age of the actual actor playing the Prince. Time and time again in *Hamlet*, the audience is confronted with the problem of making sense of the relationship between events in a fictional world and events in a 'real' world, for as we have already seen, one of the main themes of the play is theatricality itself.

The Elizabethan theatre was a notoriously self-conscious institution, which enjoyed referring to, and often making jokes about, its own theatricality. But few writers ever dealt with this notion as subtly and as comprehensively as Shakespeare did in *Hamlet*. In order to get a sense of the thoroughness of Shakespeare's playing with theatrical illusion and dramatic convention in *Hamlet*, let us look in detail at one extraordinary exchange, which takes place just before that play-within-a-play, and imagine how it must have come across to a contemporary audience in the Globe theatre near the beginning of the seventeenth century. The play is about halfway through. Hamlet is hot on the trail of Claudius, and is about to confirm his suspicions by means of the performance of *The Murder of Gonzago*. The players are ready, the court is assembling and the tension is mounting. As the members of the court take their places in the 'audience', Hamlet and Polonius have the following exchange:

> *Hamlet* My lord, you played once i'th'university, you say?
> *Polonius* That did I, my lord, and was accounted a good actor.
> *Hamlet* What did you enact?
> *Polonius* I did enact Julius Caesar. I was killed i'th'Capitol.
>   Brutus killed me.
> *Hamlet* It was a brute part of him to kill so capital a calf
>   there. Be the players ready?
>
> (III, ii, ll. 97–105)

What is the point of this short and apparently inconsequential conversation? Why does Shakespeare bother to include it at this moment in the play? These questions can be answered on a number of different levels. Firstly, on the level of theatrical technique: as noted above, the exchange comes at a point when the entire court is assembling on stage in order to watch the Players' performance. As a matter of sheer craftsmanship, Shakespeare would have found it useful to include one or more short and self-contained conversations between characters in order to 'cover' the inevitable hiatus on stage while everybody found their places and sat down.

Secondly there is the way in which the exchange contributes to the immediate dramatic action. It comes just after a rather aggressive little clash between Hamlet and Claudius, and for Hamlet to be able to turn away from the King and engage Polonius in trivial small-talk about Polonius's university career allows him, effectively, to snub Claudius.

But what of the actual words spoken? At a third level, they contribute to the character-drawing which goes on in the play. We already know that Polonius is supposed to be a bit of a buffoon – a 'tedious old fool', as Hamlet calls him earlier. Hamlet himself, on the other hand, is a rather sharp-witted young man. This exchange confirms both these characters. People reminiscing about their student days always sound a little fatuous, and Polonius is no exception. The slightly odd way in which he talks about his performance ('*I* was killed i'th'Capitol. Brutus killed *me*'), as if, significantly, he is unable to distinguish between actor and rôle, adds to our overall impression of his foolishness. Hamlet, conversely, maintains his character of wit and ironist, seizing on Polonius's words and playing with them, using them as counters in a verbal game which allows him to score off Polonius, and eventually to insult him (for 'calf' is a way of saying 'fool').

At yet another level, we might consider the specific implications of these references to Brutus and Caesar. Critics have often pointed to a resemblance between the characters of Hamlet and of Brutus in Shakespeare's *Julius Caesar*: both of them are basically honest men who get caught up in circumstances beyond their control which lead them to commit murders; both of them spend time examining their consciences about the rights and wrongs of their chosen course. So, is Shakespeare effectively asking at this point that the audience make the comparison between Hamlet and Brutus? Almost certainly – and in a very specific way. For there is a further level of irony. Twentieth-century scholars have attempted to compile cast-lists of Shakespeare's plays, and to work out which actors in his original company played which rôles. This research is incomplete and there are gaps in the findings, and yet certain agreements have been reached. From these agreements we can build the following picture: the actor playing the rôle of Hamlet is, as we noted before, the thirty-four-year-old Richard Burbage. Opposite him as Polonius is John Heminges (who was later to co-edit the First Folio of Shakespeare's plays). The same research indicates that when the Lord Chamberlain's Men first staged *Julius Caesar* a year or two earlier (and perhaps when they revived it a week or two earlier) Burbage had played Brutus and Heminges had played Caesar. So, now, during the performance of *Hamlet*, Heminges/Polonius reminds Burbage/Hamlet that they had previously played opposite each other in the rôles of Brutus and Caesar. And thus for a second or two, the actors step out of rôle, and the audience are forced for that instant, to see them not as Polonius and Hamlet, but as Heminges and Burbage, making a joke about themselves as actors and about the parts they play. And, although we need not discount all the other levels of meaning which I have suggested, what gives the moment its energy is the fact that it operates quite simply as a joke between the two actors.

The Burbage/Heminges joke is more than a theatrical in-joke, of course. First of all, it amplifies one of the central themes of the play. *Hamlet* tells a story about people whose lives are based on kinds of play-acting – Hamlet himself being a character who is obsessed with theatres and play-acting. But at another level, what Shakespeare is doing at this point is destabilizing the whole structure of the dramatic fiction. He is saying to the audience 'Don't get too involved – this is a play, remember.' And he is using a whole battery of dramatic techniques in order to do it. On the one hand, we remember, this comes at a moment when the audience is about to see a play-within-a-play, and to watch an audience on stage watching that play. This technique of showing a play-within-a-play is one of the favourite devices of Shakespeare's generation of dramatists (Shakespeare himself had already used it several times before he wrote *Hamlet*) and one of its inevitable results is to bring under scrutiny the whole business of plays and their effects on audiences. Then, as if to compound this, Shakespeare has characters in this very same scene who make reference to *Julius Caesar*, a play which he himself wrote and which The Lord Chamberlain's Men had staged comparatively recently. To add to the irony, Polonius is himself the Lord Chamberlain in Claudius's court. Even at this level the dramatic illusion is by now under some stress. And then, relentlessly, Shakespeare throws in the further level of complexity which involves two actors making a joke about the parts they play. So, at exactly the point in the play when Claudius is about to get so involved in the action of a performance that he loses control and gives himself away, Shakespeare goes to immense lengths to jolt the audience out of their immersion in the dramatic fiction, and to remind them that they are 'creatures sitting at a play'. It is not until later that the audience discover that there is yet another level of irony: just as Burbage/Brutus killed Heminges/Caesar in the earlier play, so Burbage/Hamlet will kill Heminges/Polonius in this one. The brief conversation between Hamlet and Polonius also functions as a moment of dramatic foreshadowing, preparing the way for events to come.

If we intend to acknowledge that Shakespeare's plays were written to be acted on the stage rather than to be read in the study, and if we are to do more than pay lip-service to that idea, then our interpretations of his plays must be able to accommodate such apparently trivial details as the age of a particular actor, or the fact that an actor may be recognized from one part to another – those details, in short, which have most to do with the presence of an *audience*. One of the striking features of the drama of the Elizabethan period is the way in which playwrights do address themselves directly to an audience; an awareness of that audience is an integral part of the playwright's art. It is, therefore, not in the least implausible to think of Shakespeare playing directly to an audience in such a way, allowing his actors to make jokes about themselves. We should, however, remember that there is more than one 'audience' for any play. In the case of *Hamlet* we have already identified at least two audiences from the title-page of the first quarto: there is the audience in 'the Cittie of London' and the audience 'in the two Universities of Cambridge and Oxford'. And different audiences will experience the same play in different ways. The Burbage/Heminges joke is available to the regular patrons of the Globe in a way that it may not have been to the Fellows and undergraduates who watched the play in Oxford and Cambridge. Conversely, perhaps the intellectualism of young Hamlet struck more forcible chords in the college Hall than it did in Globe performances. The drama is a very unstable form of art and a play can undergo shifts in meaning from one performance to the next. It may well be that what the Globe audience 'saw' was a play in which Hamlet came across as a rather brittle and unsympathetic figure, whereas the college audience saw in him a character whose cast of mind it found recognizable and attractive. The various arguments which twentieth-century critics have had about Hamlet's character (whether he is immature and self-indulgent, or whether he is sensitive and sympathetic) might turn out to have been contradictions which were inherent in the play from its earliest performances.

It remains to ask if there is any discernible reason why Shakespeare examines, parodies, explores and dissects the nature of theatricality so intensively in *Hamlet*? It may be, of course, that this merely represents a natural expression of his own interest in the theatre, but it may also be the case that there is some further and more specific cause. The exact date of *Hamlet* is uncertain, and so what follows can only be expressed tentatively. Nonetheless, it is probable that the play was substantially written and first performed during 1601 – the same year as The Lord Chamberlain's Men mounted their ill-judged performance of *Richard II* performed for the benefit of the supporters of the ill-fated Earl of Essex's rebellion.

The performance of *Richard II* was presumably designed to have an effect on the real world of power politics, and to make some difference to the cause of the Earl of Essex. Elizabeth herself recognized the intended identification between herself and Richard, and saw what kind of mirror was being held up to Nature there. Her subsequent leniency towards The Chamberlain's Men must have been experienced by them all with massive relief – perhaps by none more than Shakespeare, who saw his friend and patron the Earl of Southampton condemned to death for his part in the uprising. If 1601 is a correct date for *Hamlet* it says something about Shakespeare's nerve, if nothing else. There is something particularly daring about writing and performing *Hamlet* in that year. It is, after all, a play which deals with a corrupt old ruler and a rebellious young hero. In *Hamlet*, moreover, the hero rewrites an old play and puts it on in order to bring about the downfall of the old ruler. There is an uncomfortable proximity between what happens in Elsinore and what had been happening in London in 1601.

The company of Players who arrive at Elsinore are down-at-heel, their low fortunes ascribed to 'the late innovation': this is usually taken to be a reference to the ensuing theatrical in-joke about the boy actors who carry the custom of the town. However, as Harold Jenkins explains in his Arden edition of the play, the word 'innovation' could be synonymous with 'rebellion'. Although no more is made of this in the play, to accept this reading of the word immediately presents us with a picture of a company of actors who have fallen on hard times because of a recent rebellion. It is quite plausible to see in this, as some critics have, a wry reference to what might have happened to Shakespeare's own company in 1601 if Elizabeth had decided to be less lenient. The very fleetingness of the remark lends plausibility to the reading: if it *is* an allusion to The Chamberlain's Men's brush with power politics, then it is an enigmatic reference, perhaps for the benefit of only a very few hearers, which it may be best not to spell out too clearly.

Shakespeare takes chances in *Hamlet* in order to define again for himself the nature, scope and implications of his own art. The aftermath of Essex's abortive rebellion would be precisely the time when Shakespeare would need to do some serious thinking, or re-thinking, about the nature of theatre, and in particular about its relationship with the real world. At the most basic level, the relationship between dramatic illusion and reality which the play probes may refer primarily to the recent reality of Shakespeare's own career as dramatist. It seems more than probable that the intensive exploration of the nature of theatre which Shakespeare undertakes in *Hamlet* was prompted by the narrow escape which his own company of players had just had.

'Played at court'

Nonetheless, The Lord Chamberlain's Men weathered the crisis, and survived into the reign of King James, to be honoured with the patronage of the King himself in 1603. Although they held a particularly privileged position (and its attendant responsibilities) The King's Men, as they were now known, were not alone in benefiting from royal favours. Indeed, the central importance of the court in the literary and cultural life of the English Renaissance is something which modern readers tend to underrate. In fact there are very few of the writers of the sixteenth and early seventeenth centuries that we have heard of today who did not have substantial dealings with the court of Elizabeth or James. For many of them indeed, their primary careers were not as writers at all. They were statesmen, churchmen, civil servants, soldiers – men like John Donne, Walter Raleigh, Edmund Spenser, Francis Bacon and Philip Sidney – whose professional advancement was often closely tied in with court favour and court hierarchies. Professional writers, too, were cultivated by the court, and employed in the writing of masques and pageants as well as plays which might be performed before the monarch. The most prominent of them were at least partially dependent upon the court for patronage.

In such a situation, the silence against which the poet's words reverberate is a silence owned by the sovereign. We have already seen that there are plenty of stories of writers being punished for saying things that are politically unacceptable. There was even a bureaucratic structure, the Office of the Revels, which performed the function of the official censor. Yet the writer could also lay claim to a degree of freedom: if there were bounds beyond which he could not step, there was also a large area of compromise and accommodation. Many of the defences of poetry of the period claim that the poet should be a politically privileged being, whose special kind of truth-telling is of particular value to a sovereign, even if what he says is sometimes unpalatable. It must be presumed that such a situation often prevailed, for Elizabethan and Jacobean literature contains its fair share of radical criticism of the status quo. Unfortunately for the writers, however, it did not *always* prevail; the unwritten rules could be broken and the mood could change at a moment's notice – as the young Ben Jonson, among others, discovered. The Fool in *King Lear* complains:

> I marvel what kin thou and thy daughters are. They'll have me whipped for speaking true; thou'lt have me whipped for lying; and sometimes I am whipped for holding my peace.
>
> (I, iv, l. 186 ff.)

The Elizabethan and Jacobean writer who stepped into the minefield of contemporary politics must have done so with much the same trepidation.

Shakespeare, playwright to The King's Men, wrote tragedies set in courts and peopled by kings, queens, dukes and governors. The stories which he tells are tales of power, and he tells them in a theatre which is implicated in the power structures of the day. His attitude towards those power structures is difficult to assess, and Shakespeare has been claimed both as a radical and a conservative. In fact, we have comparatively little in the way of any records of Shakespeare's own political or religious convictions. What we do 'know' is largely what has been reconstructed from the plays themselves. And yet the relationship between the playwright and King James I is one which may have an important bearing on the way the plays themselves came to be written. James exerted a powerful influence on early seventeenth-century culture in general, and as playwright to The King's Men, Shakespeare himself would have been at the most sensitive point of this influence.

Shakespeare wrote, as any skilled professional playwright must, with one eye on his audience. One of the factors which decide the forms and meanings of literary works is precisely that relationship between the writer and the audience: the question 'Who is talking to whom?' is one of the most basic of literary criticism. In Shakespeare's case we must bear in mind that there is more than one audience for whom he had to write. On the one hand he was talking to the playgoing public of London, the mixed and various paying customers at the Theatre, the Globe, and later at Blackfriars. On the other hand he was talking to an élite and powerful circle of patrons, of whom the most important was England's monarch. The number of court performances which The King's Men were invited to give varied from year to year, but it was always a substantial number. The Christmas festivities were the busiest time: between Boxing Day 1607 and 7 February 1608, for example, they performed at court thirteen times. Performances would take place in various halls of the royal palaces; in the Great Hall or the Banqueting House at the Palace of Whitehall or in the Great Hall at Hampton Court. The royal invitation brought the company not merely money – although at £10 per performance it provided at least as much as a good day in a public theatre – but also prestige and security.

Perhaps Shakespeare did not, after 1603, always sit down to write with the image of the king in the forefront of his mind; probably James was not always the principal listener to whom the dramatist's words were addressed; it is impossible to tell what effect Shakespeare would have hoped his plays might have had on the king and his policies. Nonetheless, the great tragedies written during the first few years of the seventeenth century show Shakespeare engaging with contemporary issues concerning the court. This is true even of *Hamlet*, written during the last years of Elizabeth's reign. Then, in the early years of the new king's reign, Shakespeare began to turn more and more towards a subject-matter which engaged directly with King James's own obsessions, and began to tell stories which suggest that he was very conscious of James as a potential audience for his plays.

Shakespeare had always taken an interest in state affairs, of course. His sequence of history plays, an account of the factional strife in English government up to the time of the Tudors, was a massive and ambitious project, which – like all histories – put a particular construction upon the events of the past, and implied particular interpretations of the present. In his cycles of history plays, Shakespeare had already proclaimed himself, among other things, a shrewd political writer. But even shrewd political writers run risks: the affair of *Richard II* and the Essex rebellion had shown that only too vividly. The relationship between the stage and the political power structures of the day was one which was under constant scrutiny: when James claimed Shakespeare's company for his own it is possible that he did so because he understood the dangerous ideological potential of good theatre.

But Shakespeare did not stop writing history plays after 1603. Two of the plays which are traditionally thought of as 'tragedies' are also plays about the history of the British monarchy: *Macbeth* and

101

King Lear. And if their settings make them seem less immediately topical than some of the mainstream 'history plays', their subject matter made them pressingly relevant to affairs of state in Shakespeare's own time.

'King Lear' and the divided kingdom

King Lear tells the story of a king who divides his kingdom, Britain, into separate parts and thereby throws the land into chaos. Lear's original plan is to go into a peaceful retirement, dividing the rule of Britain between his three daughters and their husbands. At the ceremony, however, his youngest, Cordelia, offends him by refusing to make a public show of her love for him. Enraged, Lear disowns and banishes her and splits the kingdom instead between her sisters, Goneril and Regan. The folly of his deed pursues him through the play, as Goneril and Regan show themselves increasingly vicious towards Lear and his followers – who include his Fool and the disguised Duke of Kent, whom Lear had also banished. They also become increasingly competitive towards each other and the country is brought to the brink of civil war. Lear himself, unable to cope with the viciousness he himself has unleashed in his daughters, goes mad. Cordelia, meanwhile, has raised an army in France, and returns to try and reclaim her country for her father by force of arms. She fails, and although she and Lear are briefly united she is killed on the orders of the ambitious Edmund. Although the evil sisters and their henchmen also die, and some semblance of rule is restored, the country has been reduced to a state of ruin, and Lear's own death comes as a release from the dreadful tortures of his life.

This story of the divided kingdom, then, was played before James – a monarch who was simultaneously and separately King of England and of Scotland, and whose dearest wish at the time was to unite the kingdom of Britain into a single entity. James I's project for the Union of England and Scotland was one of the most contentious issues of the new king's political agenda. As has already been shown (see p. 22), James believed that the two kingdoms were actually already united in his own person, and all that was necessary was the constitutional ratification of this fact. His image of himself was that of a peacemaker, reconciling old factions:

> First, by my descent lineally out of the loynes of Henry the seventh, is reunited and confirmed in mee the Vnion of the two Princely Roses of the two Houses of LANCASTER and YORKE, whereof that King of happy memorie was the first Vniter . . . But the Vnion of these two princely Houses, is nothing comparable to the Vnion of two ancient and famous Kingdomes, which is the other inward

Peace annexed to my Person... Give me leaue to discourse more particularly of the benefits that doe arise of that Vnion which is made in my blood...
(In *Political Works of James I*, ed. C.H. McIlwain, Cambridge, Massachusetts, 1918, p. 271)

The theatre, even before Shakespeare wrote *King Lear* had not remained aloof from the Union debate, and James had already become accustomed to seeing his own image on the stage in this context. Contemporaries of Shakespeare, playwrights such as Thomas Middleton and Ben Jonson, had recently written pageants for James's formal entry into London, celebrating him as the spirit of peace, and elaborating on a series of myths, legends and historical accounts in order to portray him specifically as the bringer of unity to the divided kingdoms.

A series of more minor details support the hypothesis that the play about the ancient king has something to say about (or to) the contemporary one. Details such as the fact that King James I's two sons actually held the titles held by Lear's designated heirs, the dukedoms of Cornwall and of Albany (how might *that* have affected the reception of the play's first line when it was played at court?). Then there is the fact that, like Lear, James had a famous court Fool, named Archie Armstrong, to whom he was greatly attached. Like Lear, too, James was particularly fond of hunting, and his lavish treatment of followers was a particular bone of contention between him and the Commons – just as Lear's lavish following of a hundred knights is a particular source of irritation to Goneril. It is hard to imagine that the Lear story would not have had a particular resonance for the king; nor that Shakespeare, writing the play, would have been unaware that he was treading on politically sensitive ground. He had, after all, already shown his ability to imagine what it is like to put on a play in front of a king who is sensitive to the implications of a drama: in *Hamlet* he had written a scene in which a king, watching a play, recognizes a version of himself in one of the characters – thus bringing the performance to an abrupt close, and the playwright to a tragic end. Like a licensed Fool, a playwright may sometimes be whipped for speaking true and sometimes whipped for lying. Yet the conclusion that *King Lear* was a play at least partly conditioned by Shakespeare's developing relationship with the new monarch, and his attitudes towards James's policies is difficult to resist.

But if there does appear to be some connection between James and Lear, it is more difficult to say exactly what the significance of this is. Critics are still debating whether *King Lear* was written in open support of James and his policies, showing the disastrous effects of having a divided kingdom (with Lear thus becoming a kind of fictional opposite, or antitype, of James); or whether the character of Lear himself was intended as some kind of satiric comment on James's own autocratic behaviour; or whether the play was somehow designed to bring together and reconcile the two opposing parties. No firm decision has yet been reached as to which side (if any) of the Union debate Shakespeare was actually on.

It may be that the critical argument has focused on the wrong issue. The specific question of unity or division may well have exercised Shakespeare's mind, but as a play *King Lear* seems in the end to have comparatively little to say about it. If the general implication of the story is that to take a kingdom and cut it up is generally a bad thing, few of James's opponents would have been likely to disagree, in principle anyway: their argument was the rather different one that England and Scotland were historically, culturally and constitutionally two separate kingdoms, not a single one which had been artificially divided. What *King Lear* does have a great deal to say about, however, is an issue which underlay the whole Union debate: the issue of the nature of authority in general, and of kingship in particular.

James's claim to unite in his blood the two kingdoms of England and Scotland was hotly contested by the Commons, who grew increasingly suspicious of his attitude towards the authority he held. The Commons went to great lengths to try to convince James that in English constitutional law the distinction that existed between the 'body natural' of the king, and his 'body politic' meant that James's mere presence on the English throne was not enough to unite the two crowns. The subtle – almost pedantic – legal points about where the personal identity of the king begins and ends, and where his rôle as constitutional monarch takes over, became a central point in the debate about the political future of England and Scotland.

It is also, in a different way, a central issue in *King Lear*. At the beginning of the play Lear is King, and he wields the King's authority: his mistake lies in believing that once he has given up his power he can retain that authority. The limits of authority are explored in the play, and Lear's dividing of the kingdom comes to be seen not only as a foolish act but as one which is (like his disowning of Cordelia) unnatural. Lear treats both Cordelia and the kingdom as if he owned them – which is a grave misunderstanding of the rôle, the rights and the duties of kingship. In this more tangential way, *King Lear* seems to be making reference to the political situation of Shakespeare's own day, and to the king before whom the play will be shown.

'Macbeth' and the Scottish crown

Macbeth can be related even more directly to court performance. There seems to be little doubt that this play was written with King James in mind. *Macbeth* probably received its first performance on 7 August 1606, at Hampton Court, before James I and King Christian of Denmark, and in the case of *Macbeth*, there is much more involved than the usual pressures on the playwright to remember that what he was writing would probably be performed before the king. For in this play, Shakespeare deals with two subjects which were particularly close to the heart of King James: the topic of magic and demonology: and the matter of James's own ancestry and royal lineage.

King James's interest in magic and witchcraft is well-documented, and the witches in *Macbeth* seem to derive some of their central aspects from his account of the powers of devils and witches in his own treatise on devil-worship, *Daemonologie* (1597). In particular,

Woodcut of King James interrogating witches.

Shakespeare made use of what James has to say about the ambiguity of devilish prophecies:

> ... as to the devil's foretelling of things to come, it is true that he knows not all things future, but yet that he knows part ... [he makes himself] so to be trusted in these little things, that he may have the better commodity thereafter to deceive them in the end with a trick once for all; I mean the everlasting perdition of their soul and body ... he will make his scholars to creep in credit with Princes, by foretelling great things, part true, part false.

Or, as Banquo puts it:

> ... oftentimes, to win us to our harm,
> The instruments of Darkness tell us truths;
> Win us with honest trifles, to betray's
> In deepest consequence.

(I, iii, ll. 123–6)

The ghost in *Hamlet* is a self-consciously literary and dramatic device, stemming directly from Senecan traditions. In *Macbeth*, the appearance of Banquo's ghost at the feast is used to similar effect. But the witches are something different. They belong to a folk tradition, a tradition which had little to do with dramatic conventions, and much to do with the fears, anxieties, hostilities and prejudices of rural and small-town life in Shakespeare's England or James's Scotland. They represent something which exists at the edges of, or beyond the boundaries of, civilized life; something which has been marginalized and repressed – and something which is feared. Feared not just by superstitious villagers, either; in a play which addresses itself to the highest in the land, Shakespeare can use the witches as ambiguous images of the dark and terrifying energies which lie beyond the reach of rational thinking. The important thing about the influence of James's *Daemonologie* upon Shakespeare's *Macbeth*, is that James's literal belief in – and obsession with – the powers of darkness made available to Shakespeare a vocabulary for talking about these energies.

If James's interest in witchcraft offered Shakespeare certain dramatic possibilities, his interest in his own linear descent appears at first to have offered Shakespeare problems. In fact, *Macbeth* must have seemed an audacious, even a reckless, choice of story for Shakespeare to dramatize. Like so many of his plays, it is based on a pre-existing narrative, and (as he did in *King Lear*) Shakespeare here chooses to adapt for the stage an episode from early British history. As was his custom when writing of this era, he used as his prime source the Elizabethan historian Raphael Holinshed, whose

Chronicles of England, Scotland and Ireland had already provided much material for Shakespeare's history plays.

However, the story which Shakespeare tells differs in several respects from the story which he read in Holinshed's *Chronicles*. One change in particular suggests the importance of King James as an audience for the play. In Holinshed's version, Banquo is a villain and co-conspirator with Macbeth. The historian tells how Macbeth

> ... communicating his purposed intent with his trusty friends, amongst whom Banquo was the chiefest, upon confidence of their promised aid, he slew the king at Inverness or (as some say) at Botgosuane, in the sixth year of his reign. Then having a company about him of such as he had made privy to his enterprise, he caused himself to be proclaimed king ...
> (Arden edn *Macbeth*, p. 172. I have modernized spelling.)

In Shakespeare's version, of course, Banquo is an innocent and honourable man, one whose probity Macbeth fears. The change seems at first glance to be rather a minor one, and it can be explained quite adequately in terms of dramatic structure. It probably suited Shakespeare quite well to make Banquo innocent of the murder of Duncan, since this allowed him to focus more sharply on the guilt of Macbeth and his wife: if the Macbeths had had a bevy of conspirators to help them, it would have lessened the impact of their evil, and might even have suggested that if Duncan had so many enemies, perhaps some of them might have good reason to want him dead. Instead, Shakespeare gets much dramatic power out of the fact that Lady Macbeth and Macbeth are acting entirely alone, against a king who seems to command the loyalty of everyone else about him.

There is, however, another reason for the change, one which can be seen as having a contemporary political significance for Shakespeare. Earlier in his narrative, Holinshed explains that Banquo was

> the Thane of Lochquhaber, of whom the house of the Stuarts is descended, the which by order of lineage hath now for a long time enjoyed the crown of Scotland, euen till these our days ...
> (Arden edn *Macbeth*, p. 167)

In other words, Banquo was the direct lineal ancestor of James Stuart (or 'Steward'), King of Scotland and now of England. When the witches prophesy that Banquo's children shall inherit the crown, they are referring to a line of succession which ends up with James himself. From the occult depths of the fictional world which Shakespeare creates, words reach out which locate the play firmly in the contemporary political scene of King James's court.

Shakespeare makes this absolutely explicit in the play. In Act IV Scene i, Macbeth goes for a second time to the witches to seek reassurance that he will not be defeated by his enemies. They show him a series of apparitions which culminates in 'A show of eight Kings, the last with a glass in his hand'. The word 'glass' here means a mirror – perhaps some kind of magic mirror, in fact. Macbeth starts back in horror:

> What! will the line stretch out to th'crack of doom?
> Another yet? – A seventh? – I'll see no more: –
> And yet the eighth appears, who bears a glass,
> Which shows me many more; and some I see,
> That two-fold balls and treble sceptres carry,
> Horrible sight!
>
> (IV, i, ll. 117–22)

The image is of James himself, the eighth King in the procession; the glass shows the future house of Stuart, James's own successors. Their 'two-fold balls and treble sceptres' are references to the orbs and sceptres of the coronation ceremony. (The 'two-fold balls' represent the orbs of two coronations, in Scotland and in England. The sceptres are 'treble' because in the English investment ceremony two were used, and another one in the Scottish ceremony.) It is clear why Shakespeare's Banquo had to be portrayed as innocent of involvement in the murder of Duncan. If Shakespeare had followed Holinshed closely, he would have ended up writing a play which drew attention to the house of Stuart's foundation on treachery and regicide, and its complicity with the tyranny of Macbeth.

Such a story would have been contentious enough at the best of times, since before his accession James had gone to great pains to assert the legitimacy of his claim to the English throne. In 1606, however, the theme would have had an added dimension. That year saw the trials and executions of the conspirators in the Gunpowder Plot, in which Guy Fawkes and his accomplices had made an attempt on the life of James and all his Parliament in the name of international Catholicism. The Shakespeare scholar Leslie Hotson has suggested that Shakespeare may have had a particular personal interest in the events surrounding the Gunpowder Plot, since his friend and patron the Earl of Southampton was one of the intended victims; it is even possible that Shakespeare may have known, directly or indirectly, some of the conspirators themselves. The evidence for this is by no means certain; more persuasive is the scholarship which has shown that Shakespeare makes direct reference to the trial of one of the accomplices, a Father Garnet, at least twice in the play (in Act II, Scene iii, ll. 4–12, and in Act IV, Scene ii, ll. 46–57). If it is true that the Gunpowder Plot hovers around the edges of *Macbeth*, what are we to make of this?

The Gunpowder Plot and its aftermath may appear to be peripheral to *Macbeth*. Certainly, I do not intend to argue that the play has that particular historical incident as a central part of its subject-matter. But politics and literature interact in a variety of ways, and it does not seem at all unreasonable to suggest that it is significant that the play was written soon after an attempt had been made on the life of a Scottish king – who also happened to be King of England. James, as it happened, profited greatly from the backlash of public and parliamentary opinion against the would-be regicides, and was temporarily more secure in his power than he had ever been. But the spectre of contemporary treason had been raised once more, and playwrights who wanted to write plays about historical treason needed to tread carefully – especially if their narratives were likely to raise the whole question of the legitimacy of the Stuart line. It is hardly surprising that Shakespeare makes Banquo into an innocent bystander, a man who is, in many ways, the opposite of the tyrant Macbeth, and who later becomes a figure of ghostly premonition indicating Macbeth's guilt; nor is it surprising that in 1606 a writer addressing himself at least partly to the king should lay so much stress upon celebrating the house of Stuart and should show that Banquo's descendants are the very opposite of the murderous Macbeth; nor is it surprising that Malcolm, who is another opposite of Macbeth, should represent some form of alliance between England and Scotland; nor that Shakespeare should take time out to mention that the English king (historically, Edward the Confessor) at whose court Malcolm seeks refuge, was blessed with the gift of healing by touch the disease known as the King's Evil – a gift that James was believed to possess.

In the interplay, then, between what Shakespeare took from Holinshed (and other writers) and what he changed, we can discover much about why the text is as it is. Many of the changes which Shakespeare did make concern stagecraft and dramatic presentation, of course, but in some of them the boundaries between aesthetic and political desirability become blurred. In some cases, political expediency is clearly the prime consideration. For example, in Holinshed, Duncan's battle at the beginning of the story is described as being primarily against 'the Danes'. Since the royal audience for that first performance of *Macbeth* in 1606 seems to have included not only James I but also King Christian of Denmark, Shakespeare's decision to make Duncan's enemies Norwegian rather than Danish is understandable.

But it is those occasions when Shakespeare makes larger, more structural changes, rather than the changes of detail, which reveal most about the process by which the play came into being. Shakespeare's Duncan, for instance, is a more worthy king than Holinshed's; Shakespeare's Macbeth is correspondingly more evil than in the *Chronicles* – where his reign is described rather favourably:

> Macbeth, after the departure thus of Duncan's sons, used great liberality towards the nobles of the realm, thereby to win their favour, and when he saw that no man went about to trouble him, he set his whole intention to maintain justice, and to punish all enormities and abuses, which had chanced through the feeble and slothfull administration of Duncan ... These and the like commendable laws Macbeth caused to be put as then in use, governing the realm for the space of ten years in equal justice.
>
> (Arden, *Macbeth*, p. 173)

Shakespeare chooses to make Macbeth more unequivocally tyrannical and Duncan more unequivocally holy. In this he may have been following other, less well-known, historians whose account of the story differed in some details from Holinshed's. But, once more, the question is, why? It seems that Shakespeare, whose plays so often revel in ambiguities, does not want to clutter the second half of this story with problems about whether Macbeth might not actually be a better ruler than Duncan ever was. Accordingly, he simplifies the moral issues of the Macbeth story, and makes them more black-and-white than they are in Holinshed. In Shakespeare's version of events Macbeth's tyranny is not alleviated by 'commendable laws' and 'equal justice'; and while Macbeth has his ambiguities in the early part of the play, Shakespeare leaves us in no doubt that once the murder of Duncan has been committed, any sympathy we have for Macbeth cannot be founded on any suspicions that he might not be as bad as he's made out to be. He *is* bad, unequivocally so; and despite the compelling energy which the character of Macbeth generates on stage, it is an energy which derives from evil.

This is important. Shakespeare is writing a play which addresses itself directly to the king, and which deals with many of the affairs which concerned James both constitutionally and personally. He is also writing a play about a man who embraces evil and who has to live with the consequences. The two strands are closely interwoven. The focus of the play is, of course, Macbeth himself, but his deviations take place against a backdrop which suggests a possibility of goodness. Macbeth's evil is continually contrasted with the implicit goodness of Duncan, with the more dramatized goodness of Malcolm, with the innocence of Lady Macduff and her son, and with the promise of supernatural and historical retribution represented by Banquo. In particular, the witches' pageant of the eight kings, predicting the ascendancy of the House of Stuart, provides an image of future good arising out of present evil. It implies that in times to come (up to and including the 'present' in which the play was first performed) there will be a line of monarchs whose reigns will be the opposite of Macbeth's, and who will be just and merciful rather than bloody and tyrannical. It is, on one level, a conventional tribute to a monarch and a patron. On another level it is a superb moment of theatre, as the literal presence of James in the audience becomes in itself a force to set in opposition to the evil of the play's main character.

All this is not to say, simply, that Shakespeare's only aim in *Macbeth* was to flatter the Kings of England and Denmark. We need, perhaps, to guard against an excessively naïve conception of the relationship between political power and artistic licence and/or responsibility – as if a writer, confronted by political power, could only respond by flattery or else risk punishment. It is certainly true that the playwright was in many ways a socially and legally vulnerable figure: it was not unknown for eminent playwrights to find themselves in prison on account of their writings. And of course, the playwright of The King's Men held a particularly sensitive position. But rather than assuming that a writer's only recourse in such a position was to turn to servile flattery, it is more realistic to think in terms of there being certain tacit conventions concerning how far a writer such as Shakespeare might be able to go in addressing himself to the complexities of contemporary politics. Those conventions will often, but not always, stop short of allowing the writer to seem to be offering specific comments on policies, events, beliefs, etc. My own belief is that in *Macbeth*, Shakespeare is telling a story whose content inevitably has specific relevance to the political situations of his own day. In so far as he engages with that kind of subject-matter in the presence of the king himself, he is inevitably drawn towards gestures which affirm the validity of James's power. Hence those moments which celebrate Stuart authority, and the rewriting of Banquo's rôle. With a lesser writer, things may have ended there. But this is Shakespeare writing, and so, playing across the tributes to Stuart power, there is a complex and ambiguous story which deals with the relationship between a man, his kingly power, and the effects of evil.

King Lear and *Macbeth*, then, are plays whose structures derive at least in part from being written in the expectation of being performed at court. And if in *King Lear* Shakespeare presents an ambivalent (or at least ambiguous) attitude towards King James, in *Macbeth* he effectively inscribes James himself as a kind of ghostly and heroic presence within the play. It may be objected, quite properly, that to read the plays in the light of Shakespeare's relationship with King James is irrelevant to an understanding and enjoyment of them today. *King Lear* and *Macbeth*, after all, continue to entertain theatre audiences who are completely unaware of any relationship between the plays and seventeenth-century politics. This is obviously true of our own day – and may even have been true in Shakespeare's time. Shakespeare, after all, did not write *only* for a royal audience: if his theatre company was dependent upon royal approval, it was also dependent upon the continuing attendance of the paying customers at the Globe Theatre. We can only guess what percentage of that audience would have picked up the allusions in the plays to contemporary politics – or how many of them would have found them interesting. But to suggest that Shakespeare sometimes wrote for a specifically courtly audience is not to diminish the relevance of his plays for later generations. Rather it is an attempt to suggest why some of the plays are the way they are. For different audiences and different contexts inevitably provide different meanings for Shakespeare's plays: *Macbeth* played at Hampton Court in 1606 means different things from *Macbeth* revived at the Globe in 1611 – and that in turn means something different from *Macbeth* played at Stratford-upon-Avon in 1988. In *Henry V.*, the Prologue exhorted his audience to 'eke out our performance with your mind': the different kinds of 'eking out' which different audiences undertake is one of the pleasures of theatre in general, and of Shakespeare's plays in particular.

Part Three
Critical Analysis: Hamlet (*1601*)
Othello (*1604*)
King Lear (c. *1605*)
Macbeth (*1606*)

9 Hamlet

'Whole Hamlets... of tragical speeches'

In 1589 the vitriolic Elizabethan satirist, Thomas Nashe, lashed out
at the decadence of the contemporary English stage. The playwrights, he said in his Preface to Greene's romance *Menaphon*, were
'a sort of shifting companions... that could scarce Latinize their
neck-verse if they should have need'. He complained of the debased
taste of the age, which fed on translations and imitations of the
Roman dramatist Seneca, with his diet of sex, violence and bombast.
In an ironic praise of these English playwrights he went on to
describe how they ransacked the pages of Seneca for inspiration:
'English Seneca read by candle-light yields many good sentences, as
Blood is a beggar, and so forth; and if you entreat him fair in a
frosty morning, he will afford you whole Hamlets, I should say
handfuls of tragical speeches' R.B. McKerrow, *The Works of Thomas
Nashe*, vol. III, ed. Basil Blackwell, 1966, p. 315).

That pretended mistake, of saying 'Hamlets' instead of 'handfuls',
tells us something useful: that by 1589 there was a play called *Hamlet*
in existence and that Nashe at least thought of it as laughably wordy
and derivative – a typical example of the worst aspects of Senecan
tragedy. A couple of other references to the play throughout the
1590s establish that it played at the Theatre in or before 1596, and
at Newington Butts in 1594, and that it had in it a 'ghost which
cried... like an oyster-wife, *Hamlet, revenge*'.

But this *Hamlet*, which the Elizabethans seem to have treated as
rather a joke, was not Shakespeare's. As so often, we do not have an
exact date for Shakespeare's text, but it is virtually certain that the
play that we know as *Hamlet* was not written until the beginning
of the seventeenth century. The play which dates from the late 1580s
and which Nashe is ridiculing, is generally referred to as the 'Ur-
Hamlet' (from the German, meaning 'original'). It has been attributed
to various writers, notably to Thomas Kyd, the author of the
popular *Spanish Tragedy* – another 'English Senecan' play, and one
which itself has a very great number of similarities to Shakespeare's
Hamlet. And so we start with a seeming paradox: that *Hamlet*, that
rich, complex and continually challenging text which generations of
readers and audiences, actors and critics have enshrined as one of

the greatest works of literature, started life as a rewrite of someone else's old play.

Perhaps it is not so paradoxical after all. It is well known, certainly, that Shakespeare rarely made up his own stories, preferring instead to adapt tales from English and Italian romance writers, or English and Roman historians. The story of *Hamlet* itself was not invented by Kyd – or by any English dramatist, but exists in versions by the twelfth-century Danish historian, Saxo Grammaticus, and by the sixteenth-century French writer, F. de Belleforest, whose *Histoires Tragiques* included the Hamlet story in 1570. Thus it is not as if Shakespeare had simply taken over Kyd's own totally original plot. Yet the niggling feeling remains: to take a verse romance or a prose history and turn it into drama may be regarded as legitimate adaptation; to take someone else's play and rewrite it, looks very much like plagiarism.

Perhaps plagiarism is just what it was. The rival theatre companies of Shakespeare's London were, of course, continually looking for an edge over the competition, and used every trick available to present a programme of plays which would keep the customers coming in. They provided an assorted menu of original stories and adaptations of tales, new scripts and revivals of old performances. They needed a constant turnover of playscripts in order to satisfy a public which had come to expect from a theatre company anything up to six different plays in a week. Because Shakespeare was the writer-in-residence and a major shareholder in the Chamberlain's Men, and had a vested interest in their success, he was casting around for their next box-office hit. Because he also happened to be a dramatic genius, what emerged was one of the world's great plays.

The Senecan influence which Thomas Nashe found so laughable has been much discussed by literary historians. Certainly Seneca was one of the classical authors that no cultured Elizabethan could have omitted from their education – although his moral treatises held a more central place in the Elizabethan curriculum than his dramas. But his plays were, as Nashe suggests, translated, adapted and imitated, and English writers clearly admired them, and numbered Seneca among the great authors of classical times. As one writer put it, 'Seneca's tragedies, Plautus' comedies, Virgil's *Georgics* and 'Warrior'; of the Latins, for the stateliness of the matter and style, are most honoured'. There are certain stylistic and structural devices which Elizabethan playwrights, including Shakespeare, used, which may well have been learned from Seneca's tragedies. The five-act structure, the fondness for ghosts, the use of long rhetorical speeches on the one hand, and sharp one-line exchanges (called 'stichomythia') on the other – all these are to be found in

Seneca. Some of his stories (themselves borrowed from the Greeks) also exerted a fascination on the Elizabethans – especially those like *Thyestes* and the *Agamemnon* which dealt with revenge and blood-soaked family histories.

Yet much of what Seneca had to offer the Elizabethan theatre could have been learned elsewhere, and much of what he had to offer was not wanted. It is quite likely that Seneca's own plays were written not for performance in the sense that the Elizabethans understood it, but for public recitation. Thus, if some aspects of Seneca's stories and strategies appealed to Elizabethan writers, they nonetheless had to solve in their own way the problem of how to make them theatrically workable, relevant and exciting to a contemporary audience. The Elizabethan theatre was a greedy monster with a huge appetite, which took what it fancied from whatever sources were available to it and made them its own, spitting out whatever it found unpalatable, indigestible or irrelevant.

The raw Senecan influence, ridiculed by Nashe, soon found its way into the bloodstream of English drama, forming part of a developing tradition of tragedies whose plots hinge on political power, forbidden sexuality, family honour and private revenge. These plays, the 'revenge tragedies', are one of the main sources of the perennially popular story of The Revenger (see above, p. 67–70).

In writing *Hamlet*, then, Shakespeare is not only embracing, deliberately and wholeheartedly, a set of theatrical conventions which his audience would understand as being in the tradition of English Senecan/revenge drama; he is going a step further by taking an old and well-known play which is a jokey byword for the whole Senecan tradition and rewriting that. We do not know enough about that original Ur-*Hamlet*, of course, to know the exact nature of this rewrite, but we know that in his refashioning of this particular story, Shakespeare is dealing directly with one of his own culture's most often-treated myths – the myth of the hero charged with the duty of revenge. Shakespeare's Hamlet is one of many heroes of the Elizabethan and Jacobean stage who finds himself grievously wronged by a powerful figure, with no recourse to the law, and with a crime against his family to avenge. And *Hamlet* the play is firmly embedded in the dramatic conventions of its day.

But how does Shakespeare *use* the conventions of revenge and Senecan tragedy in *Hamlet*? Where does he follow them, and where does he depart from them? The interplay between acceptance of and rejection of convention is always important and revealing. To the extent that writers employ the conventions of their age, they are engaging (as writers must) with the concerns of their age; to the extent that any individual writer makes a decision to break with, vary or reject those conventions, he or she is making a statement about how he or she views those concerns. In writing a revenge play, Shakespeare announces that he intends to deal with certain subjects which are traditionally associated with the revenge play; in producing the specific text that he does, he says something specific and unique about those subjects.

In fact, Shakespeare follows convention fairly closely for a large part of *Hamlet*. In the first two scenes of the play, for example, the writer sets up a series of expectations for his audience: he provides a court setting, a ghost, suggestions of 'some foul play' committed before the play begins, and a discontented young man in black speaking in asides and soliloquies. He thus signals to the audience that 'this is a revenge play'. And during the rest of the play we see the extent to which that initial promise is carried out.

It develops initially along lines which Shakespeare's first audience might have expected – or even have found predictable. The Ghost confirms the nature of the crime – which is indeed both violent and sexual, for Claudius both killed Hamlet's father and then married 'incestuously' with Hamlet's mother. Hamlet is charged with assuming the role of revenger, and he begins to consider how to go about it – and whether to go about it. Much has been made of Hamlet's delay in exacting his revenge, but in fact *all* heroes of revenge tragedies delay their vengeance in various ways. Part of the pleasure of the genre lies in a continual suspense as to how (or even whether) the revenge will eventually be consummated. Hamlet, then, is not unusual in delaying. Indeed, his delay has rather more narrative justification given to it than is often the case in such plays. He is, after all, under the constant gaze of his enemy, and Claudius is very secure in his position of power: nobody else appears to suspect him. Claudius seems to hope at first that Hamlet's antagonism towards him is simply a matter of excessive grief, or some other 'natural' cause; he is certainly willing to be convinced that it all springs from a melancholy love-sickness. But as it becomes clearer that Hamlet suspects the truth, Claudius's ruthlessness reasserts itself. Hamlet's position is thus a very vulnerable one. Whereas an revenger-hero may often be anonymous and well-disguised, stalking an enemy who does not suspect his presence, Hamlet is engaged in a continual battle of wits with Claudius. This is one of the reasons why Hamlet, at the end of Act I, Scene v, decides to put on his 'antic disposition', his mad act, and why he charges Horatio and Marcellus not to reveal that they 'know aught of [him]': it is to a large extent a matter of self-preservation, of survival, since while he can convince Claudius that he is simply a little crazed, he has a certain amount of room for manoeuvre.

The tactic has the disadvantage that it draws attention to him even further, and increases the vigilance of Claudius's surveillance

117

of him, but it has the advantage that it is more or less in keeping with his behaviour before he heard the Ghost's words: from the very beginning of the play, Hamlet is, in Claudius's terms, acting strangely. As far as an audience is concerned, Hamlet's antic disposition has the added effect of emphasizing his ever-increasing isolation and alienation from the world of Claudius's court. (And since to distance oneself from the norms of the society in which one lives is in itself one definition of madness, the often-asked, though now rather unfashionable, question as to whether Hamlet is 'really' mad or whether he is just 'acting' is not an irrelevant one.)

Hamlet's delay has three main stages. First of all, he puts off all action until he has positive proof of Claudius's guilt, which he obtains by staging a play which finally convinces him of the truth of the Ghost's words. Secondly, he passes up the opportunity to stab the praying Claudius in the back, preferring to wait for a chance to kill him in a way more fitting. Again, he is being a conventional revenge hero here. The punishment should, if possible, fit the crime – and the fact that he envisages killing Claudius 'in th' incestuous pleasure of his bed' suggests which crime it is that obsesses Hamlet. Thirdly, however, he gets side-tracked. Forced into confrontation with his mother, he kills the eavesdropping Polonius, thinking that it is Claudius he is attacking. The fact that his revenge misfires and that the (comparatively) innocent Polonius is killed has two main effects: it makes Hamlet's own homicidal campaign lose energy – as if some sort of blood lust had been sated. It also forces Hamlet finally out into the open: from this point on Claudius *knows*, rather than suspects, that he is a threat. Polonius's death also gives Claudius an opportunity to move against Hamlet, which he does, sending him off to England to be put to death. At this point, about a quarter of the way through Act IV, Hamlet himself disappears from the stage for about half an hour. By the time he returns (presumably several weeks later in stage time, since he has had to escape from Rosencrantz and Guildenstern, make a deal with the pirates who fortuitously capture him, and return to Elsinore), the play seems to have changed gear, as Shakespeare begins to elaborate and complicate the initial revenge pattern of the play. What should be stressed, however, is that there is never any significant deviation from that pattern. The play does, however, have an unusual angle on the conventions of revenge tragedy; in fact, it emanates a certain kind of 'knowingness' about the theatrical genre to which it belongs – a knowingness which stems in part from the fact that it is a rewrite of an old piece of 'English Seneca read by candle-light'.

This is what makes *Hamlet* stand out from many other revenge plays of the period: not that it rejects the conventions of its genre but that it both enacts and analyses them. Reading a play in the light of its dramatic forebears and inherited conventions inevitably suggests particular kinds of interpretation, and there is a rather neat and tidy school of thought about *Hamlet* which more or less goes like this:

> Hamlet is a revenge play, like Kyd's *Spanish Tragedy*, and like Tourneur's *Revenger's Tragedy* and so on. The Renaissance was a violent time and their theatre's obsession with things like revenge proves it. But whereas most of Shakespeare's contemporaries assumed that revenge was a normal and proper course of action to take, and created revenger-heroes who behave accordingly, Shakespeare (being, like us, so much more humane and sensitive) creates a humane and sensitive hero who is appalled by the task appointed to him.

There may be a grain of truth in this view, but it is certainly not the whole story. First of all as we have seen above (pp 68–9) Shakespeare's contemporaries did *not* think of revenge as a natural course of action. It can be demonstrated not only that all moral and theological teaching of the day explicitly preached against revenge, but also that the playwrights who dealt with the story in the theatre took such teaching into account. They rarely presented the hero's case as unproblematic, and Hamlet is by no means unusual in feeling that the burden of revenge poses him ethical problems. (It is a common mistake, incidentally, to assume that Shakespeare's fellow playwrights and rivals were all mindless hacks, whose inadequacies merely show up the genius of the master. Shakespeare may have been a genius, but one of the things which contributed to his greatness was the intensely active and inventive community of theatre practitioners – actors, managers and writers – to which he belonged.) Secondly, while it might be attractively neat to think of Shakespeare looking back on the tradition of revenge tragedies and then writing a play like *Hamlet*, in which the hero transcends the limitations of the outdated tradition, we must remember that chronologically *Hamlet* comes, not at the end of the revenge play tradition, but halfway through it. *Hamlet* does indeed engage in examining, exploring and questioning some of the implications of Senecan tragedy, but not merely in order to reject them. And thirdly, Hamlet himself is only *sometimes* a 'humane and sensitive' hero. At other times he is melodramatically violent, cold-bloodedly callous, or even gleefully bloodthirsty, both in word and deed. Hamlet is not merely the rational man faced with the appalling burden of carrying out a revenge which is repugnant to his conscience – although he *is* that, among other things. But the important phrase is 'among other things'. For the character of Hamlet is, above all, one which seems to elude any simple description.

Indeed, after four centuries of commentary, criticism and scholarship, the one thing that may safely be said is that Hamlet the prince and *Hamlet* the play are enigmatic. Of all Shakespeare's plays, *Hamlet* is the most written about. Hundreds of books, thousands of articles, millions of words have been published purporting to explain the 'true meaning' of the play – and rarely do two explainers fully agree with each other. Depending on our point of view, this may be a cause for celebration – suggesting as it does the infinite variety which the play contains; or else it may be a cause for frustration – as if the play were like a Rorschach blot, one of those random blobs of ink which experimental psychologists ask subjects to make sense of, and to which everyone brings his or her own perceptions, seeing in the blob the outline of a horse or of a cucumber. There is a 'Rorschach' moment in *Hamlet* itself, in fact. Polonius is trying to attract Hamlet's attention, while Hamlet, playing mad, fends him off:

> *Polonius* My lord, the Queen would speak with you, and presently.
> *Hamlet* Do you see yonder cloud that's almost in shape of a camel?
> *Polonius* By th'mass and 'tis – like a camel indeed.
> *Hamlet* Methinks it is like a weasel.
> *Polonius* It is backed like a weasel.
> *Hamlet* Or like a whale.
> *Polonius* Very like a whale.
> *Hamlet* Then I will come to my mother by and by.
>
> (III, ii, ll. 365–74)

Hamlet is, of course, satirizing Polonius, and is rather contemptuous of the way in which the Chamberlain will agree to any interpretation which he, Hamlet, cares to put on the shape of the cloud. But the exchange makes the point: interpretations are various and unstable, and looked at in one light an object may seem like one thing, looked at in another light it may seem like something else.

It is fitting that *Hamlet* should have been the subject of so much intense interpretative activity on the part of critics, readers, actors and audiences, since interpretation itself, and the activity of making meanings, are central to the plot of the play. They are things which the characters in the play are obsessed with. For example, Hamlet himself shares with Horatio, Marcellus and Barnardo the problem of interpreting the meaning of the Ghost's appearance: the question of whether it is a 'spirit of health or goblin damn'd' (I, iv, l. 40) is one which haunts Hamlet well into the play. And once he has solved that particular riddle to his own satisfaction, Hamlet is left in the uniquely central position in the play which has made his character so fascinating to actors and critics alike: he is the essential questioner, trying continually to make meanings out of the events and objects around him, trying to interpret the significance of everything, from the actions of a military leader to the skull of a dead jester.

Claudius, on the other hand, is continually trying to interpret Hamlet's words and actions. For him, indeed, it is a matter of political and personal survival to find out what, if anything, they mean: whether they spring from love, from melancholia, or from a suspicion of the truth about his father's death. Acting (usually) on behalf of Claudius, nearly everyone else in the court – Polonius, Ophelia, Gertrude, Rosencrantz, Guildenstern – is set to the task of interpreting Hamlet. Meanwhile Hamlet's own objective for much of the play is to hide himself from other people's interpretations, to furnish them with false explanations for himself and to keep them guessing as to how much he knows, or what he intends to do. This, once more, is partly a matter of necessity. If Hamlet is an ambiguous character, one of the reasons is that ambiguity is, for him, a survival mechanism.

'The trappings and the suits of woe.'

Hamlet first appears in Act I, Scene ii of the play, and I want to spend some time looking closely at this scene. It is tempting to talk very generally about *Hamlet*, but – as so often in Shakespeare – it is in the details of the interactions of characters from one moment to another that the dynamic of the play most clearly reveals itself. Act I, Scene ii is a particularly useful scene to focus on in this respect since it is the point at which the action really begins. The main protagonists are introduced, and the relationships between them are established; most importantly, we can see in this scene the point from which Hamlet himself starts.

The play's first scene, Act I, Scene i, had been concerned with providing a particularly dramatic exposition of the story so far. Much of what we were told in this scene laid a false trail and concerned the preparations for battle between Denmark and Norway and the audience had been invited to read the Ghost's appearance in the light of this. It is not until later that the something which is rotten in the state of Denmark is traced to Claudius himself. We were told, however, that Horatio intends to tell Hamlet about the apparition, and the scene ended with Horatio and his companions going in search of the Prince.

When we see Hamlet for the first time, in Act I, Scene ii, it is in a scene which is initially dominated by Claudius, who addresses his court in general, and several individuals in particular. What is the occasion of this scene? It seems to have more than one function. It is the moment when the wedding celebrations of the marriage between Claudius and Gertrude are to end, and the serious business of governing the country is to begin. Play ends and work begins in this scene, as Claudius's speech brusquely marks the end of the period of festivity.

> Therefore our sometime sister, now our queen
> Th'imperial jointress to this warlike state,
> Have we, as 'twere with a defeated joy,
> With an auspicious and a dropping eye,
> With mirth in funeral and with dirge in marriage,
> In equal scale weighing delight and dole,
> Taken to wife. Nor have we herein barr'd
> Your better wisdoms, which have freely gone
> With this affair along. For all, our thanks.
> Now ...
>
> (I, ii, ll. 8–17)

Claudius, in this first speech, touches upon some of the central preoccupations which are to be followed through in the rest of the play. This is not just a matter of telling the audience 'the story so far' although Claudius does this as well. What is striking, though, is the rhetoric he employs to tell the story. The very language enacts the kinds of contradictions and tensions which exist in Claudius's Denmark: Claudius speaks in a series of paradoxes about 'a defeated joy', 'mirth in funeral', 'dirge in marriage', 'delight and dole'. Claudius, presumably, is trying to give an impression of balance and good judgement: he is, he implies, giving due attention both to mourning and to celebration, holding these emotions 'in equal scale'. That lengthy first sentence of the quotation emphasizes the way in which Claudius is attempting to use language and rhetoric to control the contradictions of his own position: the basic statement 'Therefore our sometime sister ... have we ... taken to wife' is qualified and modified by clause after subordinate clause, producing the desired effect of gravity and judgement which is so important for Claudius to maintain. But while for Claudius the rhetoric does the job well, we as audience are perhaps more struck by the number of contradictions which do exist rather than by the way in which Claudius handles them.

More generally, this is a scene which both announces and enacts one of the major themes not only of *Hamlet* but of all the major tragedies: the point at which public and private identities interact. Claudius's speech illustrates the juxtaposition of the two, as he turns from celebration of his personal life (in the form of marriage) and puts on the mask of the ruler ('Now ...'). It is not, of course, as simple as this, for the public and private are not two separate realms, as the structure of Claudius's speech might seem to suggest they are. His marriage to Gertrude and the celebration of it is hardly a private act, for a royal wedding is always a public event: the intimacy of the sexual union has meanings which reverberate in the political sphere. Any intimacy between Claudius and Gertrude is already compromised, in fact, since we learn as the play progresses that Claudius's marriage is one of convenience through and through: Gertrude is for him a property which has helped him on his path to the throne. Moreover, as we shall see, his public rôle as ruler of the kingdom will involve him increasingly in dealings which involve his family. The interweaving of the personal and the political, of the private and the public spheres, is a central theme of the play. Conventional Elizabethan political wisdom distinguished between the 'body politic' and the 'body natural' of a ruler, splitting the identity of a king or queen into two separate aspects – the public identity and the private. One of the concerns of the play is to explore and to question the validity of this distinction between the public and the private spheres, not only in the figure of the ruler, but in those of his subjects as well.

These twin themes of the tensions and contradictions within the court, and the relationship between public and private identities are given an emblematic stage presence in the figure of Hamlet himself. In these early scenes of the play, Shakespeare recurrently suggests a sense of normal life being under strain: the idea is there in the nervousness of the guards in Act I, Scene i, and it is repeated in the stage picture which comprises Scene ii. It is notoriously difficult to reconstruct Elizabethan stage effects, or to work out exactly how Shakespeare meant some of his scenes to appear on the stage, but in Act I, Scene ii of Hamlet we are given some pretty precise information as to how the scene should look. Most importantly, we are told what Hamlet himself is wearing: he is wearing an 'inky cloak', and 'suits of solemn black'. The rest of the court, it is to be presumed, are wearing clothes more fitting for a wedding celebration or for everyday affairs in the court. If much of the early part of Claudius's first speech is about moderation and balance, about giving equal weight to mourning and to celebration, the audience have in front of them, in Hamlet, a figure whose very apparel proclaims his refusal to do this. Claudius has described the progression which he wants the court to undergo, from mourning to celebration to the everyday normality of the affairs of government: Hamlet remains stubbornly and defiantly in mourning. The point is that Hamlet is foregrounded before he ever says a word. He is noticeable before we even know who he is, and his silent presence, symbolically loaded as it is with implications both of mourning and of rebellion, establishes by his very appearance that all is far from well in Elsinore.

Hamlet's appearance also touches on the theme of the public and private identities – a theme which the scene will elaborate on, once Hamlet starts to speak. But again, even as a silent presence in a scene full (initially) of Claudius's talk, Hamlet's presence has certain implications. He is ignored by Claudius for the first sixty-three lines of the scene; when he is finally addressed his first reply is an aside and his second an evasive pun. Most actors playing Hamlet have preferred to find some place on the sidelines to stand during the early part of this scene, or if they have had to go centre stage, have had to find various ways to suggest that they are trying to detach themselves from the main, communal action: It is because Claudius so obviously shows himself in control of the public domain (it is his party) that Hamlet is forced to retreat from that into some area not controlled by Claudius: the 'privacy' of his own subjectivity. In announcing that he refuses to join in Claudius's public celebration, Hamlet also announces that he himself 'really' inhabits a different psychological space from the rest of the court: they are content to join in Claudius's public world, but Hamlet, wearing black to set himself apart from the rest, signals that he has retreated 'inside himself'.

Hamlet's self-isolation is referred to explicitly in the following exchange between Hamlet and Gertrude, in which his mother attempts to persuade him to relinquish his mourning-garb, and to effect a reconciliation with Claudius:

> *Queen* Good Hamlet, cast thy nighted colour off,
>   And let thine eye look like a friend on Denmark.
>   Do not forever with thy vailèd lids
>   Seek for thy noble father in the dust.
>   Thou know'st 'tis common: all that lives must die,
>   Passing through nature to eternity.
> *Hamlet* Ay, madam, it is common.
> *Queen* If it be,
>   Why seems it so particular with thee?
> *Hamlet* Seems, madam? Nay, it is. I know not 'seems'.
>   'Tis not alone my inky cloak, good mother,
>   Nor customary suits of solemn black,
>   Nor windy suspiration of forc'd breath,
>   No, nor the fruitful river in the eye,
>   Nor the dejected haviour of the visage,
>   Together with all forms, moods, shapes of grief,
>   That can denote me truly. These indeed seem,
>   For they are actions that a man might play;
>   But I have that within which passes show,
>   These but the trappings and the suits of woe.
>
> (I, ii, ll. 68–86)

This is the only moment while Claudius is on-stage in this scene that Hamlet can be induced to respond in anything more than one-liners. His response to her question is complex but consistent: it has two elements in it. Firstly he asserts that his clothes *do* denote him truly, and that the outward manifestations correctly represent his state of mind: he doesn't just 'seem' to be grieving – he *is* grieving. He then, however, goes on to denigrate the value of the clothes (which he has chosen, presumably, in order to announce his grief to the world) as a system of communication. All outward signs of grief, he insists, can be counterfeited: they are 'actions that a man might play', and thus not to be trusted. Hamlet implies that he happens to be displaying a continuity between his outward behaviour and his inner feelings, but he implies too that that continuity is arbitrary rather than necessary.

It is a constant obsession of Hamlet throughout the play that he is always looking for some sort of truth that exists beneath the surface of things; here he is expressing what he believes to be the 'truth' about himself – that his true being exists subjectively, in some 'inner self' which comprises 'that within which passes show'. He has, in effect, split himself into two parts: there is the outer self, which is for public consumption. He happens to want to communicate his feelings, and so he wears black and moons about sullenly; but, he implies, it would be just as easy for him to 'play a part' and conceal those feelings – just as it would be possible for someone who did *not* feel grief to play the part of a mourner.

What is important, according to Hamlet, is what he 'really' feels – and he locates this reality in some deeply subjective area of his character which is not for public consumption at all. The split which it involves, between the private and public elements of one's personality, is so common a feature of traditional Western thinking about the notion of character that it seems unremarkable and commonsensical. It is precisely the 'naturalness' of this split between public and private identities which Shakespeare explores throughout the play. At this stage in *Hamlet* he is content to let it stand, and we are asked to sympathize with Hamlet's distinction between appearance and reality, and to accept his own evaluation of himself as having 'that within which passes show'.

We saw that Claudius, in his first speech, attempted to give an impression of balance by reconciling the opposites (of, for example, mourning and celebration) in a series of paradoxes. In his reply to Hamlet's outburst, too, he uses language which seems to be calculated to take into account both sides of a question. On the one hand, he tells Hamlet that it is 'sweet and commendable' of him to be so obviously affected by his father's death. On the other hand, he continues, mourning must end sooner or later and life must go on.

Thus, Claudius's answer to Hamlet appears at first sight to be the
epitome of reasonableness, a balanced combination of sensitivity
and down-to-earth common sense.

'Tis sweet and commendable in your nature, Hamlet,
To give these mourning duties to your father
But you must know your father lost a father,
That father lost, lost his – and the survivor bound
In filial obligation for some term
To do obsequious sorrow. But to persever
In obstinate condolement is a course
Of impious stubbornness, 'tis unmanly grief,
It shows a will most incorrect to heaven,
A heart unfortified, a mind impatient,
An understanding simple and unschool'd,
For what we know must be, and is as common
As any the most vulgar thing to sense –
Why should we in our peevish opposition
Take it to heart? Fie, 'tis a fault to heaven,
A fault against the dead, a fault to nature,
To reason most absurd, whose common theme
Is death of fathers, and who still hath cried
From the first corse till he that died today,
'This must be so'.

(I, ii, ll. 87–106)

When we actually look at the different weight which Claudius
gives to the two opposite parts of his argument as his speech develops,
we realize that Claudius's 'balance' is actually nothing of the kind.
To the first part of his argument, the part in which he is praising
Hamlet for his sensitivity, he accords just three phrases: 'sweet and
commendable', 'filial obligation' and 'obsequious sorrow', all of
which contain some element of approval ('obsequious' did not, in
the early seventeenth century, have some of the negative overtones
which it has now: it means in Claudius's speech, quite simply,
'having to do with funerals [obsequies]'). However, the negative
side of the argument, in which he criticizes Hamlet for overdoing
the mourning, turns into a tirade against Hamlet, and is loaded with
phrases such as 'obstinate condolement', 'impious stubbornness',
'unmanly grief', 'incorrect to heaven', 'a heart unfortified', 'a mind
impatient', 'an understanding simple and unschool'd', 'peevish
opposition', 'a fault to heaven', 'a fault against the dead', 'a fault to
nature' 'most absurd'. The seeming balance of the structure of
Claudius's speech is overwhelmed by what it actually says.

There are various interpretations we might make of this. We
might read this as evidence that Claudius's attempt to seem balanced

and controlled is actually under a great deal of strain, and that he is far less in control of the situation than he wants his audience (both on-stage and off) to believe. Or we might see it as a naked manifestation of power: Claudius, because he is in a public situation, needs to be a little tactful towards Hamlet, and thus compliments him on his sweet and commendable nature, and assures him that he regards him 'with no less nobility of love/ Than that which the dearest father bears his son' (ll. 110–11); but Claudius is, after all, king, and his power is absolute. This speech can be plausibly read as Claudius showing Hamlet the iron fist that he habitually hides beneath the velvet glove. Whichever interpretation we assign to the contradictory elements of Claudius's speech, it is important that we recognize that these contradictions do exist. My own preference is for the second interpretation, the one which reads Claudius's speech as a veiled reminder to Hamlet of the power that Claudius now wields. For if the state occasion at which Claudius is speaking marks the end of the wedding celebrations and the resumption of day-to-day business at court, it also marks the moment at which Claudius himself fully assumes the reins of government: it is his first major opportunity to flex his political muscles, and it is quite in keeping with this that he should take the opportunity to remind Hamlet where the power in the court now lies.

The confrontational aspect of the early part of this scene is, moreover, heightened by Claudius's treatment of a request which Hamlet presumably made before the scene started:

> For your intent
> In going back to school in Wittenberg,
> It is most retrograde to our desire,
> And we beseech you bend you to remain
> Here in the cheer and comfort of our eye,
> Our chiefest courtier, cousin, and our son.
>
> (I, ii, ll. 112–17)

Once more, note the contrast in tones: the first two and a half lines are brusque – almost dismissive of Hamlet. The tone changes almost immediately to one of 'beseeching' – but Claudius, as we have seen, has no need to beseech. He has, effectively, already ordered Hamlet to stay in Elsinore. Either the last few lines of Claudius's speech are grossly hypocritical or else – as I tend to believe – something quite interesting is going on here. Claudius, as we have already noted, tends to use language in a way calculated to control the world around him. Here he is doing a similar thing again: when he says that he wishes Hamlet to remain 'in the cheer and comfort of our eye/ Our chiefest courtier, cousin, and our son' he is not, of course, describing a state of affairs which exists in Elsinore at that time: there is nothing 'cheerful' or 'comfortable' about the eye which he casts on Hamlet in this scene (and we may be tempted to think that he wants Hamlet around so that he can 'keep an eye' on him in a much less friendly way than he suggests here). Moreover, while Hamlet is 'chiefest courtier' in rank, being heir to the throne, he is anything but the most loyal and benevolent of Claudius's courtiers; and, furthermore, the other titles which Claudius here bestows upon him, he has already rejected (for the family relations have left him 'too much in the sun'). So Claudius's last two lines here sound simply like lies. On another level, however, what Claudius is doing is not describing how things are in Elsinore, but how he expects them to be – what we might call expressing a wish, or, on a more sinister level, making the assumption that he only has to say something for it to become true.

Claudius's refusal of Hamlet's request has another function within the scene: it sets up the comparison between him and Laertes. It is a commonly-noted feature of the play that Hamlet is continually being compared to other characters—both characters in the play itself and characters from literature and myth. In Claudius's first speech in the scene, we were introduced to 'Young Fortinbras', who has a few similarities to Hamlet: he too is the nephew of a king; he too is an enemy of Claudius; he too is seeking some sort of vengeance following the death of his father. Some of these correspondences between Hamlet and Fortinbras are to be developed in Act IV, Scene iv and at the close of the play. But now Shakespeare offers us another character with whom Hamlet will be compared: Laertes and Hamlet are both comparatively young men in a court dominated by the middle-aged; both are described as being popular with the people of Denmark; their common love for Ophelia unites them thematically in the fourth act, and the ensuing swordfight which results in both their deaths makes clear the extent to which they are each other's opposites; both give themselves the task of avenging the death of a relative; both are spied on by their parents. At this point in the play, however, the comparison is of a more basic kind. Both have returned to Elsinore to see Claudius crowned, and both now have asked permission to return to their former occupations – Laertes wanting to go back to France, Hamlet to Wittenberg. Laertes' request is granted, Hamlet's is refused.

The first part of this scene ends with Hamlet delivering a veiled insult to Claudius: his line 'I shall in all my best obey you, madam' is directed towards his mother, and Hamlet implies that his obedience is towards her and her alone. Claudius, for his part, continues to establish his command of things by ignoring (and thus annihilating) the implied sub-text of Hamlet's remark. Taking the line at its face value, he translates it into the public sphere once more, calling it

'This gentle and unforced accord of Hamlet'. In doing so he establishes once more that he owns the domain of public discourse: at first sight the rest of Claudius's court might imagine that Hamlet's jibe was rather sullen and bad-tempered – but the King says that it is gentle and unforced accord, and so that is how the courtiers must see it. The Emperor is wearing his new clothes, and little by little, moment by moment, Claudius, like all effective tyrants, rewrites history.

'Break, my heart, for I must hold my tongue'

At this point, as Claudius and his retinue sweep off, the scene changes gear – becomes, indeed, effectively a different scene altogether. (It is sometimes suggested that we get a clearer sense of the structure of scenes in Shakespeare if we think of the French convention of making each 'scene' not so much a change of location as a significant change of personnel on stage.) Hamlet, left alone on stage, begins his first soliloquy:

> O that this too too sullied flesh would melt,
> Thaw and resolve itself into a dew,
> Or that the Everlasting had not fix'd
> His canon 'gainst self-slaughter. O God! God!
> How weary, stale, flat, and unprofitable
> Seem to me all the uses of this world!
>
> (I, ii, ll. 129–34)

Earlier in the scene, Hamlet had insisted that what the world saw of him could not 'denote [him] truly'. And now, through the convention of the soliloquy, Hamlet steps forward to confide in the audience just what it is that he is hiding from those around him. The soliloquy offers the audience an area of privileged communication with the character, a moment in which his most private thoughts are made available to them. A character speaking in soliloquy never deceives an audience – unless, of course, he is deceiving himself. Throughout the play it is possible to chart Hamlet's progress by means of his soliloquies; through them, Shakespeare draws a portrait of a man whose ideas, thoughts, and beliefs are under constant pressure, subject to constant change.

Hamlet's starting point is a rejection of the 'flesh'. Before ever he has any firm suspicion of the real nature of Denmark's rottenness, Hamlet is disgusted with his own body and wants to dissociate himself from it. The actual deed of suicide is a second thought: his first thought, his first wish is that his 'sullied (or 'solid'?) flesh' should 'melt, Thaw and resolve itself into a dew'. These two images do not merely repeat each other: indeed, there is a slight contradiction between them. The first image, of melting and thawing, suggests a total dissolution in which body and soul together metamorphose into a natural but non-human image: the dew. The second two lines, in which Hamlet laments that God had 'fix'd His canon 'gainst self-slaughter' is more orthodoxly Christian, not only in its regard for the commandments of 'the Everlasting', but also in its implied dualist assumption that the death of the body does nothing to relieve the soul of its responsibilities.

These ideas will resurface elsewhere in the play: notably, and at length, in the graveyard scene, and in the famous 'To be or not to be' speech (which is in large part a recapitulation of lines three and four of this soliloquy). These first lines of Hamlet's first soliloquy, in fact encapsulate many of the major obsessions of the play. Those words, which appear to be the death-wish of a man in a state of depression, are what a great deal of the play is 'about'. Hamlet's horror of, his desire to rid himself of, the 'flesh' has a bearing both on the play's central concern with images of death, and on Hamlet's own fixation on sexuality.

For at this stage in the play, what obsesses and disgusts Hamlet is simply this: the fact, and the speed, of his mother's remarriage to Claudius. Phrases concerned with shortness of time beat rhythmically and insistently throughout the soliloquy:

> ... within a month –
> Let me not think on't – Frailty, thy name is woman –
> A little month, or ere those shoes were old
> With which she follow'd my poor father's body,
> Like Niobe, all tears – why, she –
> O God, a beast that wants discourse of reason
> Would have mourn'd longer – married with my uncle,
> My father's brother – but no more like my father
> Than I to Hercules. Within a month,
> Ere yet the salt of most unrighteous tears
> Had left the flushing in her galled eyes,
> She married – O most wicked speed! To post
> With such dexterity to incestuous sheets!
>
> (I, ii, ll. 145–57)

The first few lines of Hamlet's soliloquy had been rational, reflective and eloquent. But as it progresses – and more specifically, as it begins to deal with the *reasons* for Hamlet's state – the speech begins to verge on incoherence. A brief comparison with Claudius's speech earlier in the scene is illuminating. There Claudius had a sentence whose basic statement was 'Therefore our sometime sister ... have we ... taken to wife' (I, ii, ll. 8–14). The sentence was rounded out by a whole series of other clauses – all of which, however, fed into the main statement. Hamlet here has a 'sentence' whose basic statement gives almost exactly the same information: 'Within a month ... she ... married with my uncle.' But this basic statement, like Claudius's, contains within it a number of other clauses. The difference is that whereas Claudius's subordinate clauses are there for amplification, to display balance and control, Hamlet's are simply a series of interruptions, which break up his line of thought and show a mind overwhelmed by ideas which it cannot control. Hamlet's language leaps off in all directions, as his syntax shows itself incapable of organizing his emotions into an orderly pattern. It is as if the statement itself – that his mother married with his uncle – were so distressing that the sentence will not form itself coherently for Hamlet. And as the coherence of his language breaks down under pressure, he resorts to addressing himself ('Let me not think on't'), citing misogynistic aphorisms ('Frailty, thy name is woman'), summoning up mythological references (Niobe), and animal comparisons ('a beast that wants discourse of reason'). Even when he has managed to come out with his statement, his language does not stop, but sends him in a circle, wheeling on through a number of further interruptions in order to repeat 'Within a month... she married.'

The importance of this first soliloquy is twofold: firstly, as suggested above, it introduces the themes of sexuality, death, suicide and heavenly decree which are to obsess Hamlet throughout the play. But secondly, in its method it presents a kind of paradigm of the play itself. The ability of language to give order to thoughts and emotions is challenged from below by a pressure of thought and emotion which is beyond its normal capacity. In a similar way, the rational and pragmatic world of the court (and the 'normality' of its everyday life, to which Claudius needs so desperately to return) is soon to be destroyed by pressures of the irrational and the supernatural, by the Ghost and by Hamlet's 'madness'. Shakespeare's tragedies – and *Hamlet* in particular – are plays in which the normal settled routine of everyday life is torn apart by forces, emotions and desires which defeat the protagonists' usual ways of making sense of the world.

The soliloquy is interrupted by the arrival of Horatio, Marcellus and Barnardo. Hamlet's first response, as he hears people approach, is to go back into his shell and become again the silent, self-protecting figure whom we saw earlier in the scene. 'Break, my heart', he says, 'for I must hold my tongue'.

In fact, once he realizes that the newcomers include Horatio, he does not hold his tongue at all. Only seconds after their meeting, the ideas which had been obsessing him throughout his soliloquy come rushing out again, now in the form of sardonic humour:

Horatio My lord, I came to see your father's funeral
Hamlet I prithee do not mock me, fellow-student.
  I think it was to see my mother's wedding.
Horatio Indeed, my lord, it follow'd hard upon.
Hamlet Thrift, thrift, Horatio. The funeral bak'd meats
  Did coldly furnish forth the marriage tables.

(I, ii, ll. 176–81)

But this air of ironic wit does not last long. As soon as the news is broken, that Hamlet's father's ghost has been sighted, the mood and tone of the scene change. Hamlet inundates Horatio, Barnardo and Marcellus with questions. These are, though, not merely the questions of a man agog to hear more. Hamlet virtually interrogates the other three, asking them questions not just to satisfy his own curiosity, but also to test the reliability of their story. Like a prosecuting counsel, his interrogation includes aggressive cross-questioning tactics:

Hamlet Arm'd, say you?
All Arm'd, my lord.
Hamlet From top to toe?
All My lord, from head to foot.
Hamlet Then saw you not his face?

(I, ii, ll. 226–8)

When he has thoroughly satisfied himself that their story is consistent, he commits himself to the next stage of the investigation, declaring 'I will watch to tonight. Perchance 'twill walk again.' He enjoins them to secrecy – as so many people are enjoined to secrecy about so many things in Elsinore – and the audience is left, with Hamlet, speculating about the meaning of the Ghost's appearance. Hamlet already suspects 'some foul play', and although he has no specific idea as to what exactly that might have been, he ends the scene with an image which says a great deal about the tragedy of *Hamlet*: 'Foul deeds will rise. Though all the earth o'erwhelm them, to men's eyes.' This idea of the past, rising through to overturn the false peace of the present, is what the Ghost represents.

By the end of this scene, we have met, not just 'Hamlet', but at least three Hamlets, each one made up of contradictions. There is Hamlet, the outsider in the court – sullen and silent, yet easily provoked to outburst by his mother, verbally uncommunicative, yet wearing clothes that make statements louder than any words, wanting to signal to people his disgust at the behaviour of the King and Queen, and yet simultaneously convinced that those signs of outward behaviour cannot 'denote [him] truly'. Then there is the speaker of the soliloquy, whose language manifests the conflicts of his situation, and whose syntax loses itself under the pressure of trying to find coherent self-expression. At precisely the moment when the audience must be expecting some kind of clear explanation or introduction to the play and its issues, they are presented with a soliloquy by someone who is in no state to soliloquize. And then there is the Hamlet who exists in the company of Horatio and his companions: at first, sardonically humorous, then acute and questioning, torn between scepticism and belief.

It is not (as Hamlet himself might claim) that there is one 'real' Hamlet and that all the rest are just masks or misconceptions: one of the things which *Hamlet* the play (and perhaps, in his own way, Hamlet the prince) explores, is the way in which personal identity is constructed and reconstructed time and again in different situations. The contradictoriness and multifacetedness of identity is a constant theme in a play which deals so centrally with ideas of plays, illusion, rôle-playing and theatricality.

'The purpose of playing'

The whole world of Elsinore is one in which people act out rôles and play parts. Characters continually set up fictional scenes: Polonius (who 'played once i'th'university... and was accounted a good actor') and Claudius, the seeming king, devise, stage and sometimes watch little dramatic tableaux in which Rosencrantz, Guildenstern, Gertrude, Ophelia and Laertes play their parts opposite Hamlet. The ceremonies of the court, be they state occasions, funerals, or fencing matches, provide one very public kind of theatre. Another, more private kind, is produced by the continual spying which ensures that nobody's intimate conversations are ever without an audience and that everyone is always on show. Laertes has no privacy even when he escapes to France; Gertrude has no privacy even in her own closet; Claudius has no privacy even as he prays! And at the centre of the play stands Hamlet himself, the most theatrical of Shakespeare's heroes, whose mind is obsessed with two questions of theatre. The first is the decision as to whether or not he wants to become the hero of a revenge drama; the second involves his continual search through a whole repertoire of rôles, in order to try and find the 'real self' which he is convinced lies somewhere in amongst them.

From an early age, we are told, Hamlet was an enthusiastic play-goer, 'wont to take... delight in the tragedians of the city'. But more than that, we see him become in turn an actor, director, playwright and dramatic theorist. He instructs the players in their craft, writes scenes for them and tells them how to play them. It is Hamlet the

playwright who finally forces Claudius to reveal his guilt. And it is
because he is a proficient actor (as a good Revenge hero must be) that
Hamlet can survive, for a while, in the claustrophobic world of the
court at Elsinore. For throughout most of the play he plays a series
of rôles which disguise from Claudius his purpose and his suspicions.

But Hamlet is also an actor in a more literal and more specific
sense, and the particular way in which this is revealed is significant.
As well as having enjoyed the performances of the tragedians of the
city, it turns out that Hamlet can remember their speeches, and even
(after some initial hesitation) perform them:

> One speech in't I chiefly loved – 'twas Aeneas' tale
> to Dido – and thereabout of it especially when he
> speaks of Priam's slaughter. If it live in your memory,
> begin at this line – let me see, let me see:
> '*The rugged Pyrrhus, like th'Hyrcanian beast*' –
> 'Tis not so. It begins with Pyrrhus:
> '*The rugged Pyrrhus, he whose sable arms*
> *Black as his purpose did the night resemble*
> *When he lay couch'd in th'ominous horse,*
> *Hath now this dread and black complexion smeared*
> *With heraldry more dismal. Head to foot*
> *Now is he total gules, horridly trick'd*
> *With blood of fathers, mothers, daughters, sons.*'

(II, ii, ll. 442–54)

After a few lines more he hands the rôle over to the Player, but the
point has been made. We have seen Hamlet becoming an actor,
performing the speech about Pyrrhus. His performance even merits
some words of praise (for what they are worth) from Polonius. And
what is particularly significant here is the specific speech that Hamlet
lights upon, the speech about Pyrrhus. It is a revealing one for him
to choose, for it is about a young man, smeared in blood, murderously
searching through the streets for an old king, Priam, whom he will
kill. Hamlet continually looks for analogies of his own position, and
he finds one in the story of Pyrrhus: what drives him to act out this
speech – and to have the Player finish it for him – is the fact that it
provides him with an image or a fantasy of himself as Pyrrhus, the
violent avenger.

Paradoxically, what makes this such powerful theatre is the fact
that the speech itself is not even particularly good poetry. It is rather
bombastic and old-fashioned compared to the dramatic verse that
Shakespeare himself is capable of writing. But what is at issue is not
the quality of the verse but its effect on the audience – or rather, one
member of the audience, Hamlet himself. Hamlet's fascination with
the theatre has some very practical motivations: here he uses the

drama in order to tell and to hear at one remove stories about himself. The sadistic streak which exists in his fantasies extends not just to Claudius but also to Gertrude, his mother. 'Say on, come to Hecuba', he urges the Player; for if the speech starts with the young man looking for the king in order to kill him, it ends with the agony of the distraught queen, and with Polonius interrupting the action because the emotional pitch has got too high: 'Look whe'er he has not turned his colour and has tears in's eyes. Prithee no more' (II, ii, 1. 515).

The tears in the Player's eyes are a problem for Hamlet, for they lead him to contemplate questions about appearance and reality. His soliloquy beginning 'O what a rogue and peasant slave am I' starts as a meditation on the relationship between stage grief and grief in real life, a comparison between the Player's 'trappings and ... suits of woe' and Hamlet's own real-life 'motive and ... cue for passion'. It soon turns into a speech of self-loathing as he blames himself for his inaction. But this, too, takes a suddenly theatrical turn

> Yet I,
> A dull and muddy-mettled rascal, peak
> Like John-a-dreams, unpregnant of my cause,
> And can say nothing – no, not for a king,
> Upon whose property and most dear life
> A damn'd defeat was made. Am I a coward?
> Who calls me villain, breaks my pate across,
> Plucks off my beard and blows it in my face,
> Tweaks me by the nose, gives me the lie i'th'throat
> As deep as to the lungs – who does me this?
> Ha!
> 'Swounds, I should take it, for it cannot be
> But I am pigeon-liver'd and lack gall
> To make oppression bitter, or ere this
> I should ha' fatted all the region kites
> With this slave's offal. Bloody, bawdy villain!
> Remorseless, treacherous, lecherous, kindless villain!
> Why what an ass am I! This is most brave ...
>   (II, ii, ll. 561–78)

Hamlet, contemplating the Player – the man who counterfeits action – tries to 'act' himself into the rôle of the man of action, the revenger, challenging imaginary critics and then working himself into a frenzy with that crescendo of adjectives: 'Remorseless, treacherous, lecherous, kindless villain'. The attempt, however, is a failure, Hamlet is too self-conscious to be really carried away by his own rhetoric: he falls back into sneering at himself and his own rôle-playing.

Simply to act out the part is not enough for him; he must 'act' in the other sense of the word, too.

Throughout the early part of the play, these two meanings of the word 'act' – to play a fictional rôle, and to accomplish something in reality – jostle against each other and impinge upon each other. It is as a consequence of this that Hamlet eventually constructs his *Mousetrap*, based on the play of *The Murder of Gonzago*. The affective power of dramatic fiction, he reasons, is so great that Claudius's conscience must be caught by it. Events prove Hamlet right, of course: the theatrical representation of his own crime proves too much for Claudius's sang-froid and he storms out, leaving Hamlet in no doubt of his guilt. For Hamlet, the theatre is never a matter of art for art's sake. He continually finds that meanings created within a fictional world (of, for example, the Player's Pyrrhus speech, or *The Murder of Gonzago*) spill out and affect the world of his reality.

This blurring of the worlds of fiction and reality is directly responsible for some of the prolems of interpretation which exist in *Hamlet*. One difficulty about the play is that it is not always possible to decide whether Hamlet is putting on an act or not. In Act III, Scene i, for example, there occurs the speech which is the most famous in the play, arguably the most famous in any of Shakespeare's plays and one of the most famous in dramatic literature:

> To be, or not to be, that is the question:
> Whether 'tis nobler in the mind to suffer
> The slings and arrows of outrageous fortune,
> Or to take arms against a sea of troubles
> And by opposing end them. To die – to sleep,
> No more; and by a sleep to say we end
> The heartache and the thousand natural shocks
> That flesh is heir to: 'tis a consummation
> Devoutly to be wish'd. To die, to sleep;
> To sleep, perchance to dream – ay, there's the rub ...
>
> (III, i, ll. 56–65)

There is no denying the power of this speech – but what does it actually mean? It is almost impossible to decide, since not only the speech itself but also its context in the scene are both enigmatic. The language is obscure and allusive, and it is not always clear exactly what it is that Hamlet is contemplating. Some people read the speech as a debate about suicide, other think he is talking about murdering Claudius, and another school of thought sees the speech as swinging between these two ideas. But even if it were possible to make firm decisions about these, the dramatic context in which the speech appears introduces further indeterminacies which make a definitive interpretation difficult.

This context is as follows. At the end of the previous scene Hamlet decided that 'The play's the thing/ Wherein I'll catch the conscience of the King (II, ii, ll. 616–17). He has decided to try to establish the truth about Claudius and although we do not know it yet, this will involve the parts that he has written for inclusion in *The Murder of Gonzago*. At the beginning of this next scene, Claudius and his courtiers are, symmetrically, still trying to establish the truth about Hamlet. The King questions Rosencrantz and Guildenstern about what they have discovered – which turns out to be very little. We are given a little bit more information about Hamlet's plans for the King to see a play, and we see Claudius take the bait.

Meanwhile, Claudius himself is busy laying traps for Hamlet. Polonius's interpretation of Hamlet is that he is distracted by love. Claudius (who presumably would be very relieved if this were all that was wrong with his nephew) wants to find out if this is the case:

> Sweet Gertrude, leave us too,
> For we have closely sent for Hamlet hither
> That he, as 'twere by accident, may here
> Affront Ophelia.
> Her father and myself, lawful espials,
> We'll so bestow ourselves that, seeing unseen,
> We may of their encounter frankly judge,
> And gather by him, as he is behav'd,
> If't be th'affliction of his love or no
> That thus he suffers for.
>
> (III, i, ll. 28–37)

Thus when Hamlet walks onto the stage in this scene it is not onto some kind of neutral area in which he is free to address the audience in a direct and unproblematic way. On the contrary, he walks into a highly-charged space which has already been commandeered by Claudius; the King has stage-managed a scene in which Ophelia is to play a part knowingly and Hamlet is to play one unwittingly. Ophelia, therefore, is already on stage as Hamlet enters; she has been given her part to play – and even a prop to play it with – by Claudius and Polonius. Claudius and Polonius are on the stage but hidden from Hamlet's view, and they constitute an on-stage audience, watching intently the small drama that is to be played out between Ophelia and Hamlet. But instead of Hamlet walking on and greeting Ophelia, he comes on and begins the famous soliloquy: 'To be or not to be: that is the question'. But before we can contemplate *that* question, there is another one to be answered: to whom does Hamlet address the speech?

It is a matter of how the conventions are being used. The straight-forward way of playing the soliloquy convention dictates simply that the speaker ignore everything else that is going on around him, and give the speech as if it were the unmediated thoughts which are going on inside his head. This is a common way of acting this scene, and there is a lot to be said for it. Against it, however, is the immense trouble that Shakespeare has already taken to ensure that when Hamlet enters he does so onto a stage which is already loaded with significance. Or, to put it more simply, if Shakespeare had wanted it to be a straightforward soliloquy, hasn't he made it unnecessarily confusing by having (a) someone already on stage – since soliloquies are usually delivered from an otherwise empty stage – and (b) two more people whom we know to be eavesdropping on everything that goes on onstage. Hence another strong possibility appears – that instead of playing this speech as a soliloquy (in which case the assumption is that nobody else can hear what is being said, since a soliloquy represents a character's internal thoughts) it should be played as a speech spoken out loud by Hamlet expressly so that Ophelia can overhear it.

If this is the case, it changes the whole way in which we, the audience, listen to the speech. If it is delivered as a straightforward and conventional soliloquy, it says one thing about Hamlet's mental state – that is to say that he is contemplating some violent action but is deterred by thoughts of retribution in the afterlife. If, on the other hand, it is spoken for Ophelia's benefit, it says something very different – that Hamlet is continuing to keep up the act which is designed to prevent anyone from knowing what is really going on in his mind. The first reading of the scene makes it a self-expressive moment in which the audience see into Hamlet's soul; the second reading makes it yet another of Hamlet's succession of rôles and masks.

My own preference is for the second of these two readings, but I cannot prove beyond any reasonable doubt that it is the right one, and that the more conventional reading is wrong. One can make appeals to even more general contexts, of course, and in favour of the straightforward reading is the very fact that it *is* straightforward: people have been playing this speech as a soliloquy for years; there is no reason to make things more difficult by speculating about whether Hamlet is aware of Ophelia's presence, and so on. On the other hand, in favour of the second reading is the argument that, at this particular point in the play it seems very odd for Hamlet to be particularly obsessed with the immediate prospect of either suicide or murder, since he is busy concocting his plan to trap Claudius with *The Murder of Gonzago* and settle his guilt once for all; thus it is more in keeping to assume that in this scene Hamlet is simply continuing to do what he does throughout the rest of the play and put on an act for the benefit of the rest of the court.

Thus Hamlet's rôle-playing, and the audience's uncertainty as to when he *is* playing a rôle and when he is not, serves to compound the sense of Hamlet's impenetrability. An audience is given the illusion of intimacy with Hamlet; we seem to know all about his 'inner being' by virtue of his large number of soliloquies. But actually, we know comparatively little about him, since what he presents to an audience is a series of consciously-adopted rôles and masks. Even at the moments when characters in plays are traditionally at their most honest and open, we cannot be sure that Hamlet is not simply hiding behind yet another mask.

'The image of my cause'

Thus rôle-playing lies at the centre of Hamlet's strategy for survival. Both his interest in the stage and his assumed mask of madness offer him the possibility of playing a variety of parts. As we have seen in Act I, Scene ii there is his initial adoption of the rôle of Malcontent, later to turn into Revenger. He parodies the Unworldly Scholar, both to Horatio and to Polonius. For Ophelia's benefit, and for Polonius's too, he becomes the Distracted Lover, with 'his doublet all unbraced, no hat upon his head'. And perhaps for Ophelia's benefit, too, and for the benefit of anyone else who may be listening, he becomes the Melancholic Man, contemplating suicide in the 'To be or not to be' speech.

But there is another aspect to Hamlet's continual adopting of various rôles. This consists of the way in which Hamlet is repeatedly compared or contrasted, implicitly or explicitly, with other characters in the play. For example, faced with the sight of Fortinbras leading his army into battle, Hamlet immediately begins to draw comparisons between Fortinbras and himself, projecting himself in his own imagination into the rôle of military hero, for whom 'Rightly to be great Is . . . to find quarrel in a straw When honour's at the stake'. But the parallels between Hamlet and Fortinbras go beyond Hamlet's envying Fortinbras his military capacity. Fortinbras, like Hamlet, is nephew to a king; his late father and Hamlet's were military opponents; like Hamlet, he opposes Claudius at the beginning of the play; at the end of the play he takes over Hamlet's function as head of state in Denmark. As we have seen, parallels have also been drawn between Hamlet and Laertes, between Hamlet and the Player who can weep so easily 'For Hecuba', and between Hamlet and 'the rugged Pyrrhus'. In the dumbshow of *The Murder of Gonzago* the murderous Lucianus is primarily a representation of Claudius killing Old Hamlet with his poison – but Lucianus is also described as being, specifically, 'nephew to the King': it may well be that like Pyrrhus he functions, at least in part, as an image of Hamlet's own fantasy of killing his uncle. Moreover, the fact that Lucianus refers simultaneously to Claudius and Hamlet opens up the possibility that similarities exist even between these apparent opposites. And if Lucianus, Pyrrhus, Laertes and Fortinbras represent that unfulfilled side of Hamlet which wants merely to 'drink hot blood' (III, ii, 1.398), there is also a character who mirrors and parodies his habit of 'thinking too precisely on th'event': the Gravedigger's comic pedantry matches Hamlet's own logic-chopping.

The whole play, in fact, seems structured precisely in order to reflect kaleidoscopically a variety of images of Hamlet – images which are sometimes embodied by Hamlet himself and sometimes by other people. Even Ophelia provides a reflected image of Hamlet. For while it is Hamlet who, in the early part of the play, seems to contemplate 'self-slaughter' and who appears to go mad, it is eventually Ophelia whose real madness leads to her actual suicide. And in fact what the later parts of the play show is a series of functions which had orig-inally been attributed to Hamlet being displaced onto other characters. Thus on the one hand the audience sees Hamlet himself trying out and experimenting with a variety of rôles; and on the other hand it sees other characters taking over some of the rôles which he discards or is unable to maintain. And so it is Ophelia rather than Hamlet who goes mad and kills herself – and note the additional correspon-dence between her death by drowning and the death at sea which Hamlet escapes! It is Fortinbras, not Hamlet, who comes to assume the crown of Denmark; and Laertes, not Hamlet, who plays out to the full the rôle of determined and bloody revenger which Hamlet had been contemplating from the earlier scenes of the play.

It is this last transfer of rôles which is the most significant, for it signals the change which takes place in Hamlet towards the end of the play. It has often been remarked that the Hamlet who returns to Denmark after his escape from the pirates is a different figure from the Hamlet of the first three and a half acts. His overall mood, it is said, has changed: his stoical assertions to Horatio that 'There's a divinity that shapes our ends, rough-hew them how we will', and that 'There is special providence in the fall of a sparrow' are both statements of this new mood. It has been interpreted by critics in a variety of ways: as a transcendence, as a kind of despair, as a new determination, as regeneration, or as defeat.

In fact the extent of the change in his 'character' is debatable, since the keynote of Hamlet was always changeability, and he shows himself to be as multi-faceted in the final stages of the play as he was in the earlier scenes of it. Even in the final scene of the play, he is still playing the same game of hide-and-seek, hiding his own identity behind his 'antic disposition'. His 'apology' to Laertes is typically evasive:

Was't Hamlet wrong'd Laertes? Never Hamlet.
If Hamlet from himself be ta'en away,
And when he's not himself does wrong Laertes,
Then Hamlet does it not, Hamlet denies it.
Who does it then? His madness. If't be so,
Hamlet is of the faction that is wrong'd;
His madness is poor Hamlet's enemy.

(V, ii, ll. 229–35)

What has changed, however, is Hamlet's function in the play. What the audience now knows, but Hamlet himself does not, is that he now has a dual rôle in the structure of the narrative. Before he left the stage to be sent to England, his task as he saw it was to reconcile himself to playing the part of the revenger. Now that he has returned, however, things have moved on: his killing of Polonius has changed everything. Two revenge plots are now in progress, and they overlap each other. In one of them Hamlet is the hero, the revenger set on avenging his father's death. In the other, however, it is Laertes who takes on that rôle, whereas Hamlet inherits the rôle of the villain and eventual victim – the rôle which in Hamlet's own story Claudius has to play. The irony is that Hamlet has, in a sense, become Claudius.

Hamlet himself is barely aware of this. He does admit that

... I am very sorry, good Horatio,
That to Laertes I forgot myself;
For by the image of my cause I see
The portraiture of his.

(V, ii, ll. 75–8)

but beyond that he seems not to have thought through the ominous implications of the similarities between himself and Laertes. The audience, however, is only too aware of the shift which the play has undergone. Hamlet is no longer merely the potential revenger: he is also the potential victim. As the two plots converge, Hamlet the actor finally completes the playing-out of his rôle of revenger and is simultaneously overtaken by a revenge plot not of his own making. Like all revenge plots, it ends in multiple slaughter: the impulse towards revenge which is initially located in a single individual spreads out and overwhelms the whole political structure of the kingdom. Ironically, it provides yet another example of a 'staged show' which spills over into reality, as the fencing match which Hamlet believes to be merely in play turns out to be in deadly earnest. The final image of the play is that of a stage littered with dead bodies; surveying it all is Fortinbras – another character against whom Hamlet had once measured himself. The play had begun against the backdrop of the threat of a Norwegian invasion: now it is the Norwegian Fortinbras who will assume the throne of Denmark.

10 Othello

'Honest Iago'

One of Shakespeare's themes – it was the theme of so many play-wrights of the period – was that of the changing times. The old hierarchies of the fifteenth and sixteenth centuries were breaking down (went the cry) and nowadays everything is in disorder.

> Preferment goes by letter and affection.
> Not by the old gradation, where each second
> Stood heir to the first...
>
> (I, i, ll. 36–8)

This is Iago talking, bemoaning the evils of the times. Iago and Hamlet have more in common than is sometimes recognized. Both have much of the revenger about them: they are adept at changing shapes, they have a privileged relationship with the audience, and they are out of sympathy with the times, taking on themselves the rôle of satirist. In fact, the plot of *Othello* might be described as a revenge tragedy seen from the point of view of the victim. Thus the vengeful Iago becomes, (as Laertes did in his way) not hero but villain, as he plots and plans away against Othello, speaks satirically to the audience in the rôle of the traditional malcontent, and finally effects his complex revenge upon Othello.

But if Iago bears some of the hallmarks of the revenger, quite what is it that he is revenging? What drives Iago to do what he does? For some critics, it is enough to label him as a 'Machiavel'. To an Elizabethan Englishman the writings of Niccolò Machiavelli, the Italian political theorist, characterized all that was evil about foreigners in general and Italians in particular, and when Marlowe introduced the figure of 'Machevill' into the drama in *The Jew of Malta*, he provided audiences with a readily-identifiable villain whose villainy needed no further motivation. This is, certainly, one context in which to understand the character of Iago. Coleridge's famous phrase about Iago's 'motiveless malignity' has been echoed (out of context) in order to support such a reading. But Shakespeare – as Coleridge himself knew – does not present his audience with a character who is without his own reasons for what he does. Indeed, he shows Iago as a man who feels himself wronged by Othello, not on one count but on two. First of all we are told that Iago's anger stems from having been passed over for promotion in favour of Cassio:

>   ... three great ones of the city,
> In personal suit to make me his lieutenant,
> Oft capp'd to him, and by the faith of man,
> I know my price, I am worth no worse a place.
> But he, as loving his own pride and purposes,
> Evades them, with a bombast circumstance,
> Horribly stuff'd with epithets of war:
> And in conclusion,
> Nonsuits my mediators: for 'Certes', says he,
> 'I have already chosen my officer',
> And what was he?
> Forsooth, a great arithmetician,
> One Michael Cassio, a Florentine.
>
> (I, i, ll. 7–20)

The point is, not that Iago has no motives, but that he has one, and we can see that it is essentially trivial. It is the imbalance between Othello's slighting of Iago and the kind of revenge which Iago eventually takes for it that is significant.

Not that the relationship between Iago's motive and his action remains static. Both his resentment against Othello and the deeds which result from it grow in intensity through the play. Iago's part in the narrative is constructed as a crescendo of malevolence. At the beginning of the play he has not formulated a plan which is likely to lead to Othello's – or anybody else's – death. Indeed, in the first act of the play, he seems more intent on annoying Othello than on destroying him, and his plots and machinations tend towards simply attempting to get the marriage between Othello and Desdemona annulled. It is only at the end of Act I, with the failure of this first attempt on Othello, that the more complex 'double knavery', which will strike both at Othello and at Cassio, begins to be hatched. Secondly, as this takes shape, Shakespeare begins to provide Iago with a second motive – one which he does not confess to Roderigo, but only to the audience.

>   ... I hate the Moor,
> And it is thought abroad, that 'twixt my sheets
> He's done my office; I know not if't be true...
> Yet I, for mere suspicion in that kind,
> Will do, as if for surety...
>
> (I, iii, ll. 384–8)

What are we to make of this? Compared to the way Iago talked about the previous wrong, that of being passed over for promotion, the language of this is almost throw-away. Iago's information is not certain but is only a suspicion. Iago, however, does not seem to care whether it is true or not: he simply seizes on it as a convenient fuel for the anger towards Othello, which he already feels. We could read this as suggesting that Iago's primary motive is his jealousy of Cassio's promotion, and that this sexual jealousy towards Othello is merely secondary. Or else, we might decide that since Iago tells the audience about his suspicions in a soliloquy and hides them from Roderigo, it is being indicated that this sexual jealousy is actually very important – the essential motive for his hatred of Othello, for which the 'promotion' issue is only a blind.

Yet if we were not meant to place a lot of emphasis on the sexual jealousy that Iago has for Othello, why would Shakespeare have included the speech in Act II, Scene i, where Iago not only repeats what he said before, but does so in terms which make it clear that the thought of Othello's cuckolding him has shifted from being a useful pretext to being an absolute obsession?

> ... I do suspect the lustful Moor
> Hath leap'd into my seat, the thought whereof
> Doth like a poisonous mineral gnaw my inwards,
> And nothing can, nor shall content my soul,
> Till I am even with him, wife, for wife:
> Or failing so, yet that I put the Moor,
> At least, into a jealousy so strong,
> That judgement cannot cure.
>
> (II, i, ll. 290–7)

Previously, Iago had resented the fact that there were rumours; here he seems disturbed by the possibility that the rumours may be true. Note that here, too, Iago's plot is not yet a fixed one – and that one version of it which appeals to him is quite simply seducing Desdemona and getting even with Othello that way – 'wife, for wife'; the plot involving Cassio and Othello's jealousy is still a secondary, contingent plan.

Do Iago's 'motives' matter? Some schools of criticism would argue that they do not, and that to concentrate upon them amounts to treating a character in a play as if he were a character in a novel (or worse, as if he were a character in real life!). It is true that certain ways of approaching character in the drama, both academic and theatrical, have over-stressed notions such as 'motive'. Yet there are a number of reasons for examining the motivations of characters: firstly, they are part of the implied information with which the dramatist provides us. We need to establish some sort of agreement concerning them if only to ensure that we have understood the story. Action in the drama consists or characters doing and saying a number of things for a number of reasons. If we misunderstand those reasons then we may well misunderstand the logic of the whole play's action. Certainly if the reasons are unclear, ambiguous or subject to a variety of interpretations, then that too is a matter for examination. Secondly, it is probably the case that readers and audiences will find themselves more interested in a play whose actions spring from human protagonists, people motivated by recognizable emotions such as jealousy, rather than from 'motiveless malignities' or embodiments of evil. Iago, in the reading I propose, is not an embodiment of evil: he is an ambitious and sexually insecure young man who resents Cassio's professional successes and Othello's sexual ones, real or imagined. Thirdly, this attribution of the motive of sexual jealousy to Iago makes structural sense within the play. Iago's machinations focus upon Othello's sexual jealousy. This is appropriate not only because Othello is highly vulnerable here, but also because Iago is counter-attacking in precisely the domain in which he believes himself to have been wronged. Othello's marriage to the beautiful Desdemona is another instance of precisely that sexual success which Iago resents. And since, like so many revengers, Iago's end is best served if the 'punishment' fits the 'crime', his assault on Othello is necessarily by means of Desdemona. Since he cannot get even with Othello 'wife for wife', he turns to the more complicated, intricate and interesting plot which has the added advantage of allowing him to implicate and destroy the other object of his resentment, Michael Cassio.

It should be noted that this reading of the play need not compromise our attitude towards Othello himself: we do not have to assume (or even suspect) that he has actually had an affair with Emilia. Shakespeare makes it clear that Iago has no better foundation for his suspicions than the gossip of the town, and although Iago becomes more and more convinced that the gossip is well-founded, there is no need for us to draw the same conclusion. So to read Iago as a character driven by sexual jealousy need not involve us in reading Othello as a sexual philanderer. But it does change the way we understand the relationship between Iago and Othello.

The basis of that relationship is that Othello believes Iago to be honest. He is not alone in this, of course. Everybody in the play repeatedly asserts the belief that Iago is honest. From the very beginning of the play (where Roderigo talks about his trust in Iago) the notion of Iago as being trustworthy is hammered home again and again. 'A man he is of honesty and trust', says Othello of Iago in Act I, Scene iii; he repeats himself ten lines later, addressing his ensign as 'honest Iago', and continues to use this phrase, and variations on the theme, throughout the play. By the end of the play, in fact, the word 'honest' has been used so many times by so many people, in so many different contexts, and has been given such a variety of connotations, that we may wonder quite what it means. Indeed, to a great extent, this continual harping on a single word may be seen as a deliberate ploy to draw our attention to its being problematic: we might want to conclude that one of the central issues of the play is the very nature of honesty itself. But it is not the complexity of the word as it relates to Iago which is important, but its simplicity. People like Othello and Cassio usually mean something quite straightforward when they praise Iago for his honesty. They mean that they believe him to be a plain dealer, one who does not dissemble but who speaks the truth as he sees it whatever the cost, and whose loyalty to his friends and comrades-in-arms is limited only by the demands of his conscience.

The audience, of course, knows that none of this is true. We are made aware from very early on that Iago is a liar, a plotter, a malcontent and a hypocrite. He openly admits to Roderigo that what he shows on the outside and what he feels on the inside are two entirely separate things:

> ... others there are,
> Who, trimm'd in forms, and visages of duty,
> Keep yet their hearts attending on themselves,
> And throwing but shows of service on their lords,
> Do well thrive by 'em, and when they have lin'd their coats,
> Do themselves homage, those fellows have some soul,
> And such a one I do profess myself...
>
> (I, i, ll. 49–55)

Like Hamlet when he talks about his 'inky cloak', Iago stresses a concept of personality which has two distinct levels: on the one hand there are the 'forms and visages' – those things which others may see, the outward show. And on the other hand there is the 'heart' – that interior self which is, in Iago's and in Hamlet's terms, the 'real' personality. Iago's description of himself is that of a person in which the inner man is very different from the outer. Here he does not mean that the inner man is in conflict with the outer: it is rather that the outer man is a deliberate disguise, a deception practised knowingly in order to further the interests of that 'real' Iago, the one tucked away inside. And central to Iago's vision of personality is this notion of deliberateness. According to Iago, a man deliberately constructs his own personality, whether for good or ill. The image he uses is that of a garden:

> 'tis in ourselves that we are thus, or thus: our bodies are gardens,
> to the which our wills are gardeners, so that if we will plant nettles,

or sow lettuce, set hyssop, and weed up thyme; supply it with one
gender of herbs, or distract it with many; either to have it sterile
with idleness, or manur'd with industry, why, the power, and
corrigible authority of this, lies in our wills.

(I, iii, ll. 319–26)

Iago has a supreme belief in the power of man to fashion his own self,
his character, his personality and his destiny. He locates this power
in his concept of the 'will'. What he does not go on to say in this
speech – for he is talking to Roderigo, whom he continually manipulates – is that in the hands of a ruthless man, that will also includes
the power and the ability to manipulate *others*, to mould them and to
fashion *their* characters, personalities and destinies. And it is the
ruthlessness of his own will that Iago conceals beneath his mask of
honesty.

It has often been noted that *Othello* contains a great number of
contrasts – both in terms of plot and in terms of imagery. Black and
white, light and darkness, love and hate – all seem to be stressed as a
series of oppositions which contribute to the tragic outcome. If we
take this idea of contrasts into the realm of character, we might see
that the opposite of Iago is Desdemona. One of the functions of the
exchange between the two in Act II, Scene i, when Iago shows off his
wit to Desdemona in a series of anti-feminist satires, is to point up
the contrast between them:

Desdemona O heavy ignorance, that praises the worst best: but
what praise couldst thou bestow on a deserving woman indeed?
one that in the authority of her merits did justly put on the vouch
of very malice itself?
Iago She that was ever fair and never proud,
Had tongue at will, and yet was never loud,
Never lack'd gold, and yet went never gay,
Fled from her wish, and yet said 'Now I may;'
She that, being anger'd, her revenge being nigh,
Bade her wrong stay, and her displeasure fly;
She that in wisdom never was so frail
To change the cod's head for the salmon's tail;
She that could think, and ne'er disclose her mind,
See suitors following, and not look behind;
She was a wight, if ever such wight were –
Desdemona To do what?
Iago To suckle fools, and chronicle small beer.
Desdemona O most lame and impotent conclusion: do not learn
of him, Emilia, though he be thy husband.

(II, i, ll. 143–62)

147

Iago's evasive, barbed and paradoxical language is contrasted with Desdemona's clear, direct and logical speech; his aggressive, witty cynicism is contrasted with her gentler optimism. It should be noted that there is a sub-text to this scene which springs directly from Iago's sexual jealousy of Othello. Desdemona is engaged here in a kind of verbal fencing match with Iago, who is at this point in the play still trying to get even with Othello 'wife for wife'. Iago's comments on women's dishonesty are not idle banter: they form part of an erotic battle of wits, in which Iago's aggressive cynicism is also an invitation to Desdemona. It would be a mistake to assume that Desdemona's response is a naïve one. Here, as elsewhere in the play, she is portrayed as a woman who knows her own mind, who is willing to go against convention, who is intelligent and determined. It would be truer to say that she is – honest.

The two people closest to Othello himself throughout the play are Iago and Desdemona, balanced as a pair of opposites, and affecting Othello as surely in their two opposite ways as any Good and Bad Angel from an old morality play or interlude. And what Iago continually attempts, and finally achieves, is to put Othello's own character under such stress that the contrarieties and contradictions – the opposites in Othello's own soul – enforce Othello's breakdown. For Othello seems to be another character with whom to contrast Iago – he seems to be someone whose outer and inner man are in harmony – an honest man. But it is Iago's technique to recognize the disunity of his own personality, and to use that as a tool to activate the disunity which he is convinced exists in others. Iago knows that what lurks inside him is not the same as that which appears on the outside, and his knowledge of this in himself makes him certain that the same is the case for other people. His way of evil consists in finding the contradictions in others and using them to their destruction. His first successful attempt is on Cassio, behind whose upright and proper outward show Iago detects a man whom drink can transform into one who will 'squabble, swagger and swear'. His second is on Othello himself, in whom Iago sees a man whose love can readily be turned into hate.

Much of the action of the play involves demonstrating how people can be turned into the opposite of what they seem, or what they believe themselves to be. It is important to recognize that Iago's plotting involves a reversal not only of how we see characters but of how they see themselves. Cassio sees himself as a man of moderation and virtue – and so he is until Iago's machinations turn him into a drunken brawler. Othello sees himself as a fond husband and generous lover – and so he is until Iago's plotting turns him into a murderously jealous tyrant. It is Iago's peculiar function to liberate in other people the suppressed 'other', that opposite of their constructed 'selves' which is also a potential self of each of them.

'The story of my life'

Hamlet, at the start of his story, is a comparatively unknown quantity. He may be a prince, and heir presumptive to the throne, but he seems to have been away in Wittenberg for many years, and is not well known to the court; he does his best to distance himself emotionally from most others in the court, and has little in the way of a reputation which precedes him. The continual attempts of other characters to 'interpret' him, and his continual attempt to defy interpretation, enhance this sense of mystery. But in this, Hamlet is unusual among Shakespeare's tragic heroes: Othello, Macbeth and Lear (as well as Coriolanus and Mark Antony) all arrive centre stage with their reputations full-blown: each one of them is known in his society as a public figure before we begin to explore their private tragedies. Images, reputations, legends and myths surround the characters of 'Brave Macbeth' (*Macbeth* I, ii, l. 16), whose legend we see in the making, and Lear who, is in the public gaze and surrounded by all the trappings of power, 'hath ever but slenderly known himself' (*King Lear*, I, i, l. 295). Othello, when we first encounter him, is already a national hero. In all three of these plays we watch the gradual disintegration of a man to whom we were first introduced at the height of his powers. We meet Macbeth immediately after his finest hour in battle, when rewards and honours are being heaped upon his head. Lear we see just before his abdication, at a moment when (from his own point of view at least) a long and peaceful reign is reaching a dignified and civilized conclusion. Othello we meet on his wedding night, as he combines the two roles of soldier and lover.

In fact, the first three scenes of Othello constitute a little comedy of their own: it is a perfect comic plot, indeed, of the kind which Shakespeare elaborated in earlier plays such as *A Midsummer Night's Dream*. Two lovers with the odds stacked against them elope to get married. Despite parental disapproval and the machinations of some villains, they finally succeed, and sail off to live happily ever after. The rest of *Othello* is about the way in which that 'happy ever after' fails to work out.

Comic plots in Shakespeare tend to be about the constructing of identities in a social context which is, in the end, benevolent. The lovers start out at odds with society, running away to the Forest of Arden or to a wood outside Athens, or else twins get confused so that identities are mistaken, but sooner or later the plot untangles itself and people settle down (usually, but not necessarily, in marriage) knowing who they are and what their place is in the world which they inhabit. Shakespeare's tragic plots, on the other hand, tend to show the destruction of the identities which people start out with: the hero is brought face to face with realities with which he is unable to cope, and his world collapses. In *Othello*, in fact, we get both movements: the comic for the first two-and-a-half scenes, and the tragic thereafter. By halfway through Scene iii, we have seen Othello's courtship of Desdemona socially validated, as the Duke gives it his blessing and Brabantio gives up his claims to his daughter. The rest of the play is given over to the tragic plot in which Othello's own sense of himself, his identity, is torn apart.

So what is this 'identity' which is destroyed during the course of the play? If Othello suffers what one critic has called 'a complete collapse of the personality' (Michael Long, *The Unnatural Scene*, Methuen, 1976, p. 38) how are we to describe this personality which collapses? Over the last few decades, productions and readings of the play have tended to polarize into two camps, each of which responds differently to the character of Othello, and thus produces a different interpretation of *Othello* the play. One way of seeing Othello was summed up at the beginning of the century by A.C. Bradley: 'Othello is so noble... and his sufferings are so heart-rending, that he stirs... in most readers a passion of mingled love and pity which they feel for no other hero in Shakespeare' (*Shakespearean Tragedy*, 1904, reprinted Macmillan 1960, p. 155). The opposing camp, while not disputing Othello's nobility, suggests that Shakespeare's attitude towards that nobility is a much more ironic one. This was most vigorously propounded by F.R. Leavis, in an essay entitled 'Diabolic Intellect and the Noble Hero: or The Sentimentalist's Othello': 'Othello, in his magnanimous way, is egotistic... a habit of self-approving self-dramatization is an essential element in Othello's make-up' (in *The Common Pursuit*, 1952, reprinted Chatto and Windus 1972, p. 142). The Bradleyan reading of Othello's personality makes the play into the story of a thoroughly good man tricked into a moment of evil by the malevolent genius of Iago. Leavis's reading produces an Othello whose own egotism and lack of self-knowledge drives him towards catastrophe.

Another way of describing the choice is to say it is between Othello as victim and Othello as at least partial author of his own downfall. At one point in the history of the play, it looked as if the second view had won out convincingly over the first. Leavis's notion of Othello as a self-dramatizing egotist seemed to have dispensed with Bradley's 'sentimental' reading of Othello as a good man brought low by Iago's duplicity. As recently as 1976, it was possible for Michael Long to say that 'I don't think it is possible seriously to deny the force of [Leavis's and his supporters'] readings; and I certainly think that any attempt to return to the Coleridgean–Bradleyan sentimentality of the "noble hero" is unlikely to bear much fruit. Leavis's moral case ... cannot be reversed'. (In *The Unnatural Scene* (Methuen, 1976) pp. 38–39). The suggestion is that to see Othello as anything other than a self-deluded egotist is sentimental and old-fashioned. Throughout the 1970s and 1980s, however, theatrical productions began to stress the potential racial issues which are involved in the play; this has produced an Othello who is a victim not merely of Iago's machinations, but of a set of attitudes in Venetian society which we have no trouble in recognizing as an early manifestation of racism. Certainly, the language of Iago and his comrades often reeks with racial hatred: 'the thick-lips', they call Othello, and 'an old black ram' and 'a Barbary horse'. In the face of such discourse, to see Othello as a certain kind of victim does not, after all, seem so out-of-date.

This is something to which we can return presently. First of all, however, let us consider the extent to which the idea of Othello as a self-dramatizing character might be illuminating. The earliest point at which we have an instance of this, is in Act I, Scene iii. It is the point at which Othello, accused by Brabantio of bewitching Desdemona away from him, is justifying himself before the Duke and senators of Venice. This is how he describes the way in which Desdemona fell in love with him:

Her father lov'd me, oft invited me,
Still question'd me the story of my life,
From year to year; the battles, sieges, fortunes,
That I have pass'd:
I ran it through, even from my boyish days,
To the very moment that he bade me tell it.
Wherein I spake of most disastrous chances,
Of moving accidents by flood and field;
Of hair-breadth scapes i' th' imminent deadly breach;
Of being taken by the insolent foe;
And sold to slavery, and my redemption thence,
And with it all my travel's history;
Wherein of antres vast, and deserts idle,
Rough quarries, rocks and hills, whose heads touch heaven,
It was my hint to speak, such was the process:
And of the Cannibals, that each other eat;
The Anthropophagi, and men whose heads
Do grow beneath their shoulders: this to hear
Would Desdemona seriously incline;
But still the house-affairs would draw her thence,
And ever as she could with haste dispatch,

She'ld come again, and with a greedy ear
Devour up my discourse...
She lov'd me for the dangers I had pass'd
And I lov'd her that she did pity them.
This is the only witchcraft I have us'd:

(I, iii, ll. 128–50, 167–69)

It is a complex moment. Othello, describing his courtship, tells the council how he used to tell stories of his own adventures as a soldier and a traveller. These stories, he says, are what won Desdemona's love. Othello seems to regard this as unremarkable; we may wonder why Shakespeare makes such a point of stressing that what Desdemona fell for was not the living man in front of her, but a mythologized and glorified version of himself, constructed through the stories he tells of his past exploits.

Here, even as Othello describes his courtship, he re-enacts it, now telling again (in summary at least) the stories he told Desdemona. With evident pleasure he relives both the adventures themselves and the wooing of Desdemona through his story-telling. In this passage he certainly seems to enjoy talking about himself. The suspicion that Othello has 'a habit of self-approving self-dramatization' is clearly not without some kind of foundation. And this suspicion is strengthened when we consider the kind of story he tells about himself. 'My travel's history', he calls it, and the Othello with whom Desdemona falls in love is a character in a story: specifically, he is the hero of a traveller's tale.

Travellers' tales, in the Renaissance, were often tales of adventure and descriptions of distant lands – but they frequently contained elements of fantasy and make-believe, tales of strange customs and fabulous beasts and strange, semi-human creatures. And this is precisely what Othello's story is like. He recalls that he told Desdemona of 'The Anthropophagi, and men whose heads/Do grow beneath their shoulders'. The 'story of my life' which Othello tells contains some elements which to us are rather questionable. How did Shakespeare expect an audience to respond to such details? Did he himself simply believe the more fantastical elements of the old travellers' tales of writers like Mandeville and Pliny? It is quite possible: we have evidence that well-educated and well-travelled men like Sir Walter Raleigh gave credence to such accounts. But it is also possible that Shakespeare was more sceptical, that he found tales of Anthropophagi and their like rather far-fetched, even amusing, and that he included them here in order to give Othello's traveller's tale precisely that air of unreality, of fictionality, which I believe it has. For *Othello* is a play in which the making of fictions is a central issue. The great fiction-maker in the play is, of course, Iago – who makes up a deadly story to bring about Othello's downfall. But Othello himself is fascinated by stories. His 'habit of . . . self-drama-tization' is not merely a symptom of his egotism; that may have something to do with it but the matter does not end there. For Othello shares with Hamlet a tendency to construct his own identity in terms of stories. (He has, as we shall see, specific reasons for doing so.) From the first time we see him, he is engaged in constructing plots – not malevolent plots against other people like Iago's, but literary plots. He writes himself into various kinds of stories: in Act I he writes himself into a traveller's tale; by Act V he has written himself into a tragedy.

'An old black ram'

It has often been said that one of the things that makes Shakespeare the great writer that he is, is his ability to subvert, at crucial moments or in crucial ways, the expectations of an audience. Leavis's reading of the play, I suspect, has its roots in a conviction that the 'sentimen-talist's' view of Othello as 'noble hero' is simply too one-dimensional. So Leavis emphasizes a subversive counter-current in the play, by which the expectations of an audience – that the hero of a tragedy should be uncomplicatedly noble – are undermined. These, at least, are the terms in which I was first introduced to the play.

The question is, however: what audience are we talking about? Certainly not Shakespeare's. There is little in the drama of the time to suggest that Shakespeare's contemporaries expected anything of the kind from the hero of a tragedy – or if they expected it, they very rarely got it. Perhaps A.C. Bradley's generation of late Victorians expected tragic heroes to be one-dimensional, (though Bradley him-self was more sophisticated than that). In general, I think it is true to say that Shakespeare is good at surprising an audience, at doing the unexpected, and at subverting expectations. But for this idea to make any sense, we must think in terms of Shakespeare's relationship to his own audience.

In *Othello*, we need to take into account a Jacobean audience's expectations concerning a hero of a tragedy who is also a Moor; for in this play, the subversion of expectations has to do, not with Othello's egotism, but with the colour of his skin.

In choosing a black hero for his tragedy, Shakespeare was, on one level, simply following his sources. He found the story for the play in a collection of Italian tales called *Gli Hecatommithi* by Giovanni Battista Giraldi Cinthio (published 1565), which he may have read in the original Italian. He follows Cinthio's plot very closely until near the end, when he tightens everything up. In the Italian story,

'The Moor' (Othello) employs 'The Ensign' (Iago) to batter 'Desdemona' to death with a stocking full of sand; they then disguise her death as an accident by making her bedroom ceiling collapse on top of her. Othello later turns against Iago in remorse, but Iago manipulates 'The Corporal' (Cassio) into publicly accusing Othello of Desdemona's murder. Although he is tortured, Othello denies everything, and is sentenced to perpetual exile, only to be eventually killed by Desdemona's relatives.

Dramatizing prose narratives is about finding theatrical solutions to narrative problems, about finding ways of dealing in stage terms with the story which the prose tale tells. The essential problem that Shakespeare had to deal with in translating into theatrical language this tale from *Gli Hecatommithi* was not to do with the clumsiness of the original story's ending so much as with the central character. The very idea of a tragedy whose hero is a Moor carries with it, for Shakespeare's theatre, certain problems.

When reading *Othello*, it is possible, for much of the time, to forget that the central character is black. On stage, the fact simply cannot be missed: Othello's blackness is a constant visual element of the play, and one which the players of Shakespeare's theatre would go to some lengths to present. We know a little about the traditions of make-up which were current at the time and which were used by actors (all white, of course) to personate Africans: they would involve 'A Box of black painting' for the complexion and 'Corled hed sculles of blacke laune' for the 'fleece of woolly hair' which was part of the stereotyped image of the African. Since Othello is specifically referred to in the play as 'the thick-lips', it may be that this feature too was represented by make-up. The point is that by the time that Shakespeare wrote *Othello*, there was a tradition of the portrayal of Moors on the English stage: the physical conventions for their representation had evolved, and the stereotypes had accrued a series of meanings.

The meanings of these stereotypes had, of course, a social basis. Black Africans were hardly common in seventeenth-century London, but neither were they completely unknown. The Age of Elizabeth was also the great Age of Exploration. English seamen such as Drake, Hawkins and Raleigh made great voyages of discovery arround the coast of Africa and across to the new World. This opened up commercial and diplomatic relationships with some North African countries, and as a result the courts of Elizabeth and James occasionally played host to Moorish ambassadors. At a less exalted social level, too, these voyages initiated contact between white and black. Since a voyage of discovery was, inevitably, a somewhat hazardous venture, it was not always possible to raise sufficient funding at home; consequently, in order to make ends meet, it was often necessary to combine voyages of discovery with voyages of commerce, and to do a little trading on the way. Usually that trading was in slaves, picked up on the North or West African coast and sold (often illegally to Spanish buyers) in the Caribbean. From the middle of the sixteenth century it had been common practice for seamen to bring back to England some of these exotic creatures, a few of whom took up residence in London. Records from the parish of All Hallows, London, indicate that three African women and one African man were living there in the 1590s. By 1601, in fact, Queen Elizabeth decided that the situation was getting out of hand, and let it be known that she was 'discontented at the great number of "Negars and blackamoors" which are crept into the realm'. Her solution was simple, predictable and familiar: she appointed an officer to transport many of them out of the country.

Shakespeare's contemporaries, then, were not necessarily completely unacquainted with the sight of a black African. It was even becoming possible to recognize that not all Africans looked alike or were the same colour. While 'Moor' was the generic term for North African, 'Negro' came to denote the natives of southern Africa. On stage these fine distinctions were rarely observed, however: Africans in general were portrayed as black, and the word 'Moor' could be used to refer to any African, regardless of place or origin. In the middle of the sixteenth-century, when the merchant-adventurers, the explorers and the slave-traders had only just begun to bring back a few exotic slaves from their North African voyages, figures of Africans were occasionally intro-duced into plays, masques or pageants in order simply to add novelty, glamour and strangeness to the spectacle. By the turn of the century, when Elizabeth had decided that the 'Negars and blackamoors' were a threat or a nuisance, and was initiating the first 'repatriation' pro-gramme, the Moor in English drama had developed into a figure which was nearly always portrayed as evil.

For the theatre of Shakespeare's day was the theatre of an increas-ingly confident emergent nation state, and if one result of England's growing international stature was a new cosmopolitanism of English culture, another almost inevitable corollary was an occasionally jingoistic patriotism, a long with a streak of xenophobia. The more obviously alien a figure, the more easily it may be used to symbolize everything that is 'un-English': a Jew is more convenient than an Italian, and a black is more convenient than a Jew – especially since black was in any case a colour traditionally associated with evil or deformity. According to Elizabethan stage convention, therefore, the character of the black Moor was expected to be lecherous, violent, jealous, treacherous, servile and crude. In plays such as Robert Peele's *The Battle of Alcazar* (1588–89), and the anonymous *Lust's Dominion* (1598–99) the figure of the villainous Moor had already been established as an image of oriental inferiority and infamy.

It should be noted that Shakespeare himself was not above exploiting this kind of racial stereotype in his plays: one of the most blatant examples of the 'villainous Moor' is to be found in Shakespeare's early work. In *Titus Andronicus* (probably written about 1590), Aaron the Moor emerges as a melodramatic villain of grotesque proportions. Here is what he has to say about himself:

> ... I curse the day – and yet, I think,
> Few come within the compass of my curse –
> Wherein I did not some notorious ill:
> As kill a man, or else devise his death;
> Ravish a maid, or plot a way to do it;
> Accuse some innocent, and forswear myself;
> Set deadly enmity between two friends;
> Make poor men's cattle break their necks;
> Set fire on barns and haystacks in the night,
> And bid the owners quench them with their tears.
> Oft have I digg'd up dead men from their graves,
> And set them upright at their dear friends' door
> Even when their sorrows almost was forgot,
> And on their skins, as on the bark of trees,
> Have with my knife carved in Roman letters
> 'Let not your sorrow die, though I am dead'.
> Tut, I have done a thousand dreadful things
> As willingly as one would kill a fly;
> And nothing grieves me heartily indeed
> But that I cannot do ten thousand more.
>
> (*Titus Andronicus*, V, i, ll. 125–44)

Having exploited the stereotype in *Titus Andronicus*, Shakespeare now, in *Othello* works against the stereotype, by presenting a Moor who is not servile but noble – a great warrior and leader of men; not lecherous and violent but courtly and civilized.

This is the joke of Othello's proclaiming himself to be an unskilled speaker. He is not, of course: in fact, he uses language very well indeed – as can be seen in the very speech in which he claims to be a rough, plain speaker:

> Most potent, grave and reverend signiors,
> My very noble and approv'd good masters:
> That I have ta'en away this old man's daughter,
> It is most true: true I have married her,
> The very head and front of my offending
> Hath this extent, no more. Rude am I in my speech,

And little blest with the set phrase of peace,
For since these arms of mine had seven years' pith,
Till now some nine moons wasted, they have us'd
Their dearest action in the tented field,
And little of this great world can I speak,
More than pertains to feats of broil and battle,
And therefore little shall I grace my cause,
In speaking for myself: yet, (by your gracious patience)
I will a round, unvarnish'd tale deliver,
Of my whole course of love . . .

(I, iii, ll. 76–91)

Not only is Othello a story-teller – he is also a rhetorician. His sentences are elegantly constructed; his command of balance and parenthesis, of sound and rhythm, is sophisticated. Far from being 'rude . . . in [his] speech', Othello is conspicuously, almost flashily, eloquent: consider how elaborately he makes the point that he is not much of a speaker! Othello clearly enjoys using words, and this is one of the reasons why he has been thought of as self-dramatizing. But his 'self-dramatization' has a specific social context, and Othello's mastery of the Venetians' language has more than a touch of triumph in it. For while the stereotype of a Moor, like a typical soldier, might be expected to be 'rude . . . in [his] speech', Othello is neither a typical soldier nor a stereotype of a Moor. Othello's eloquence is something which he uses to establish an identity which is in direct and conscious opposition to the expected stereotype. He is showing the Venetians that he is as cultured and as educated as they – even while he claims, with false modesty, to be nothing more than a rough soldier.

Othello's personality, in fact, exists in terms of what he is not. His character is constructed in resistance to the stereotyped expectations of what 'Negars and blackamoors' are like – expectations held not only by the theatre audience, but also by some of the Venetians in the play. In the second scene of *Hamlet* the prince's black clothes proclaimed his alienation from the court. In *Othello*, the general's black skin proclaims him an alien in Venice. But although Othello is an alien, he is by no means alienated. On the contrary.

Othello's marriage to Desdemona seems on one level to represent the culmination of the process of his assimilation into Venetian society. Venetians such as the Duke are, on the whole, willing and even eager to accept him as a Venetian. He is, after all, a military hero. Venice was one of the most important Mediterranean seaports of the sixteenth century, just as London was becoming one of the most important Northern seaports of the seventeenth century. Like London, Venice depended for its wealth on trade; it was cosmopolitan, civilized and sophisticated. It also needed a strong and efficient military force to protect its trade routes and trade links. This is what Othello has helped to provide. He has been an invaluable and loyal servant of the state, and in the process he has assimilated the customs, the values and the language of Venice. His appearance before the Duke in Act I, Scene iii, his total and assured victory over Brabantio, the support he receives from the Duke, and the public ratification of his marriage to Desdemona all show how successfully he can function as a member of Venetian society.

It takes a certain amount of effort, it is true: Othello speaks more correctly, more formally, more eloquently than most of the Venetian nobility precisely *because* he himself is not a native-born Venetian. He has to work harder in order to be accepted. And although on one level he is a respected member of Venetian society, we are aware from the very beginning of the play how vulnerable his position is.

There is no single 'voice of Venice' in the play: Venice is made up of a diverse multitude of voices. Now if one of those voices is that of the Duke, eager to see justice done, and unwilling to antagonize so valuable a servant of the state as Othello, another is the voice with which Roderigo and Iago speak: the voice of malice which reverts almost automatically to racial insult. 'The thick-lips . . . [the] lascivious Moor', says Roderigo; 'an old black ram . . . a Barbary horse', adds Iago. The old stereotype is always there, lurking in the background, ready to be used against him as soon as someone has a grudge against him.

We should note, too, that the voice of malice and of racial insult is not one which will be heard only in the mouth of 'evil' characters like Iago. It can be heard, too, when normally decent and tolerant folk come under stress. We are given an illuminating instance of this in the character of Brabantio. Brabantio is, perhaps, the epitome of the respectable Venetian citizen, confident in the values of the city. (When Roderigo and Iago disturb him in the middle of the night to tell him of Othello's 'theft' of Desdemona, his instinctive reaction is 'Tell'st thou me of robbing? This is Venice': such things, in Brabantio's world view, simply do not happen in Venice.) He is a governor of the city, one of the 'potent, grave and reverend signiors' of the Council who are so accepting of Othello; moreover, he seems to have been one of those who had most thoroughly welcomed Othello into Venetian society. As Othello reminds him, it was Brabantio who regularly invited Othello to his house, questioning him about the 'story of [his] life'. And yet, when he discovers that Othello has 'stolen' his daughter from him, his liberalism and tolerance collapse into hysteria:

O thou foul thief, where hast thou stow'd my daughter?
Damn'd as thou art, thou hast enchanted her,
For I'll refer me to all things of sense,

(If she in chains of magic were not bound)
Whether a maid, so tender, fair and happy,
So opposite to marriage, that she shunn'd
The wealthy curled darlings of our nation,
Would ever have (to incur a general mock)
Run from her guardage to the sooty bosom
Of such a thing as thou? to fear, not to delight.

(I, ii, ll. 62–71)

Othello is no longer a man but a 'thing'; a damned and demonic thing associated with black magic and witchcraft, a thing which Desdemona must surely fear. The notion that Desdemona might simply have fallen in love with Othello does not even occur to him (and so, later on, when he learns that she has been 'half the wooer', he is totally crushed by the fact). The whole idea seems to Brabantio to be 'Against all rules of nature' because to Brabantio, 'nature' is simply another word for the normal customs, behaviour and beliefs of his class, his generation. The rest of Brabantio's logic follows from this simple and erroneous proposition, that the beliefs he happens to hold about the world are 'natural'. It is 'natural', in Brabantio's terms, for Desdemona to obey her father's wishes, and for her, after having flirted with the pick of the republic's noble young men, finally to settle down with one of them. For her to refuse them in favour of Othello is unnatural – all the more so since Othello is now sub-human, a 'thing'; and therefore, since she is acting 'against all rules of nature', she must be under a spell, and subject to 'unnatural' forces. When Brabantio turns against Othello, he does so not just in terms of skin colour; it is not merely the 'sooty bosom' which disgusts him, but the whole series of associations between blackness and devil-worship which Brabantio's conceptions of what is 'natural' call into play.

Othello, therefore, lives in a constant state of ambiguity. His life and his character are predicated on his being a living proof that Moors may be as noble, loving and civilized as any Venetian; and yet he is not allowed to forget that the old stereotypes are always there ready to be used against him. Throughout the play, Shakespeare both works against the stereotyped image of the villainous Moor – and also works with it! The pattern of the play is not just that Othello seems noble but is actually tragically flawed by being self-dramatizing and egotistical. It is that the stereotyped blackamoor turns out to be (surprisingly!) civilized and noble, but that his civilized nobility is actually very vulnerable to the machinations of one who wants to undo it. The great achievement of Iago's villainy is that he manages to turn Othello into a stereotype of himself – jealous, volatile, and eventually remorselessly, murderously violent.

Part of the way in which Shakespeare brings out this vulnerability is by using another stock dramatic device. It was suggested earlier in the chapter that *Othello* starts out as a comedy, but then turns into a tragedy. But even the main part of the play – the 'tragic' part – is effectively a comedy turned sour.

This may well have been the way Shakespeare conceived it in the first place, for *Othello* seems to owe a large debt to an early comedy by Shakespeare's great contemporary, Ben Jonson. Jonson's *Every Man in His Humour* was first performed in 1598 by the Lord Chamberlain's Men, and was revived for a court performance just a few months after the first known performance of *Othello*, and we know that Shakespeare acted in it. *Every Man in His Humour* was originally set in Italy – although Jonson rewrote it in an English setting before publishing it anew in 1616 – and in this 'Italian' version one of the story-lines concerns a jealous husband called Thorello. In addition to the name itself – which is almost an anagram of 'Othello' – Shakespeare's play contains enough specific echoes, resemblances and allusions to make it quite reasonable to assume that Shakespeare consciously took Jonson's comic plot, and grafted it onto the story from *Gli Hecatommithi*. The Moor in the Italian tale had no name, so Shakespeare invented one which was a near-anagram of Jonson's Thorello. And having turned the character's name inside out, he then did the same to the plot, making a tragedy out of Jonson's comedy. Whereas Jonson's tale of the jealous husband ends with a reassuring reconciliation, Shakespeare's ends with the death of both the husband and the wife.

Thus the ghost of a specific comic play haunts the tragedy of *Othello*. And so, in fact, does a basic comic situation. Perhaps only a few members of Shakespeare's first audience who were particularly avid theatre-goers and followers of The Lord Chamberlain's Men would have picked up some of the specific allusions to Jonson's play which exist in *Othello*. But many more would have recognized the more general comic situation against which Othello's tragedy is played out. For Othello is an old man, and Desdemona is young. Othello, moreover, has a young and handsome assistant, Michael Cassio, of whom the older man becomes jealous. There is a stock comic plot, which is the story of the suspicious, possessive but ultimately gullible old husband (the *senex*, as he was known in Latin comedy) and his unfaithful young wife. This story appears in Latin comedies, in the popular tradition of the Italian *Commedia dell'Arte*, in medieval fables and in *The Canterbury Tales*. Chaucer tells it as the story of 'January and May' in 'The Merchant's Tale', and again as the story of Alison and Nicholas in 'The Miller's Tale'. It is precisely this stock situation that Iago presents Othello with later in the play; Iago's whole strategy is to offer Othello enough bits and pieces of evidence for Othello to see himself as a *senex*, and effectively to write himself into the role of the cuckolded old man. And it is only when Othello has done this – and effectively replaced his first self-dramatization as glorious traveller, military hero and successful Venetian, with another self-dramatization as cuckolded old man – that the civilized structure of his personality begins to crack.

So Shakespeare manages to have it both ways. On the one hand he subverts the stereotype – presenting a paradoxically noble Moor, and a *senex* who is not silly but sympathetic. And on the other hand, he exploits the stereotype. Othello is noble – but he is also capable of manifesting precisely those elements which he most seeks to deny in himself – the violence and sexual obsession of the stock Moor, the gullibility and jealousy of the stock *senex*. Thus the collapse of personality which Othello undergoes is a collapse into the very stereotypes which he is most concerned to avoid. Like all of Shakespeare's tragic heroes, Othello's crisis is described as a loss of identity: 'My lord is not my lord', says Desdemona, when she first gets an inkling of Othello's jealousy. Othello refers to himself after the murder of Desdemona as 'he that was Othello'. The final part of the play shows a strange attempt by Othello to put himself back together again before he dies.

Death and Venice

Shakespeare plays a fine trick on the audience with the death of Othello; we remember that when we first knew Othello he was telling travellers' tales, recounting to the Venetian court how he had won Desdemona's love with his own tales of heroism. I suggested then that Othello is a man who quite blatantly constructs stories about himself, and who sees his own career, character and life in terms of stories. His tragedy lies at least in part in that he was too easily convinced of the story told by Iago, and too ready to interpret that story in the way Iago desired. Here, at the end of his story, he consciously returns to the idea of story-telling. Turning to the rest of the characters on stage he says to them.

> I pray you in your letters,
> When you shall these unlucky deeds relate,
> Speak of them as they are; nothing extenuate,
> Nor set down aught in malice;
>
> (V, ii, ll. 341–4)

If this seems at first to be a demand that they simply tell the truth as they see it, we are soon disabused: Othello has no doubt as to the correct way of telling the story, and in telling the characters on stage he also tell the audience in the theatre how he thinks his story should be interpreted.

> then must you speak
> Of one that lov'd not wisely, but too well:
> Of one not easily jealous, but being wrought,
> Perplex'd in the extreme; of one whose hand,
> Like the base Indian, threw a pearl away,
> Richer than all his tribe: of one whose subdued eyes,
> Albeit unused to the melting mood,
> Drops tears as fast as the Arabian trees
> Their medicinal gum; set you down this . . .
>
> (V, ii, ll. 344–52)

The extent to which we want to accede to Othello's own interpretation of his story will differ from reader to reader. It has been argued vigorously by many critics that we are meant to take an ironic stance towards Othello at this point; that his formula 'one that lov'd not wisely but too well' is rather glib and unsatisfactory, coming as it does from a man that has just killed his wife, and that there is something blatantly self-dramatizing about what Othello is doing here; he is already writing the story with himself (rather than Desdemona) as the tragic victim who is most to be pitied; he is making fine phrases out of a messy situation.

My own opinion is that if this were all there were to this speech, I would be entirely persuaded by that reading. But there is more to it than that. Othello's eloquence (and this the man, we remember, who continually denies being any good with words!) has a point to it which goes beyond mere phrase-making. After his description of his own tears, Othello seems – ludicrously – to be about to revert to stories about his own past acts of valour.

> And say besides, that in Aleppo once
> Where a malignant and a turban'd Turk
> Beat a Venetian, and traduc'd the state,
> I took by the throat the circumcised dog,
> And smote him thus.
>
> [*Stabs himself.*]
>
> *Lodovico* O bloody period!
> *Gratiano* All that's spoke is marr'd.
>
> (V, ii, ll. 353–8)

At precisely the moment when he seems to be most self-indulgently reminiscing about old times, Othello turns the situation around, and it becomes suddenly clear that he was telling his story in order to distract the hearers (both on stage and off) from his main purpose. It is still, of course, a self-dramatizing moment in a way, for Othello writes his own real death into the story he is telling, but this is a very different kind of self-dramatization from the kind that Othello

162

has usually been accused of. This is more than just self-indulgent versifying, for the audience has been lulled into a false sense of security, led to believe that they are about to hear some kind of 'noble' speech. But speech is replaced by action as the story from Othello's past suddenly turns into the story of Othello's present, and Lodovico and Gratiano are left to comment lamely on the relationship between the story Othello seemed to be telling and the one he was actually enacting.

It is a great *coup de théâtre*. Othello's story collapses in on itself, and as it does so we see that the story was about Othello himself. It had seemed that he was talking about a confrontation between himself, the Venetian soldier, and someone else – a Turk, an enemy, a heathen. At the climax of the story, however, we discover that it is Othello himself who is simultaneously the Venetian and the Turk, the civilized man and the barbarian. Othello's own death is effected by a deliberate schizophrenia: Othello the Venetian executes Othello the heathen, and he does so both in defence of and in the name of the Venetian state!

For Othello is, of course the Moor *of Venice*. He has constructed an identity on this fact: his rôle has been that of the faithful and well-nigh indispensable servant of the state. As an alien who has been accepted into that state, he is fierce in its protection as he has sought to bind himself closer and closer to the ideal of Venice through his own military prowess, through his mastery of the Venetians' language, and finally through his marriage to Desdemona, daughter of one of Venice's most stalwart families. The integration of these various strands is an important element in the obsessive and protective love Othello feels for his wife. It is no coincidence that one of Othello's cries of pain on hearing of Desdemona's 'treachery' is 'Othello's occupation's gone'. It is the cry of a man whose world is beginning to fall apart.

Venice and Venetian values are an integral part of the backdrop of the play. Thriving on commerce, the Venice of Shakespeare's Europe attracted men of various nationalities. There they found themselves both accepted – as necesary to the financial stability of the city and the state – but also in a variety of ways also excluded, for Venice contained a powerful patrician class who were keen to maintain the traditional boundaries. (Shakespeare had already dramatized some of the conflicts of such an environment in *The Merchant of Venice*, a play which shows comparatively little sympathy towards the outsider – in this case a Jew; Ben Jonson later used the same setting for his satire on a money-obsessed society in *Volpone*). In *Othello* Venice's own self-image (and comparisons with London spring easily to mind) is that of a centre of peace and prosperity, a home of civilized values. But, as we have already seen in the case of

Brabantio, the civilized values of Venice are fragile, vulnerable and subject to collapse. Under stress, Brabantio, the senator and leader of men rants hysterically against Othello's supposed witchcraft, and ends by viciously rejecting his daughter: 'I had rather to adopt a child than get it... I am glad at soul I have no other child' (I, iii, ll. 191, 196). We see a similar pattern at work with Michael Cassio, the successful and upwardly mobile young Venetian. He is courteous and civilized, but he has 'very poor and unhappy brains for drinking' (II, iii, l. 30), and a few cups of wine, plied by Iago, make him drunk. What is more significant, though, is the way in which he later reacts to his drunkenness.

> O God, that men should put an enemy into their mouths, to steal away their brains; that we should with joy, revel, pleasure, and applause, transform ourselves into beasts!... It hath pleas'd the devil drunkenness to give place to the devil wrath; one unperfectness shows me another, to make me frankly despise myself.
>
> (II, iii, ll. 281–284, 287–9)

If the drunkenness was one form of excess, Cassio's self-disgust is another. His fall from grace into drink showed one kind of fragility; his inability to come to terms with the fact that he *did* get drunk is another. Venice's rigid code of courtesy – of which Cassio's self-pitying self-hatred is one manifestation – is something which Iago knows well how to manipulate. Othello is not the only character in the play to be faced with an inverted image of himself.

But if Venetian civilization provides the controlling cultural backdrop for the play, the specific setting for most of the action is the island of Cyprus – an island which is protected by the city-state of Venice but whose traditional and mythical associations are all to do with love: it is significant in this context that the only native Cypriot in the play is Bianca, the whore. If Othello goes to Cyprus in the first place as a defending general, he also (once the Turkish threat has disappeared) goes there with Desdemona on honeymoon. But love has its dark side too, and once again it is Iago who liberates the darker powers of love. Love, in Iago's eyes, is reducible to the animal power of sexual coupling, the 'old black ram... tupping your white ewe', the 'Barbary horse' and the 'beast with two backs'. The idea that beautiful and apparently virtuous women; might be 'prime as goats, as hot as monkeys' is a natural one for Iago: for Othello it threatens the whole structure of his constructed belief, for the civilization that is Venice has no room for this earthiness. The phrase 'goats and monkeys' preys on Othello's mind and returns to haunt him. For Michael Cassio it is drink which serves to shatter the fragile veneer of Venetian civilization. For Othello, as for Brabantio, it is the violence of sexuality.

Othello's self-dramatizing is important not because it shows him up to be egotistical and therefore deserving of his fate (as some readings of the play seem to imply), but because it is part of a Venetian cast of mind which depends upon idealizing the real world. Such idealizations make the Venetians and Othello particularly vulnerable. When Iago presents them with a 'reality' which is the opposite of their idealized and courteous picture of the world, and the ideals break down, Brabantio, Cassio and Othello swing to the other extreme, and tragedy ensues.

11   King Lear

'To plainness honour's bound'

The opening scene of *King Lear* bears a structural similarity to Act I, Scene ii of *Hamlet*. Both are occasions of a royal proclamation and state ceremony – and are in fact mirror images of each other in this respect. In the earlier play Claudius addresses the court on the occasion of his taking up the reins of office; here Lear is making his retirement speech, as he is about to pass his crown on to the next generation. In both scenes it is initially the monarch who is speaking and controlling the scene; in both scenes that control is challenged by another character who seems at first to be a minor actor in the scene – another member of the royal family. Hamlet wears his inky cloak to point out his disaffection with his step-father, and his words are spiky and bad-tempered; Cordelia seems to want to sink into anonymity and reveals only reluctantly her feelings towards her father. Yet Hamlet through his aggression and Cordelia through her pained silence both challenge the authority of the King, and in the end Cordelia's challenge is the more damaging of the two.

The event which sets *King Lear* in motion is the division of the kingdom by the old king whose intent it is

> To shake all cares and business from our age,
> Conferring them on younger strengths, while we
> Unburthen'd crawl toward death.

(I, i, ll. 38–40)

The competition of love which he urges on his daughters is clearly the self-indulgent egotism of an old man so used to flattery that he cannot discern it from true love or friendship. Goneril and Regan play the game according to Lear's rules, but in the eyes of the audience their proclamations are immediately qualified, for even as they speak we are made aware of Cordelia, dismayed because of her own inability to match their flattery. Her first words are asides, meant for the ears of the audience, but not for anyone else on stage:

> What shall Cordelia speak? Love, and be silent...
> ... Then poor Cordelia!
> And yet not so; since I am sure my love's
> More ponderous than my tongue.

(I, i, ll. 61, 75–7)

As in the court scene at the beginning of *Hamlet*, a central concern of this scene is the relationship between what may be shown and what goes on in a person's heart. Goneril and Regan are good at displaying the trappings and the suits of love; Cordelia has that within which passes show, but is unable to 'heave [her] heart into [her] mouth' in order to express it. The problem is one of language: Lear, Goneril and Regan are playing an elaborate language-game – no less deadly for its being a game, but a game even so. They are speaking the language of pomp and ceremony, and going through a series of ritualistic moves which are part of the discourse of such ceremony. Cordelia's unwillingness to join in the game may spring from the best of motives: it may be the result of her scrupulosity about language and meaning which generates a dislike of seeming to promise more than can be delivered; it may be a reaction against the translation of affection into financial and economic terms, the setting a price on love which Lear proposes and which her sisters connive at; it may spring from a more general sense that any kind of flattery debases the truth of her actual love for her father. But whatever the motives, the effect of her refusing to join in the ritual is catastrophic.

The public nature of this scene cannot be stressed too much. It is a state occasion and the participants are speaking the language appropriate to rituals of state. Cordelia refuses to participate because she does not recognize, in this public language, any kind of personal truth: the language of state violates her own sense of selfhood. But does she recognize the extent to which her own language violates the ritual of state? When Lear turns to her and says

> Now, our joy,
> Although our last, and least; to whose young love
> The vines of France and milk of Burgundy
> Strive to be interess'd; what can you say to draw
> A third more opulent than your sisters? Speak.
>
> (I, i, ll. 81–5)

her response is devastating:

> *Cordelia* Nothing, my lord.
> *Lear* Nothing?
> *Cordelia* Nothing.
>
> (I, i, ll. 86–8)

The silences around her 'nothings' are deafening. The ritual has been shattered, and Cordelia has, with her few words, with her refusal of words, brought Lear's great ceremony grinding to a halt. For when she refuses Lear her words, it is in a context where the whole kingdom, symbolically, is watching her. She speaks from the heart, but she does so at a state ceremony where every nuance is

167

charged with public meaning. Cordelia's honesty, her faithfulness to her father and the truth of her love are never in the play brought into question: her goodness is a given value in the equation of the drama. But her ability to harm is commensurate with her ability to love, and Lear's sense of rejection is not without foundation; for however pure Cordelia's motive, the effect of what she does is to deliver Lear a painful public rebuff.

Cordelia calls a halt to the language of ceremony, but what replaces it after she has spoken is a discourse even more devoid of human kindness. Lear, cheated of the linguistic dignity which gives him the right to bestow blessings on his children, reverts instead to curses. The curse is a form of language which is simultaneously heartfelt and ritualistic, and at different points in the play Lear curses all three of his daughters. What he utters here against Cordelia is mild when compared with his later outburst against Goneril. Nonetheless the language with which he disinherits Cordelia is vehement:

... by the sacred radiance of the sun,
The mysteries of Hecate and the night,
By all the operation of the orbs
From whom we do exist and cease to be,
Here I disclaim all my paternal care,
Propinquity and property of blood,
And as a stranger to my heart and me
Hold thee from this for ever. The barbarous Scythian,
Or he that makes his generation messes
To gorge his appetite, shall to my bosom
Be as well neighbour'd, pitied, and reliev'd,
As thou my sometime daughter.

(I, i, ll. 108–19)

The scene had been set up as one in which he was formally to divest himself of his public office, his public identity, and transform himself into a private person. But here we see Lear stripping Cordelia of her identity, both as his successor and as his kin, 'Better thou Hadst not been born than not t'have pleased me better', he tells her, and everything else that he does to her in this scene is an attempt to negate her very being. He assumes that in denying her inheritance he is effectively reducing her, too, to 'nothing'. For Lear's own thinking about human relationships is inextricably bound up with financial matters, with possessions and property. In this scene his very language betrays this, as he plays on the double meaning of 'dear', meaning on the one hand 'beloved' and on the other hand 'of high price'; 'When she was dear to us', he says to Burgundy, 'we did hold her so, But now her price is fallen.'

Throughout the early part of the play, in fact, Lear continually attempts to quantify and measure love. In Act II, Goneril and Regan attempt to put limits on the number of his knights they are willing to entertain, Goneril allowing him no more than fifty, Regan no more than twenty-five. Lear reacts predictably: to Goneril, he says

> I'll go with thee,
> Thy fifty yet doth double five-and-twenty
> And thou art twice her love.

> (II, iv, ll. 256–8)

Cordelia expressly rejects such valuing of affection, and in the King of France she finds a suitor who is of a like mind. Because France, like Cordelia, believes that 'Love's not love when it is mingled with regards that stands Aloof from th'entire point', she is rescued, Lear's annihilation of her is only temporary, and she leaves the scene with a promise of being restored to something like her former status as the future Queen of France.

No such hope is offered to Kent, when he, too, speaks words which offend the King. Kent, the plain-speaker, takes up the argument in defence of Cordelia and addresses Lear in terms which ironically underpin the paradox of Lear's position in the play.

> *Kent*   Royal Lear,
>   Whom I have ever honoured as my king,
>   Lov'd as my father, as my master follow'd,
>   As my great patron thought on in my prayers –

> *Lear* The bow is bent and drawn; make from the shaft.

> *Kent* Let it fall rather, though the fork invade
>   The region of my heart: be Kent unmannerly,
>   When Lear is mad. What would'st thou do, old man?

> (I, i, ll. 138–45)

The abruptness of Kent's change from courtesy to insolence, from 'Royal Lear, Whom I have ever honoured' to 'What would'st thou do, old man', is devastating – all the more so since the point of the ceremony in the first place is to mark that precise change in Lear's own position, from being 'Royal Lear', the King, to being simply an 'old man'. Lear's response to Kent is as swift and as ruthless as his response to Cordelia, and Kent too, is banished.

Kent, like Cordelia, is one whose use of language is uncongenial to Lear. But whereas Cordelia is silent, Kent is outspoken. Lear speaks of Cordelia's 'pride, which she calls plainness'; later in the play, Cornwall will sarcastically cast similar aspersions on the disguised Kent's plainness:

This is some fellow
Who, having been prais'd for bluntness, doth affect
A saucy roughness, and constrains the garb
Quite from his nature: he cannot flatter, he;
An honest mind and plain, he must speak truth:
And they will take it, so; if not, he's plain.
These kind of knaves I know, which in this plainness
Harbour more craft and more corrupter ends
Than twenty silly-ducking observants,
That stretch their duties nicely.

(II, ii, ll. 92–101)

Cornwall has the 'unruly' Kent put in the stocks – but it is not only in Cornwall's court that men are punished for their plainness. Throughout *King Lear* courts are places where plain-speaking is dangerous, and Lear's own court is no exception. Cordelia's 'tardiness' leaves her 'dow'red with [Lear's] curse'. Kent's plainness of speech earns him banishment, and before he can take up again his rôle of plain-speaker and counsellor to Lear, he must, paradoxically, disguise himself; in order to say true things, he needs to put on a false identity. In the courts of *King Lear*, in fact, any kind of discourse has to be hedged around with circumspection. Lear's Fool states the problem in comic terms:

They [Goneril and Regan] 'll have me whipp'd for speaking true, thou'lt have me whipp'd for lying: and sometimes I am whipp'd for holding my peace.

(I, iv, ll. 179–81)

Lear's Fool is another kind of plain-speaker. But he, too, needs to wear disguises in order to be able occasionally to speak plainly. His rôle of Jester is one form of disguise and protection, for it affords him both official licence and the protection of anonymity. A second kind of disguise is his tone. The harsh truths that he tells Lear are surrounded by oblique remarks, jests and nonsense-rhymes. Occasionally his gibberish will turn out to be plain-speaking after all; at other times it will turn out to be indeed nonsense. The Fool's 'plainness' wears the mask of obscurity, for like Kent, it is only through a mask that he can speak truth.

The opposite of the plain-speaker is the hypocrite – or rather the person whose plainness of speech is selective and self-serving. Edmund speaks plainly enough to the audience: in fact, like Iago, his attraction lies in the way he is completely open to the audience in his evil. Goneril and Regan, too, can be plain enough when they are talking behind Lear's back:

Goneril You see how full of changes his age is; the observation we have made of it hath not been little: he always lov'd our sister most; and with what poor judgment he hath now cast her off appears too grossly.

Regan 'Tis the infirmity of his age; yet he hath ever but slenderly known himself.

Goneril The best and soundest of his time hath been but rash...

Regan Such unconstant starts are we like to have from him as this of Kent's banishment.

(I, i, ll. 287–95, 299–300)

The fact that we are likely to be convinced that they are speaking the truth about Lear is not the point: more significant is the discrepancy between what they will say to Lear's face and what they will say behind his back. Thus is their dishonesty signalled from the start. It is not until much later in the play that they grow into creatures of positive evil.

In the first scene of the play, then, three people are stripped of their rank, their status, their public identity – Lear voluntarily, and Cordelia and Kent as punishment for plain-speaking. A repeated motif in *King Lear* is the story of men and women displaced from their usual identities in society, trying to come to terms with their new rôles. In the character of Lear himself, this process is carried to its logical and terrible conclusion. For bit by bit the trappings which he had assumed were his by right are stripped away from him. His political power is the first thing to go – he gives that away along with his crown. His closest friendships and kinships he throws away by disowning and banishing Cordelia and Kent. Then his other daughters take charge, denying him his hundred knights. Then Goneril and Regan refuse him their hospitality at all. Then he is denied the right to find shelter in any civilized habitation. By the time he meets up with the blinded Gloucester he is dressed wildly and talking like a madman. He has been cut loose from his place in society and the end result is that his very sanity disintegrates. It is a complete collapse of the personality. And although there are moments of respite, nonetheless when, at the very end of the play, he loses Cordelia for the second time (having thought he had regained her) the dismantling of Lear is finally completed.

It starts in a small way – in the pettinesses of everyday running of a household, in Goneril's irritation at Lear's boisterous followers, in minor insolences by minor characters. 'Who am I, sir', Lear imperiously asks Osric. 'My lady's father', replies Osric, and Lear is forced for the first time to face up to his new reduced status as an appendage of his daughters. As his Fool taunts him, saying 'Now thou art an O without a figure... thou art nothing' (I, iv, l, 189), he himself rounds on Goneril's court:

> Does any here know me? This is not Lear:
> Does Lear walk thus? speak thus? Where are his eyes?
> Either his notion weakens, his discernings
> Are lethargied – Ha! Waking? 'tis not so.
> Who is it that can tell me who I am?
>
> (I, iv, ll. 223–7)

The tone at this point is in part ironic – he is putting on an act, pretending not to know Goneril, and challenging her household for a specific effect. But as the story proceeds, and as petty malice turns into a crescendo of evil, that question, 'Who is it that can tell me who I am?' becomes the most pressing one he has to answer.

'For which I razed my likeness'

Yet it is not only Lear who undergoes this process of displacement from a previously secure identity. The story is enacted in other characters too: Kent and Cordelia, Gloucester's son, Edgar, and eventually Gloucester as well, all go through a variation of this process of alienation from their accustomed identities and positions. Some of them survive the experience; some do not. Prominent among the survival strategies which characters adopt is the strategy of disguise. Indeed, it is more than just a strategy: it features strongly in the structure of imagery which informs the play. Disguise provides a tangible visual image for two of the central ideas of the play: the dismantling of an individual's public identity, and the relationship between flattery and plain-speaking. And if Kent is one character who wears a disguise in order to survive, another is Edgar.

In fact Edgar wears a whole variety of disguises in the play; he puts on one identity after another. He begins as 'Poor Tom', the Bedlam beggar gibbering his nonsense on the heath. The scenes in which Lear is brought face to face with Poor Tom (Act III, Scenes iv and vi) are extraordinary ones. Lear is already beginning to lose his reason when he first encounters the disguised Edgar; they are in the middle of the storm on the heath and the scene is almost surreal in its composition. What goes on on the heath is a picture of a world turned upside down. The former king, without shelter and reduced to the status of a beggar, is attended only by a Fool and a 'ruffian' (the disguised Kent). They are confronted by a 'madman' who is again a nobleman in disguise. Of the four of them, only the Fool is not displaced from his true identity – and the Fool is a character whose

Woodcut of 'The Ship of Fools'

identity is characterized by displacement. A woodcut illustrating the famous fifteenth-century satire called 'The Ship of Fools' shows a collection of different kinds of fool adrift in a boat (see above) and the Scottish poet Alexander Barclay wrote a satire of the same title based on a fifteenth-century German work. The scenes on the heath and in the farmhouse portray a similarly distorted world comprised almost entirely of different kinds of folly.

173

Kent, protected by his disguise, continues to be the plain-speaker. Assiduous in his protection of Lear, he says nothing in his disguise that he would not say in his own person, but he has to speak in borrowed accents in order to say anything at all. The Fool continues to speak a language which hides a cynical good sense under the cover of levity or nonsense. Lear's own language contains both sense and nonsense, but in a different way from that of the Fool. What Lear says swings back and forth between madness and lucidity. Continually harping on daughters, often rambling and illogical, nonetheless his speeches contain moments of terrifying clarity. Contemplating Edgar, he asks, appalled:

> Is man no more than this? Consider him well. Thou ow'st the worm no silk, the beast no hide, the sheep no wool, the cat no perfume. Ha! here's three on's are sophisticated; thou art the thing itself; unaccommodated man is no more but such a poor, bare, forked animal as thou art. Off, off, you lendings! Come; unbutton here.

> (III, iv, ll. 100–7)

Lear's momentary insight collapses into chaos as he struggles to tear off his own clothes, to reduce his state still further towards that of 'unaccommodated man'. Lear has come to recognize that his former power, and the trappings of honour that went with it, had prevented him from seeing all but a narrow band of what went on in the kingdom. His response is to divest himself of everything. Tearing off his clothes is his way of severing all links with the world of civilized behaviour. It is both a consequence and a symbol of his growing madness, which he now embraces in his search to find some kind of meaning in what is happening to him.

But Lear is wrong. 'Poor Tom' offers no insights or wisdom. The language spoken by the disguised Edgar is pure gibberish. It is a nonsensical language, in stark contrast to the gnomic utterances of the Fool, which are often packed with oblique meanings. This is a stark reminder that while there is such a thing as a divine madness – one which reveals insights only available when the protection of 'sane' perception is stripped away and which leads eventually to a more enlightened state – there are also forms of madness which have no enlightenment in them. Lear's new-found insights may yet be bought at the terrible price of the collapse of all coherence.

This is only on one level, however. On another, we are forced to remember that 'Poor Tom' does not actually exist: that this is merely Edgar playing a role – one which is as necessary to his survival as Kent's is to his. At one point in Act III, Scene iv the parallel between the two is vividly underlined as Gloucester comes on stage and we see both Kent and Edgar confronted by the person who, if their disguise was seen through, would have them put to death.

Poor Tom is only one of the five different disguises which Edgar assumes during the course of the play. In fact Edgar is a chameleon figure, shifting in various forms through the play's different levels. He can step in and out of the world of the play, for like Edmund he frequently acts as a choric commentator, addressing the audience directly. Indeed the two half-brothers, as the similarity of their names might lead one to expect, comprise reversed images of each other as they comment upon the action of the play, Edmund cynically, Edgar compassionately.

In the storm with Lear Edgar takes on the rôle of Poor Tom, and at first he continues to play this part when he comes across his blinded father. The conventions of disguise are easier to manipulate when Edgar has only the sightless Gloucester to deceive; he need only change his voice, for his appearance is irrelevant. And, in a scene which is, among other things, a most brilliant piece of theatrical trickery, he exchanges the 'Poor Tom' disguise for another. He leads Gloucester to what his father believes to be the top of a cliff, where Gloucester leaps to what he assumes will be his death. This is a moment of great complexity of tone. The sight of a blinded and desperate man trying to kill himself by jumping off what turns out to be a small hummock of grass makes for a terrible kind of black humour. The intensity of the moment is increased by the fact that the audience does not know, until the trick has actually been played, that it is a trick at all. Shakespeare's stage was, of course, non-illusionistic: details of landscape and topography would be established not by building sets to represent a cliff but by language which told the audience that the characters were on a cliff. This is precisely what happens in this scene, and the language in which Edgar creates the 'setting' is vivid and convincing.

> Come on, sir; here's the place: stand still. How fearful
> and dizzy 'tis to cast one's eyes so low!
> The crows and choughs that wing the midway air
> Show scarce so gross as beetles; halfway down
> Hangs one that gathers sampire, dreadful trade!
> Methinks he seems no bigger than his head.
> The fishermen that walk upon the beach
> Appear like mice, and yond tall anchoring bark
> Diminish'd to her cock, her cock a buoy
> Almost too small for sight. The murmuring surge
> That on th'unnumber'd idle pebble chafes,

> Cannot be heard so high. I'll look no more,
> Lest my brain turn and the deficient sight
> Topple down headlong
>
> (IV, vi, ll. 11–24)

Edgar, incidentally, is still assuming the character of Poor Tom at this point, although the disguise has begun to wear thin. He no longer attempts the rhythms of a madman, and even Gloucester has commented on the fact that his 'voice is alter'd' (IV, vi, l. 7).

The audience is as deceived about the setting as Gloucester is. As far as the audience is concerned, Edgar and Gloucester might well be on top of a cliff at this point. At any rate, there is no reason, apart from an ambiguous remark by Edgar, to assume that they are not. It is not until Gloucester has supposedly thrown himself to his death that the true nature of the setting is made apparent. For at that point Edgar immediately puts on a different disguise – that of a passer-by at the bottom of the cliff who 'saw' Gloucester fall from the top and float down to earth, provoked by a terrible monster. It is in this rôle that he continues to aid Gloucester until finally revealing himself to be his loyal son.

Even while he continues this rôle for Gloucester's benefit he modifies it for other people, to the extent that it becomes almost a different disguise altogether. When Gloucester is threatened by Oswald, Edgar interposes to protect him. As he does so he shifts from the character he had assumed while talking privately with Gloucester and becomes a caricatured country bumpkin, speaking that brand of yokel dialect which has been nicknamed 'Mummerset':

> And 'chud ha' bin zwaggered out of my life, 'twould not ha' bin zo long as 'tis by a vortnight. Nay, come not near th'old man; keep out che vor' ye, or ise try whither your costard or my ballow be the harder. Chill be plain with you . . . Chill pick your teeth, zir, Come; no matter vor your foins.
>
> (IV, vi, ll. 235–9, 241–2)

The rough-speaking countryman that he impersonates here serves to reinforce once more the link between Edgar and Kent, whose function in the Lear plot is to a large extent parallel to Edgar's own in the Gloucester sub-plot. Both of them assume a disguise, not just to escape from, but also to return to and anonymously take care of the person who rejected them.

However, Edgar has a larger rôle to play, in the end, than Kent. For Kent is basically Lear's servant, while Edgar also becomes a martial hero, a knight in shining armour who appears at the end of the play to dispense (in a limited way) justice with the sword. Once more, this happens by way of disguises. When he first approaches

Albany with the letter explaining the circumstances of his challenge, Edgar is dressed in the clothes of a poor but respectable man – presumably having changed costume since Act IV, Scene vi, when he was still dressed as a Bedlam beggar. Moreover, he intimates openly to Albany that he *is* in disguise and that there is more to him than meets the eye. And when he finally appears to challenge Edmund to a trial by combat, he is wearing yet another disguise: armed and helmeted so that his half-brother does not know him, he announces himself with the sentence 'Know, my name is lost.' It is not until he has fatally wounded Edmund that he can reclaim that name, which has been buried under a variety of disguises. For before this point, the world of *King Lear* is a world in which goodness can only survive in disguise – and sometimes not even then.

The variety of rôles in which Edgar appears is symptomatic of this rapidly-moving play. Lear, too, appears in a slightly different guise each time we see him. King, peevish old man, victim, man of insight, incoherent madman: he plays each of these parts in turn, and the play presents a kaleidoscope of images of him. Moreover, Shakespeare often generates more than one perspective on Lear at any one time. In the same way that Gloucester's 'suicide' is both funny and painful at the same time, so Lear himself often appears to be simultaneously a monster and a sympathetic figure, a man of heroic stature and 'a very foolish, fond old man'. But the difference between Lear and Edgar is that Edgar plays out his set of rôles, if not from choice, at least deliberately. Lear has no such deliberation. The different Lears that we see are not consciously-assumed rôles: they are the result of a personality undergoing a collapse.

'The great image of authority'

When the banished Kent disguises himself and goes incognito to seek service with his old master, so that he can watch over him, he and Lear engage in the following exchange.

> *Lear* What wouldst thou?
> *Kent* Service.
> *Lear* Who would'st thou serve?
> *Kent* You.
> *Lear* Dost thou know me, fellow?
> *Kent* No, Sir; but you have that in your countenance which I would fain call master.
> *Lear* What's that?
> *Kent* Authority.
>
> (I, iv, ll. 22–30)

177

Two senses of the word 'Authority' are at work here: on the one hand there is the sense of personal authority, of dignity or nobility which pertains to Lear the man and which Kent tells him he perceives in his countenance. Then there is authority in the stricter sense of the word – the power to give commands and be obeyed. Lear has the first, perhaps, but not the second – a point which is made repeatedly in the first two acts of the play. The voice which makes the point most frequently belongs to Lear's Fool, who plays on the word 'crown' in order to highlight the same disjunction between person and office: 'Thou hadst little wit in thy bald crown when thou gav'st thy golden one away', he scolds. The theme is one of Shakespeare's obsessions – the relationship between a man in his private capacity and the rôles and functions which he fulfils in society. In particular, Shakespeare returns time after time to the authority-figure, the Duke, the king, the Prince, to explore the gap he perceives between the man and his rôle. In *King Lear* the specific treatment of the theme is that Lear had renounced his public identity, thinking that he could retreat into his private one and relax, and 'unburthened crawl towards death' (I, i, 1. 43). What he discovers, however, is that the future image he had of himself does not in any way match the reality. In a sense, he has no private identity. He had never intended to divorce himself from the throne entirely, in any case. In his abdication speech to Cornwall and Albany he had himself unwittingly articulated some of the contradictions of his position.

I do invest you jointly with my power,
Pre-eminence, and all the large effects
That troop with majesty. Ourself, by monthly course,
With reservation of an hundred knights
By you to be sustain'd, shall our abode
Make with you by due turn. Only we shall retain
The name and all th'addition to a king; the sway,
Revenue, execution of the rest,
Beloved sons, be yours...

(I, i, ll. 129–37)

To Lear it seems a simple matter to take with him only those elements of kingship which it suits him to take: the name and 'th' addition', plus the right to maintain a small private army (to be paid for by Albany and Cornwall), the position without the responsibility. What he has yet to discover is that the rôle is not so easily divisible, and that it is not up to him to decide which parts of it are his by right. The most terrible thing he will discover is the extent to which his own identity is invested in his office as if his name is King-Lear, and that once he is cut off from the rights and duties which accrue to him as king, he is lost. The personal 'authority' which Kent claims to discern in Lear's face has been etched there by years of genuine authority of the kind which depends upon the very real political power of kingship. Once that power is lost, the personal authority which is left to Lear turns out to be terribly fragile, terribly short-lived.

One of the discoveries which most shocks Lear concerns the relationship between these two kinds of authority. The disguised Kent had expressed what Lear had always assumed, that there was a natural relationship between the personal and moral authority of the man and the authority of office. Lear in Kent's eyes retained that authority even when no longer a ruler; by implication, those people who do hold office, who have political authority, do so by virtue of some natural right – or at least rightness. They hold power in the world because they deserve to, because of their goodness, their wisdom, their integrity – their 'authority'. What Lear comes to believe is the exact opposite of this – that the relationship between the person and the power they wield is at best completely arbitrary, or at worst based upon nothing more than brute force:

> *Lear* Thou hast seen a farmer's dog bark at a beggar?
> *Gloucester* Ay, sir.
> *Lear* And the creature run from the cur? There thou might'st behold
>   The great image of Authority:
>   A dog's obey'd in office.
>   Thou rascal beadle, hold thy bloody hand!
>   Why dost thou lash that whore? Strip thy own back;
>   Thou hotly lusts to use her in that kind
>   For which thou whip'st her. The usurer hangs the cozener.
>   Thorough tatter'd clothes small vices do appear;
>   Robes and furr'd gowns hide all.
>   (IV, vi, ll. 152–67)

It is not the individual hypocrisy of the 'rascal beadle' or the 'usurer' which Lear finds so appalling; it is the arbitrariness of the power. If a dog is indeed obeyed in office, then what follows is that the robes and furred gowns are not merely the outward signs of an inward authority, but that they themselves constitute the authority. The golden crown that Lear gave away was not merely a symbol of his power, it was the source of it!

This speech about Authority wanders off into seeming inconsequentiality. Edgar, standing by and looking on, comments aside 'O matter and impertinency mixed! Reason in madness' – but refrains from saying which is which. Shakespeare may well have needed such a comment from someone on stage, for Lear's speech about 'the great image of authority' turns the conventional world picture of the Elizabethan upside down. The subversive impact of his words is immense, for they dismantle the whole structure of 'natural authority'. Given the context in which *King Lear* was written, and the audience to whom it would have been played, the risks being taken in such a speech should not be underestimated. For the issue of authority has a specific cultural context in the early Jacobean political scene, and recent Shakespeare scholarship has made a powerful case for seeing *King Lear* as an intervention in the seventeenth-century debates concerning the nature of the king's authority.

Lear's confident assumption throughout the early part of the play was that because he had been king, the kingdom, along with all its laws and institutions, belonged to him. (When Goneril later says to Albany 'The laws are mine, not thine', she is expressing the same misplaced sense of ownership which reveals the extent to which she is her father's daughter.) One of the things which Lear discovers in the course of the play is the extent to which, in his kingdom, authority went hand in hand with ownership: land, laws and people could all be reduced to mere possessions. In his speech on the heath in Act III, Scene iv, as he comes face to face with propertylessness, he acknowledges the injustices to which this has led. Reduced to near-beggary himself, he declares

> Poor naked wretches, wheresoe'er you are,
> That bide the pelting of this pitiless storm,
> How shall your houseless heads and unfed sides,
> Your loop'd and window'd raggedness defend you
> From seasons such as these? O, I have ta'en
> Too little care of this. Take physic, Pomp;
> Expose thyself to feel what wretches feel,
> That thou mayst shake the superflux to them,
> And show the Heavens more just.
>
> (III, iv, ll. 28–36)

This speech comes as a moment of lucidity in Lear's decline towards insanity. It shows Lear, suddenly, full of sense and compassion; he is a more sympathetic and impressive figure than at any previous point in the play. In a comedy or a tragicomedy, this speech might have marked a turning point which started Lear on the road towards redemption, towards becoming a better man or a better king. In Shakespeare's play, however, the moment of recognition is buried beneath Lear's increasing agony. For *King Lear* is a play without a happy ending. And this simple and obvious statement is one which bears some examining.

'The promised end'

The story of Lear belongs both to folklore and to history. The folk-tale 'Love Like Salt' or 'Grasscape', found throughout Europe, contains the story of the faithful daughter whose honest reply to the question 'How much do you love me?' incurs her father's wrath. But the figure of Lear himself was part of England's mythology long before Shakespeare wrote his version of the story. He was the tenth king of Britain after Brutus the Trojan, who founded Britain itself. The story of the division of the kingdom is an ongoing saga which can be traced back to Brutus's own reign. According to the legends, it was he who first made the tripartite division of the island, sepa-rating it into dominions roughly equivalent to England, Scotland and Wales. The Lear of legend inherited from his own father, Bladud, a reunited kingdom, but repeated Brutus's original mistake when he once more divided the kingdom amongst his daughters, letting loose anarchy and destruction.

The original story was to be found in various history books, from the Elizabethan Raphael Holinshed's *Chronicles of England, Scotlande and Irelande* (1577) back to the medieval *Historia Regium Britanniae* of Geoffrey of Monmouth (*c.* 1135). It was one of those stories, some-where between Celtic history and English national mythology, which to the Elizabethans and Jacobeans comprised the early history of Britain. This is one reason why the setting of the play seems so strange. The action appears to belong simultaneously to two distinc-tive historical eras. It takes place in a pre-Roman Celtic Britain, somewhere between 1200 and 500 BC, long before the Arthurian England of Merlin's time, as Lear's Fool points out. It also takes place, however, in a distinctly bourgeois society, akin to that of Shakespeare's own age and peopled with courtiers, beadles, monopoly-holders, justices, lawyers and schoolmasters.

The writers of romance and allegory had dealt with the story, too: Edmund Spenser includes it in *The Faerie Queene* (Book II, Canto 10), and the Gloucester sub-plot is to be found in Sir Philip Sidney's *Arcadia*. But, like *Hamlet*, *King Lear* is more than just a play which relies on a variety of published sources; it is a reworking by Shakespeare of earlier dramatic material. The anonymous *True Chronicle Historie of King Leir* probably dates back to 1594, more than ten years before Shakespeare wrote his version of the story. Unlike the mysterious Ur-*Hamlet*, however, the text of the original Lear play has not disappeared. It was published in 1605, quite possibly in response to the publicity surrounding a recent legal case, involving one Brian Annesley and his daughter Cordell, which bore an un-canny and coincidental resemblance to some of the events in the story

of Lear. (The original documents relating to this case, and a brief
account of it, are to be found in Geoffrey Bullough's *Narrative and
Dramatic Sources of Shakespeare* (Routledge & Kegan Paul, 1973,
pp. 270–1 and 309–11).

The following quotation from the earlier play gives a sense of the
difference between *King Leir* and *King Lear*. In *King Leir*, the King of
France presides over the reunion of Leir and his daughter Cordella.

King [*Of France*] Let me break off this loving controversy
  Which doth rejoice my very soul to see.
  Good father, rise, she is your loving daughter,

                                                        (*He riseth*)

  And honours you with as respective duty
  As if you were the monarch of the world
Cordella But I will never rise from off my knee
  Until I have your blessing, and your pardon
  Of all my faults committed any way,
  From my first birth unto this present day.
Leir The blessing, which the God of Abraham gave
  Unto the tribe of Juda, light on thee,
  And multiply thy days, that thou mayst see
  Thy children's children prosper after thee.
  Thy faults, which are just none that I do know
  God pardon on high and I forgive below.

                                                        (*She riseth*)

Cordella Now is my heart at quiet, and doth leap
  Within my breast, for joy of this good hap:
  And now (dear father) welcome to our court...
        (*True Chronicle Historie*, Scene xxiv. In Bullough,
    Narrative and Dramatic Sources, pp. 393–4. My modernization.)

It is, as Geoffrey Bullough has put it, an 'affecting recognition-
scene'. There is a sense of quiet dignity about the meeting of Leir and
Cordella which audiences must have found moving; Leir, in particular, is seen to regain his former stature and power as he solemnly
bestows his paternal, royal and almost-heavenly blessing upon
Cordella. Compare that with the corresponding recognition scene in
Shakespeare's *King Lear*.

Cordelia Sir, do you know me?
Lear You are a spirit, I know; where did you die?
Cordelia Still, still, far wide.
Doctor He's scarce awake; let him alone awhile.
Lear Where have I been? Where am I? Fair daylight?
  I am mightily abus'd. I should e'en die with pity,
  To see another thus. I know not what to say.

I will not swear these are my hands: let's see;
I feel this pin prick. Would I were assur'd
Of my condition!
Cordelia   O! look upon me, Sir
And hold your hand in benediction o'er me.
No, Sir, you must not kneel.
Lear Pray do not mock me:
I am a very foolish fond old man,
Fourscore and upward, not an hour more or less;
And, to deal plainly,
I fear I am not in my perfect mind.
Methinks I should know you and know this man,
Yet I am doubtful: for I am mainly ignorant
What place this is, and all the skill I have
Remembers not these garments; nor I know not
Where I did lodge last night. Do not laugh at me;
For, as I am a man, I think this lady
To be my child Cordelia.

                              (IV, vii, ll. 48–70)

The difference in tone between the scenes serves to remind us of some of the things that make Shakespeare not just a great poet but a great playwright. To put it at its simplest, the language which Shakespeare uses for his recognition scene is a private one, whereas the language of *The True Chronicle Historie* remains throughout rather formal, suited to a public demonstration or oration. Shakespeare's Lear is feeling his way with words, and what he says charts a growing awareness of what is happening to him, as he is torn between hope and fear. His early declaration that Cordelia must be a 'spirit' sounds like the kind of aggressive self-confidence he had shown earlier when talking to Gloucester, but now it serves a different purpose. This scene is between a father and a daughter he thought he had lost for ever, and what we see is Lear's terror of submitting to the interpretation he most wants to be true, his fear of believing that she is actually there in person. He puts off saying it, puts off believing it, until the last possible moment, concentrating instead on his own confusions. His awareness of these confusions is not unmixed with a certain amount of self-pity – 'I am mightily abus'd', he says, and the old querulous Lear resurfaces for a moment. But eventually, having tried not to say it for so long, and hedging it round with qualifications, he finally commits himself – not even speaking directly to her, but addressing someone else in middle distance: 'I think this lady to be my child Cordelia'.

In *The True Chronicle Historie*, the reunion of Leir and Cordella is dignified and noble, but it is also comparatively static. Shakespeare, in contrast, develops Lear's recognition scene through a series of painful stages, culminating a final moment of release as Cordelia acknowledges Lear's words. In this scene, words are not easy for Lear to come by; the tension of the relationship is continually heightened as Lear puts off the final moment of confrontation; and his relief when he discovers that he has not, after all, deluded himself, is palpable. Most significantly, dignity, which is the key-note of *The True Chronicle Historie,* has nothing to do with Shakespeare's Lear. We are asked to concentrate not on his dignity but on his pain.

It is all too easy to set up comparisons between Shakespeare and one of his contemporary dramatists in order to illustrate Shakespeare's superiority. That is not the main point of this exercise, although it is occasionally instructive, in order to appreciate how a great writer works, to look at the way in which a lesser hand deals with the same or similar material. But it should be borne in mind that these two scenes are trying to do two very different things, each in its way appropriate to the function of the scene in the play as a whole. For although there have already been all sorts of differences between the two treatments of the Lear-story up to this point, the most important difference between them occurs after the reunion of Lear/Leir and Cordelia/Cordella. In the *True Chronicle Historie,* the recognition scene marks the final turning point of Leir's fortunes. Reunited emotionally with Cordella and politically with the King of France, once more every inch a king, Leir marches against Gonorill and Ragan, defeats them with ease, regains his throne, and has a happy ending which promises that he will live happily, if not ever after, at least to a ripe old age, looked after by his loving daughter Cordella.

Shakespeare's great coup in *King Lear,* the black joke which he plays on the audience, is that the happy ending which the recognition scene seems to promise never materializes. The reunion of Lear and Cordelia takes place at the end of Act IV. It turns out to be, not the point from which Lear's resurgence can be charted, but a momentary flash of false hope which is offered to both Lear and the audience; hope that there is some consolation, some happy ending possible after the sorrows and the horrors that Lear has experienced. It is a hope which is almost immediately snuffed out. Throughout Act V Lear's tortures continue, made only the more poignant by that brief moment of happiness which Shakespeare presented in such an emotionally-charged way. Far from marching to victory at the head of Cordelia's army, Lear, Cordelia and the French forces are swiftly and efficiently defeated and Lear and Cordelia taken prisoner. Lear's reconciliation with Cordelia has given him new strength, and his response to his captivity shows him to be the epitome of stoicism. Comforting Cordelia, he says,

> Come, let's away to prison;
> We two alone will sing like birds i'th' cage:
> When thou dost ask me blessing, I'll kneel down,
> And ask of thee forgiveness: so we'll live
> And pray, and sing, and tell old tales, and laugh
> At gilded butterflies, and hear poor rogues
> Talk of court news; and we'll talk with them too,
> Who loses and who wins; who's in, who's out;
> And take upon's the mystery of things,
> As if we were Gods' spies: and we'll wear out,
> In a wall'd prison, packs and sects of great ones
> That ebb and flow by th' moon.
>
> (V, iii, ll. 8–19)

This is a poignant speech of renunciation of this world with all its attendant joys and miseries, a speech in which Lear affirms that he has finally found peace of mind, and cannot be touched by reversals of his earthly fortunes. The picture that Lear paints is of himself and Cordelia, having transcended the cares of the world, existing in a state of loving tranquillity even in their prison cell, unaffected by their imprisonment, able both to laugh at the transient details of everyday life and also to peer into the deepest mysteries of the universe. It is a speech that is beautiful and moving. It is also one which will be proved catastrophically wrong, for Lear has not yet grasped what Edgar knows, that 'the worst is not, So long as we can say "This is the worst..."'   (IV, i, ll. 28–29).

The audience already knows that the chances of Lear and Cordelia being left alone to sing like birds in the cage are slight, for the comparatively humane Duke of Albany, who intends to treat his royal prisoners with respect, is about to be outmanoeuvred by the vicious Edmund. As Lear and Cordelia are led away we see Edmund's villainy at work, as he gives his Captain some unspecified instructions; we do not know precisely what the Captain has been told to do – but we can guess. It will lead, of course, to the death of Cordelia, the culminating incident which will shatter Lear's hopes of peaceful transcendence, and finally break his spirit for ever. This death is all the more appalling for the casualness with which it happens: Cordelia is killed by an act of almost negligent malice repented too late. Once more hopes are briefly raised that the happy ending is possible: Edgar, once more disguised, arrives to challenge Edmund to single combat and defeats him. Goneril has poisoned Regan, but seeing Edmund defeated kills herself. Edmund – in an uncharacteristic death-bed repentance – decides to do one good deed before he dies and revoke his order to have Lear and Cordelia murdered. It is all rather melodramatic and rather messy: but what cuts through the melodrama with a terrible clarity is the image of Lear, stumbling onto the stage with the dead Cordelia in his arms, howling his grief.

Because of the expectations that we learn to have about Shakespeare's tragedies and about tragedy in general, it is perhaps rather easy to underestimate the shock value of this incident as it must have appeared to audiences who first saw the play. And not only the first audiences either: Dr Johnson reported himself 'so shocked by Cordelia's death that I know not whether I ever endured to read again the last scenes of the play till I undertook to revise them as an editor'. Nahum Tate, the Restoration poet and dramatist, found the ending unbearable and his contemporaries agreed: in 1681 he rewrote Shakespeare's play in order to give it (among other things) a happy ending, and his version of the play became the standard acting text, the one that audiences saw, for the next 140 years. It was once customary merely to sneer at Tate, but the point is that in an important way he is quite right. It is Shakespeare, not Tate, who has radically altered the story of Lear, for according to all the earlier versions, the story ends as it does in the *True Chronicle Historie* – happily. Cordelia and Lear, reunited, reclaim their kingdom, and Lear lives to rule Britain once more. In *King Lear*, Shakespeare does not merely adapt his sources, he makes a violent and shocking alteration to them. The deaths of Lear and Cordelia should never have happened, and by making them happen Shakespeare flies in the face of historical, moral and dramatic expectations.

To know that Shakespeare was working against his source material in this way offers some important insights into why the play is the way it is. The story that Shakespeare inherited was one in which forgiveness, accommodation and reconciliation led to a final state of enlightened happiness. The miseries through which Leir and his friends passed had some purpose: they were there to lead the protagonists towards a greater knowledge, integrity or wisdom. The function of the happy ending is to affirm that these goals have been attained, and that the suffering has been worthwhile. It is a traditional narrative pattern whose recurrent popularity in world literature testifies, perhaps, to a widespread desire to give meaning to the sufferings of 'the human condition'. It may be an indication of how very powerful this narrative pattern is that many readers and audiences assume it to be operative even when it is quite deliberately not! Shakespeare's *King Lear* is a case in point. Many writers on *King Lear* have talked about Shakespeare's play in precisely the terms which actually best describe *The True Chronicle Historie:* they have stressed the pattern of redemption in the play, laid emphasis on Lear's growth in knowledge and spiritual stature, and even discussed the nobility of his death. But if knowing about *The True Chronicle*

Historie does nothing else, it surely illustrates with remarkable clarity the extent to which this response to Shakespeare's play is an inappropriate one, the extent to which Shakespeare chose *not* to treat the story in such a way as to imply a sense of consolation. As the end of the play approaches, Shakespeare, with the *True Chronicle Historie* before him, takes every possible opportunity to avoid the conclusions to which the earlier play comes. Not a happy-ever-after old age, but death for Lear and Cordelia, Kent and Gloucester. And for Lear a death, not like Gloucester's (whose heart 'burst smilingly' at the moment of reconciliation with his lost son), but an anguished death, seeking refuge in delusion as he tries to convince himself that the dead Cordelia still has breath. Not even a death marked by eloquence, but one heralded by the failure of language: by inarticulate sounds, by disconnected phrases and by bleak words repeated as if in an attempt to reduce them to meaninglessness. 'Howl, howl, howl, howl . . . Never, never, never never never', weeps Lear, and his subjects stand helplessly by, hoping only that he will die soon.

The bleakness of the play's last few moments makes it difficult to take seriously those readings which insist that the play's meaning resides in Lear's discovery of the values of love and forgiveness. This kind of reading is often based on an *a priori* assumption, that what happens in a tragedy is that the protagonist learns a moral lesson and dies in a state of enlightenment. This is not to imply, however, that Lear does not go through some sort of learning process in the play: he clearly does – though in reality the word 'learning' sounds too tame and settled for what happens to Lear. As the protective shell of his rank is stripped away, and Lear is left exposed 'to feel what wretches feel' he 'learns' more and more. He learns that he is 'not ague-proof', he learns about 'unaccommodated man', and about the 'great image of authority', and he learns to humble himself before his wronged daughter. Lear, in fact, is continually learning, even as he forgets what he learned before. But that process of learning is a double-edged blade, with its negative aspect as well as its positive. Lear's madness is the result of a learning process which has become unbearable. For all his learning is still capable of self-delusion, even at the very end, as in the 'birds i' th' cage' speech, and in his desperate final attempts to believe that Cordelia lives. And if his madness enables him in some ways to see more clearly, it also imbues him with a searing disgust of humanity. This is expressed in a vitriolic outburst which encompasses both an obsession with sexuality in general, and a disgust of female sexuality in particular:

> The wren goes to 't, and the small gilded fly
> Does lecher in my sight.
> Let copulation thrive; for Gloucester's bastard son

Was kinder to his father than my daughters
Got 'tween the lawful sheets. To't, Luxury, pell-mell!
For I lack soldiers. Behold yond simp'ring dame,
Whose face between her forks presages snow;
That minces virtue and does shake the head
To hear of pleasure's name;
The fitchew, nor the soiled horse goes to 't
With a more riotous appetite.
Down from the waist they are Centaurs,
Though women all above:
But to the girdle do the Gods inherit,
Beneath is all the fiend's: there's hell, there's darkness,
There is the sulphurous pit – burning, scalding,
Stench, consumption; fie, fie, fie . . .

                                                (IV, vi, ll. 114–31)

It is hardly surprising that some recent evaluations of *King Lear* have expressed unease about the linguistic violence against women which is found in the play. From the specificity of his first disowning of Cordelia, through his cursing of Goneril and Regan and his bitter obsession with the ingratitude of daughters, through to this outburst against women in general, his tirades against women are increasingly misogynistic.

Once Lear's illusions begin to crumble, there is no stopping them. In this rapidly moving play, nothing ever stands still, and moments of disgust such as the above are stages in the process rather than the end-product of his experiences. But neither his conventionally acceptable lessons of humility, nor his moments of misanthropic and misogynistic despair do him any good. If the happy endings of the earlier Leir stories implied that the learning of lessons might lead to happiness, what Shakespeare's *King Lear* enacts is a tale in which no lesson learnt is ever learnt finally, and in which knowledge offers no protection from misery.

12 Macbeth

'Brave Macbeth'

All Shakespeare's tragic heroes kill people. Different emphases are placed on their various homicides, and different responses are required from the audience. At one extreme lies the downright approval that we are clearly meant to feel when Lear kills the anonymous soldier who had hanged Cordelia. In the middle are the more ambiguous killings carried out by Hamlet and Othello; their various murders are hedged around with extenuating circumstances. Othello's murderous attack on Desdemona has been orchestrated by Iago to the extent that it is at least arguable whether Othello is in his right mind. Hamlet actually commits a variety of killings which range from death by mistaken identity (Polonius), through cold-blooded plotting in his own defence (Rosencrantz and Guildenstern), to unwitting manslaughter (Laertes) and finally justified and almost judicial revenge (Claudius). But the killings which Macbeth carries out, either directly or indirectly, have no ambiguity about them. He is under no compulsion or misapprehension as he murders, or orders the murders of Duncan, Banquo and Lady Macduff and her children. He may feel guilt, terror, despair and even occasional remorse, but we are never asked to see any of them as justifiable homicide. They are acts of unambiguous evil.

However, there is pressure on an audience to 'sympathize' with the central character of a play – especially a tragedy. And so, if that central figure is committing evil acts, there is an immediate complexity in the audience's response. Dramatic 'sympathy' can take various forms, of course: the word does not mean quite the same thing as it does in everyday life, when we talk about 'sympathizing' with someone's problems. On stage, 'sympathy' with a character means no more than 'being engaged with' that character. Thus in *Richard III* Shakespeare created a figure of evil to whom an audience feels drawn because of his brilliant, witty and energetic holding of the centre stage. *Macbeth*, however, demands more than that. The intensity of the play's vision seems to draw an audience towards Macbeth's own point of view – towards 'sympathy' in the fullest sense with Macbeth and his situation. This is a central contradiction in the play; that the straightforwardness of Macbeth's evil distances him from the audience, whereas the intensity of the play's language focuses itself upon him in a way which draws us towards him and his point of view. The play generates, in effect, a double perspective on Macbeth himself.

The kind of tragedy which Shakespeare explores in *Macbeth* resembles, at first glance, the pattern he had already used in *Othello*. *Othello* is a play about a man who believes himself to be securely in command of his own identity, who has a strong belief in his own goodness and nobility, but who is driven by a series of circumstances (orchestrated by Iago) to commit a seemingly unthinkable crime – the murder of someone he loves. The plot of *Othello* is centrally concerned with the processes by which he is driven to do the deed; in particular, it explores the mental and emotional pressures to which Othello himself is subjected, and which lead to the breakdown of his own sense of himself. Once Othello has finally killed Desdemona, the play moves abruptly to its conclusion: Othello quickly finds out that he was wrong in believing in Desdemona's unfaithfulness; the truth of Iago's villainy is revealed; Othello is brought face to face with the monstrousness of his crime, and, unable to live with it, he kills himself.

Macbeth's progression is not unlike Othello's. He, too, appears at the beginning of the play as a character secure in his own identity – a trusted servant of the king and a military hero upon whom rewards are about to be heaped. The unthinkable crime to which Macbeth is driven (or led) is that of regicide; he kills the king who trusts him so absolutely. In *Macbeth*, as in *Othello*, we are shown the way in which the crime changes in the hero's mind from being unthinkable to being inevitable. But there is a major structural difference between the two plays; in *Macbeth*, Shakespeare spends far less time than he does in *Othello* on carefully examining the steps that lead up to the crime. To put it at its simplest – the murder in *Othello* takes place in Act V, Scene ii; in *Macbeth* it is over by Act II, Scene ii. Whereas in *Othello*, the hero's committing of the murder is the climax of the plot, this is not the case in *Macbeth*. Othello undergoes a mental and emotional collapse which opens the door to the possibility of killing Desdemona but which simultaneously destroys Othello himself. It is almost incidental that Iago's villainy is unmasked; having killed Desdemona, Othello's death seems inevitable. Macbeth also undergoes some kind of collapse; but from Act II, Scene ii onwards, however, the play is about *living* with the aftermath of this collapse. Desdemona's murder involves Othello's madness, but Macbeth's story is the more terrible, for he undergoes the collapse of personality, and yet retains his sanity. He is fully conscious during the operation, and he observes and analyses, as well as experiences, his own descent into hell.

The first act and a half of *Macbeth* contains, in effect, a compressed version of the action which takes up the entire five acts of *Othello*. First of all, an apparently unproblematic identity is established for the hero: he is, we are told, 'brave Macbeth', and the Captain who so describes him emphasizes how appropriate that adjective seems to be:

> For brave Macbeth (well he deserves that name),
> Disdaining Fortune, with his brandish'd steel,
> Which smok'd with bloody execution,
> Like Valour's minion, carv'd out his passage,
> Till he fac'd the slave;
> Which ne'er shook hands, nor bade farewell to him,
> Till he unseam'd him from the nave to th'chops,
> And fix'd his head upon our battlements.
>
> (I, ii, ll. 16–23)

In retrospect, when we have read or seen the whole of the play, and look back at this almost comically gruesome description of Macbeth's martial prowess, we can see that it contains in it some hints as to Macbeth's future developments – hints which turn out to be ironic foreshadowings of events to come. Macbeth's identity is defined from the beginning as being steeped in blood; his sword 'Which smok'd with bloody execution' might be emblematic of his later career as regicide and tyrant. But there are no clues, on first acquaintance, which encourage us to read such irony into this description. Certainly the speaker and listener in the scene, the Captain and the King, read no dark meanings into the imagery. For them both, Macbeth's unseaming of Macdonwald 'from the nave to th'chops' confirms their idea of him as 'valiant', 'worthy' and 'noble'. Macbeth's initial identity is established in terms which appear unequivocal.

'My black and deep desires'

Before long, however, this seemingly unproblematic identity is put under pressure. Macbeth encounters the three witches and is straightaway encouraged to think of himself as a natural successor to the throne. His almost immediate reaction is to start fantasizing about 'murther'. Informed that he has indeed been made Thane of Cawdor, in accordance with the witches' prophecy, he soliloquizes:

> This supernatural soliciting
> Cannot be ill; cannot be good: –
> If ill, why hath it given me earnest of success,
> Commencing in a truth? I am Thane of Cawdor:
> If good, why do I yield to that suggestion
> Whose horrid image doth unfix my hair,
> And make my seated heart knock at my ribs,
> Against the use of nature? Present fears

Are less than horrible imaginings.
My thought, whose murther yet is but fantastical,
Shakes so my single state of man,
That functioning is smother'd in surmise,
And nothing is, but what is not.

(I, iii, ll. 130–42)

During this scene and the next, Macbeth swings between a fatalistic acceptance of whatever the future happens to have in store, and a frenzied calculating of the various steps he will have to take in order to get the crown. At one point, he rejects his own 'horrible imaginings' and concludes, 'If Chance will have me King, why, Chance, may crown me, Without my stir . . . Come what come may'. Soon after, however, he is speaking the language of hardened assassin; reminded that the King has a legitimate heir in Malcolm, Prince of Cumberland, Macbeth speaks aside, saying,

The Prince of Cumberland! – That is a step
On which I must fall down, or else o'erleap,
For in my way it lies. Stars, hide your fires!
Let not light see my black and deep desires;
The eye wink at the hand; yet let that be,
Which the eye fears, when it is done, to see,

(I, iv, ll. 48–53)

Macbeth's first reaction is severely practical; he has the Prince of Cumberland blocking his path to the throne, and he must decide what to do about it. By the end of the short aside he has decided; 'let that be, Which the eye fears, when it is done, to see'. He is (for the moment at least) resolutely fixed on a course of murder.

When we next see him for any length of time, however, he is undecided again. The soliloquy which begins Act I, Scene vii ('If 'twere done, when 'tis done, then 'twere well it were done quickly') shows him arguing against his earlier certainty and veering from one resolution to another. In fact, throughout the early part of the play Macbeth is portrayed as a man who is almost literally in two minds. In Act I, Macbeth has been characterized by other people in two apparently contradictory ways. Firstly there is the image provided by the Captain of Macbeth the warrior 'with his brandish'd steel, Which smok'd with bloody execution'. Secondly there is Lady Macbeth's judgement of him; she sees Macbeth as being 'too full o'th' milk of human kindness'. These two Macbeths are in conflict right up until the moment when he kills Duncan. In a way he is a little like Hamlet, looking for 'himself' in a series of responses to a pressure which will eventually lead him to homicide. But if Hamlet's responses are couched in a dramatically self-conscious and witty style as he approaches his task through play-acting, Macbeth is never less than deadly serious.

'If 'twere done . . .'

The conflict between these two Macbeths is vividly dramatized in Macbeth's soliloquy in Act I, Scene vii. This speech takes place against a background of celebration. Stage directions instruct us that 'divers Servants with dishes and service' pass over the stage. Elsewhere in the castle, a banquet is taking place in honour of Duncan and in celebration of the peace of the realm; it is a scene of festivity from which Macbeth is excluded – or rather, from which he has excluded himself. Instead, he sits alone with his thoughts, isolated. In *Macbeth*, Shakespeare twice uses the image of the banquet to suggest the civilized celebration of a king's reign – and both times he does so ironically, showing the celebration to be sham. Later in the play, Macbeth's own attempt to celebrate with a feast soon after his coronation is interrupted by the appearance of the murdered Banquo's ghost. Now here in Act 1, Scene vii, while Duncan feasts, his host sits outside, contemplating his assassination.

> If 'twere done, when 'tis done, then 'twere well
> It were done quickly: if th' assassination
> Could trammel up the consequence, and catch
> With his surcease success; that but this blow
> Might be the be-all and the end-all – here,
> But here, upon this bank and shoal of time,
> We'd jump the life to come. – But in these cases
> We still have judgement here; that we but teach
> Bloody instructions, which, being taught, return
> To plague th'inventor: this even-handed Justice
> Commends th' ingredience of our poison'd chalice
> To our own lips.
>
> (I, vii, ll. 1–12)

The language of this soliloquy is difficult – and this difficulty is significant. In broad terms what seems to be happening is that the speaker is trying to use language to sort out the complexity of his situation, and to impose some kind of order on his thoughts. But as he speaks, his language slips away from him. Macbeth's words take on multiple meanings, and the sound of one word generates another ('surcease' – 'success'). His syntax fails him and he has to stop and start; 'If it were done . . .'; 'if th' assassination could . . .'; 'that but this blow might be . . .'. All these are different assaults on one idea – but then, as he stops and starts again the idea itself changes subtly, moving from the practicalitites of getting on with the task in hand, to an almost metaphysical meditation on 'the life to come'. Macbeth repeats himself, trying to clarify things; 'here, But here', he says, attempting to insist upon a single idea, and yet finding himself talking in ambiguities. (Does the second 'here' refer to the same place as the first? Does 'But' mean 'only' or 'on the other hand'?) Macbeth's metaphors breed further metaphors, often at levels too deep for conscious attention; in the original Folio texts of *Macbeth*, 'bank and shoal' appears as 'bank and Schoole' (an acceptable alternative spelling), suggesting not only the shallows of a river, but also the judicial bench and the schoolroom – concepts picked up later in the phrase 'We still have judgement here; that we but teach Bloody instructions'. Throughout the speech Macbeth finds his words leading him into unexpected areas. In the end, his syntax does not hold in check the confusion of his thoughts but generates new and disturbing thoughts. His words do not nail down single ideas, but set up echoes and reverberations in which meaning slips away from the speaker, or returns in new and unwelcome forms. Language in this speech is speaking Macbeth.

From the beginning of the soliloquy, the syntax is strange. Macbeth's sentence wavers between 'if' and 'when'. On the one hand he seems to be picturing the actuality of the murder, the practical details of the deed, which 'when 'tis done' should be done quickly. On the other hand he is staving off any final commitment to the decision through his use of the conditional tense and that word 'if'; 'If 'twere done', he says – as if he were still dealing with a mere abstract possibility. But clearly, in this first part of the soliloquy, Macbeth is not deciding *whether* to kill Duncan; rather, he is obsessed with the wish that he could do the deed without there being any consequences to his action.

This is an important moment in the play, for it signals the beginning of the process of breakdown which the rest of the tragedy will chart. Already in Macbeth's mind, images of disintegration and dissociation are beginning to appear, and here they present themselves to him as optimistic possibilities – ways of having perhaps literally, the best of both worlds. To be able to limit the evil to a single moment, to dissociate it from any long-lasting effects on his body or soul: this is what Macbeth is fantasizing about. And so he tries to picture a situation in which 'this blow Might be the be-all and the end-all'. But as yet, Macbeth's sense of isolation from the rest of the processes which govern heaven and earth is not sufficiently strong for him to uphold this idea for long. Against his wish-fulfilling fantasy is set what Macbeth feels to be the reality of the situation; a deed is not free of premiss and consequence. On the contrary, a person's every action is part of a complex web of cause and effect – on two levels. First of all, there is the inevitable Christian scheme of retribution, and it is an awareness of this which he seems at first to be trying to shake off as he wishes he could 'jump the life to come'. But the metaphysical implications of his evil are given comparatively short shrift here; the justice which Macbeth focuses upon at this point is earthly rather than heavenly. Macbeth's vision of the 'Bloody instructions, which, being taught, return To plague th' inventor' is practical and pragmatic, for Macbeth is speaking out of self-interest, and calculating the likely effects of a cycle of violence upon himself. But as he speaks, Macbeth unconsciously gestures towards what might be called quite accurately 'poetic justice'. The idea of evil leading to its own retribution is one which is continually dramatized in the history plays and the tragedies of the English Renaissance. And when this develops into an image of the 'even-handed Justice [which] Commends th' ingredience of our poison'd chalice To our own lips', the final scene of *Hamlet* is conjured up, and Macbeth, just for a second, turns into Claudius.

The next section of the soliloquy sees him more successful in his attempt to order his thoughts. He begins to list, as rationally as he can, arguments against killing Duncan;

> He's here in double trust;
> First, as I am his kinsman and his subject,
> Strong both against the deed; then as his host,
> Who should against his murtherer shut the door,
> Not bear the knife myself. Besides, this Duncan
> Hath borne his faculties so meek, hath been
> So clear in his great office, that his virtues
> Will plead like angels, trumpet-tongu'd, against
> The deep damnation of his taking-off;
>
> (I, vii, ll. 12–20)

But as this line of thought continues, Macbeth finds himself once more caught up in a swirl of metaphors, which outstrips his intended coolheadedness.

> And Pity, like a naked new-born babe,
> Striding the blast, or heaven's Cherubins, hors'd
> Upon the sightless couriers of the air,
> Shall blow the horrid deed in every eye
> That tears shall drown the wind,
>
> (I, vii, ll. 21–5)

In a startling series of transformations, images of innocence and vulnerability become interwoven with images of power and violence.

Duncan's 'virtues' have already been compared to 'angels, trumpet-tongued'. They are pleading on Duncan's behalf, but the trumpets also suggest something military and forceful. Now the abstract notion of Pity is personified, first as the weak and helpless 'naked new-born babe' – an object of pity or tenderness. But then that is seen as 'Striding the blast' – perhaps a storm, or the blast of the trumpets from the previous line. That in turn generates the phrase 'heaven's Cherubins', picking up the earlier 'angels'. This word 'Cherubins' focuses the double sense of innocence and power; on the one hand it contains the implications of baby-faced innocence that is still retained in the modern sense of the word 'cherubic'. On the other hand, according to authorities such as Stephen Batman (or Bateman), writing in 1582 'Cherubins' were 'the highest companies of Angelles' – the most powerful in the heavenly host. And as the metaphor unfolds, it is the military aspect which predominates as the Cherubins are seen as 'hors'd' – riding into battle, not upon ordinary horses but upon 'the sightless couriers of the air'. The metaphor of the storm, first introduced with the word 'blast' here reappears as the winds themselves are brought into battle against Macbeth. Then, in a further series of transformations, the 'sightlessness' of the air rebounds on human perceivers, whose eyes are blinded and made tearful by the 'horrid deed', and who in return 'drown the wind' with their tears. The passage begins and ends with ideas of sorrow and pity, and yet the overwhelming impression is of some violent cosmic retribution. The teeming creativity of Macbeth's language here leads him into areas of imaginative apprehension which go beyond the customary logical opposition of weakness and strength; for Macbeth at this moment weakness and strength are not opposites at all, but interconnected – a fact which is relevant to the ensuing debate between him and Lady Macbeth.

It is the imagery of the horse which stays with Macbeth as he turns to his own situation.

> – I have no spur
> To prick the sides of my intent, but only
> Vaulting ambition, which o'erleaps itself
> And falls on th' other –

(I, vii, ll. 25–8)

Again, the image is an ambiguous one. 'Vaulting ambition' may refer to a horse leaping a fence too eagerly and falling on the other side; or, more comically, it may be intended to conjure up the picture of a rider trying to vault into the saddle but ending up on the floor on the other side of the horse. Either way, by this stage, Macbeth's thoughts have led him to a state of deep doubt about his own ability. It is at this point that Lady Macbeth enters.

'All that may become a man'

The entrance of Lady Macbeth signals a shift in dramatic strategy.
The first twenty-eight lines of the scene show the problem being
handled by Macbeth in soliloquy; he is effectively arguing with himself, and this argument dramatizes the division in his own personality.
At the point when Lady Macbeth enters – to find out why her husband
is drawing attention to himself by his absence from the banquet – it
is difficult to tell what stage Macbeth has reached in his self-exami-
nation. He seems to be veering towards a decision against killing
Duncan, yet his soliloquy is interrupted, and he is never given time
actually to come out with a resolution. For once Lady Macbeth is on
stage, the rules change. We are no longer overhearing a soliloquy;
we are watching a scene in which two characters argue about something from two different points of view.

Macbeth immediately and positively declares his opposition to
the murder.

> We will proceed no further in this business:
> He hath honour'd me of late; and I have bought
> Golden opinions from all sorts of people,
> Which would be worn now in their newest gloss,
> Not cast aside so soon.
>
> (I, vii, ll. 31–5)

With a sudden burst of resolution, he confronts his wife with a firm
decision; they will not go on. Not only does he himself sound resolute,
he is giving orders, assuming the role of the lord and master handing
down his decision to his wife. An audience has seen enough of Lady
Macbeth to know how unlikely she is to acquiesce meekly to her
husband's decision. At this point, Macbeth and his wife are in direct
conflict one with the other. And it is Lady Macbeth who must provide the energy in this confrontation. It is up to her to find a way to
change Macbeth's direction back to what it was previously. In actor's
terms, she 'drives' the scene, which is constructed as a battle of wills,
with Lady Macbeth trying out a series of strategies in order to break
down the resistance of her husband. The audience, of course, already
expects her to take on this rôle; when she first received Macbeth's
letter telling her of the witches' prophecy, she expressed her fears of
his irresoluteness, and said

> Hie thee hither,
> That I may pour my spirits in thine ear,
> And chastise with the valour of my tongue
> All that impedes thee from the golden round,
> Which fate and metaphysical aid doth seem
> To have thee crown'd withal.
>
> (I, v, ll. 25–30)

She has already expressed her willingness to be Macbeth's Bad Angel, and this is precisely what she is called upon to do in this scene. Her first attempt to deal with her husband's sudden about-turn is by reacting with scorn:

> Was the hope drunk,
> Wherein you dress'd yourself? Hath it slept since?
> And wakes it now, to look so green and pale
> At what it did so freely? From this time
> Such I account thy love. Art thou afeard
> To be the same in thine own act and valour
> As thou art in desire?
>
> (I, vii, ll. 35–41)

She attacks him for what she calls his cowardice, and for his inability to translate desire into action. But this is a poor strategy. The direct attack on Macbeth merely allows him to entrench himself in his position. He even assumes a momentary dignity:

> Pr'ythee peace.
> I dare do all that may become a man;
> Who dares do more, is none.
>
> (I, vii, ll. 45–7)

On the face of it, Macbeth's answer is a good one. But it also provides precisely the handle that his wife needs. His insistence on what 'may become a man' offers her something on which she can work. She then turns Macbeth's argument back against him in such a way as to provide an alternative definition of what it is to be 'a man':

> When you durst do it, then you were a man;
> And to be more than what you were, you would
> Be so much more the man.
>
> (I, vii, ll. 49–51)

Macbeth's implied definition of 'a man' focuses on following the civilized codes of behaviour which forbid murder and regicide. Lady Macbeth's focuses on the ability to translate desire into action – to play the rôle of the man of action for which Macbeth was initially renowned. She is offering him a definition of manliness which is in keeping with his identity as a warrior. Her next persuasive strategy locks that idea into place:

> I have given suck, and know
> How tender 'tis to love the babe that milks me:
> I would, while it was smiling in my face,
> Have pluck'd my nipple from his boneless gums,

And dash'd the brains out, had I so sworn
As you have done to this.

(I, vii, ll. 54–9)

Having elevated a narrowed-down definition of manhood for her own rhetorical purposes, Lady Macbeth now commits imaginative sacrilege with its supposed opposite. Earlier in the play, she had said something similar in soliloquy:

> Come, you Spirits
> That tend on mortal thoughts, unsex me here,
> And fill me, from the crown to the toe, top-full
> Of direst cruelty! make thick my blood,
> Stop up th'access and passage to remorse;
> That no compunctious visiting of Nature
> Shake my fell purpose, nor keep peace between
> Th'effect and it! Come to my woman's breasts,
> And take my milk for gall, you murth'ring ministers.

(I, v, ll. 40–8)

That speech had a similar theme, and the rhetoric of the curse gave it a ritualistic grandeur which was impressive. But now, speaking to Macbeth, she is no longer dealing with abstract 'Spirits' and 'murth'ring ministers': she is envisaging killing her own suckling child. What makes her speech to Macbeth so powerful is the precision with which the image of tenderness is first envisioned and then destroyed. Lady Macbeth is not simply vaunting her own callousness and brutality here; rather she is conjuring up the tenderest moment she can imagine in order to bring home the urgency of her appeal to Macbeth. The image works better than she could have known. A minute or so earlier, Macbeth himself had personified Pity as being 'like a naked new-born babe'; with her unconscious echo of his image Lady Macbeth achieves a level of brutality which is specifically and consciously dependent upon the denial of her own capacity for pity. What she says to Macbeth is so shocking, not simply because it is an image of 'unnatural womanhood' but because what she is rejecting and shutting out of her life is so vividly and precisely imagined.

From this point on, Macbeth's resistance collapses. All he has to offer now is the desperate 'If we should fail?' – a question easily disposed of by Lady Macbeth's iron-willed determination. He is finally won over by the specific details of her plan to murder Duncan and to lay the blame on his sleeping guards.

> Bring forth men-children only!
> For thy undaunted mettle should compose
> Nothing but males. Will it not be receiv'd,
> When we have mark'd with blood those sleepy two

199

Of his own chamber, and us'd their very daggers,
That they have done't?

(I, vii, ll. 73–8)

Macbeth's compliment to his wife is a wry one. The tender 'babe' at the breast from Lady Macbeth's own earlier image is turned here into 'men-children' who represent not tenderness but hardness and ruthlessness – the ruthlessness he recognizes in her. With this speech, Macbeth accepts the terms his wife had set for gender differentiation – and then obliquely turns them back on her. She had told him what it was to be 'a man': now he attributes to her precisely those qualities which she had defined as manly. But this kind of paradox is all that Macbeth has left: from now on he is 'settled', and his course is decided.

There are a variety of ways, of course, in which actors can play this scene. It can be played to show an iron-willed woman bullying a weak man into action, or as a guileful temptress persuading a less intelligent man into evil. Macbeth can end the scene in reluctant compliance or in enthusiastic admiration of his wife's brilliance. Whichever way the scene is played, it is inevitably dominated by Lady Macbeth; whether by force or by persuasion she wins the argument and gets her way. And yet, if Lady Macbeth is consciously manipulating Macbeth, then there is a reciprocal, if unconscious manipulation of Lady Macbeth by Macbeth.

Compare the definiteness of Macbeth's rhetoric when he announces to his wife that 'We will proceed no further in this business' to the language he was using in soliloquy – language which was running away with itself, producing further confusions and further complexities. He suddenly sounds uncharacteristically confident of his own decision. It is the arrival of his wife that enables Macbeth to speak so certainly all of a sudden. While he is by himself he needs to hold both sides of the question in his head: once she arrives, he need not do so any longer. She can be relied upon to carry the burden of arguing for Duncan's death, while he can take refuge in his conscience: his task now is simply to oppose her.

Naturalism and allegory in Macbeth

The confrontation between the two carries some echoes of a temptation scene from an old morality play, in which a character or characters representing Vice or vices, would urge the hero to leave the paths of virtue and turn to wickedness; elsewhere in the play, corresponding figures of virtue would attempt to persuade him not to listen to the corrupting voices (see p. 73). In the morality play tradition, what was presented was often a form of *psychomachia*, in which all the different characters actually represented different warring elements of the protagonist's soul or personality, or past history. This is one reading of the play as a whole: to see Lady Macbeth and the witches merely as parts of Macbeth himself, as functions or aspects of his own personality. As a reading, it certainly has the advantage of moving away from the rather simple Aristotelian reading of Macbeth as 'a basically good man with the fatal flaw of ambition', and moving towards a model of personality which is much more fluid, paradoxical, conflict-ridden and complex. On the other hand, it fails to do justice to the psychological realism of the play, which is a powerful element in *Macbeth*. If the play was originally sketched in terms of morality-play allegory, it comes to life as psychological realism.

Urged in one direction, the undecided person will often react by swinging to the opposite extreme. Urged by Lady Macbeth to kill Duncan, Macbeth's initial reaction is to respond 'We will proceed no further in this matter'. In particular it is typical of Macbeth that he should react in this way, for there are specific advantages to him to play the part of the reluctant man. Throughout the play, one of Macbeth's main aims is to find ways of distancing himself from the evils which he commits, 'Let ... the eye wink at the hand', he says when first he contemplates the problem of the Prince of Cumberland – as if his hands could commit evil and his 'eye' (meaning his conscience, his soul, his intellect or his rational self) could somehow remain ignorant of the fact. After Duncan's death he says 'To know my deed, 'twere best not know myself' – again, looking for some way of dividing up the person who did the deed from the deed itself. When Banquo's ghost appears to him later in the play, he attempts to defend himself by insisting that it was not actually his hand that wielded the knife which killed Banquo: 'Thou canst not say I did it', he cries, taking desperate refuge in a kind of literalism. A similar kind of distancing is going on in this scene. Before the actual deed is done, Macbeth is putting some distance between himself and it. Unable to take for himself the decision to continue, he constructs a situation in which Lady Macbeth will *persuade* him to go on. He uses Lady Macbeth to objectify one side of the argument which is going on in his soul – to objectify his guilt and his acquiescence in the murder of Duncan.

In a way *Macbeth* has a double structure, for it contains both a naturalistic story and an allegorical one. On the naturalistic level a man meets some witches, hears their prophecies, doubts what to do, is urged by his wife to murder the king, and gives in to her persuasions. On the allegorical level, the contradictory desires and impulses of a central figure (Macbeth) are represented and embodied by a series of characters: his hopes for the future are spoken by the witches; his latent cruelty is expressed by Lady Macbeth, and so on.

Most readings of the play operate somewhere between these two models – including the one I have suggested above, in which Macbeth is effectively provoking his wife into a situation where she will argue him into doing what he partly wants to do anyway. In different parts of the play, however, there seem to be different kinds of balance between the naturalistic and the allegorical. When Macbeth and Lady Macbeth are on stage together, the naturalistic element seems to be at the forefront: they sound too much like a man and wife quarrelling to be thought of as allegorical representations of anything. The witches, however, are a different matter. They do not seem to belong to the world of naturalistic drama: they are, after all, supernatural.

If Lady Macbeth represents one kind of objectification of Macbeth's guilty desires, the witches represent another. Their function is to liberate his desires in the first place, by giving them a name. There is a deliberate ambiguity as to whether these witches should be seen as the direct cause of his ambitions, or whether they are in a sense the effect of them. The witches themselves have many of the qualities of a dream, in which the repressed unconscious desires find a mode of expression which exculpates the dreamer from the responsibility of those desires.

This is not to suggest that the witches should be thought of as *merely* projections of Macbeth's own imagination. Clearly they are not. Banquo sees and hears them; they exist in scenes by themselves, without Macbeth there to see them or to conjure them up. Thus they are clearly distinguished from the ghostly dagger of Act II, Scene i, which clearly *is* a projection of Macbeth's imagination: Macbeth himself is unsure whether it is there, and the audience do not see it at all. Similarly, they are distinguished from Banquo's ghost in Act III, who can be seen by Macbeth and the audience, but by nobody else. But in this play the boundaries between reality and unreality are continually being blurred, and the witches are part of that blurring process. Macbeth projects enough of his 'black and deep desires' onto their words to release in himself the possibility of action. Whether we wish to see the weird sisters as nightmare figures from a suppressed world of dream and fantasy, as demonic messengers of Macbeth's fate, or as mad old country-women talking a mixture of gibberish and guesswork, their effect on Macbeth is what matters. They put into words Macbeth's own hidden fantasies. And perhaps to say that is also to say that in a way they were a 'cause' of his evil. Perhaps the very act of verbalizing what was previously left unsaid may be enough to drag it from the world of dreams into the world of action.

'The frame of things disjoint'

From the moment that he first entertains the thought of kingship, Macbeth talks of a sense of losing control of his body: the very suggestion 'doth unfix my hair, And make my seated heart knock at my ribs'. As the notion lodges deeper in his mind, he himself begins to try to make the division of his identity. Contemplating the problem of Malcolm, Prince of Cumberland he says 'Let . . . The eye wink at the hand': 'the hand' is of course the hand which will do terrible deeds. More generally, perhaps, it is that part of him which endorses the 'black and deep desires'. 'The eye' is all within him that is opposed to these desires: the seeing part of him – his soul, his conscience, his intellect or his rational self. It is another example of Macbeth's attempts to distance the deed from 'himself'. Macbeth, in fact, is already at war with himself, and the imagery which expresses this is the image of a body divided against itself. Throughout the play we will find this image, and similar ones to it, being developed and elaborated, images concerned with the dissociation of these senses, and of bodies being split into various parts, compartmentalized or rebelling against each other. At this stage in the narrative, the idea of the 'eye winking at the hand' is, if anything, a comforting thought, as if the hand might be able to do the deed by itself, without ever troubling the 'rest' of Macbeth. As the play develops, however, the image turns into a nightmare one: when Macbeth emerges from killing Duncan the hand–eye opposition becomes a hallucination in which his own body turns destructively against itself: 'What hands are here?' he cries, 'Ha! They pluck out my eyes.'

It is not surprising, perhaps, that in a tragedy the hero should be associated with images of disintegration, division and fragmentation. The tendency of a tragedy to dramatize the collapse of personal identity makes imagery such as this totally appropriate. 'Let the frame of things disjoint' cries Macbeth as he resolves to persist in his evil course, but it is a cry which rebounds on Macbeth himself: the play charts the 'disjointing' of his own personality. When in the final moments of the play Macduff returns from the off-stage fight bearing Macbeth's head, it is the grotesque literal culmination of the metaphor of dismemberment which has been playing through the text.

But although Macbeth is the focus for many of these images of dismemberment and dissociation, they are picked up in the speech of other characters, too – as if to emphasize that the general frame of things is indeed disjointed. Macduff himself is implicated in this chain of imagery, for example: the man who eventually puts an end to Macbeth's reign is one whose own birth was a form of violent and bloody dismemberment, since he was 'from his mother's womb

Untimely ripp'd'. This is often glossed as 'born by Caesarian section', and that in all likelihood is the main purport of the phrase, but the clinical modern phrase says so much less than the Shakespearean one. When Macduff speaks, what stays in the mind is the violence of his phrase.

Lady Macbeth, as we have already seen, has used the idea of cutting away parts of herself in one of her most powerful speeches, where her desire to be pitiless and impervious to remorse is expressed in an image in which she distances herself from her own sexual identity, summoning the dark spirits of her imagination to 'unsex me here . . . and take my milk for gall'. This speech is ritualistic–an invocation and a self-directed curse of fearsome intensity. In Act II, Scene iii the Porter's bawdy speech about the effect of drink is as different from this in tone as can be imagined: if Lady Macbeth is a dark priestess, the Porter is a stand-up comic. However his material also concerns bodily dissociation, and like Lady Macbeth he talks about sexuality. He talks about those times when a man is unable to control his own body.

> *Porter* . . . drink, Sir, is a great provoker of three things.
> *Macduff* What three things does drink especially provoke?
> *Porter* Marry, Sir, nose-painting, sleep, and urine. Lechery,
> Sir, it provokes and unprovokes: it provokes the desire, but it
> takes away the performance. Therefore much drink may be said
> to be an equivocator with lechery: it makes him and mars him;
> it sets him on, and it takes him off; it persuades him, and
> disheartens him; makes him stand to, and not stand to: in
> conclusion, equivocates him in a sleep, and, giving him the lie,
> leaves him.
>
> (II, iii, ll. 25–35)

The most frequent images of dissociation, however, concern the senses, and particularly the sense of sight. What breaks down in the play is not just the relationship between mind and body, or between various parts of the body, but the whole system of visual signification and meaning. What the eye appears to register as 'there', sometimes turns out not to exist at all. The hallucinatory dagger which Macbeth sees just before he murders Duncan is a good example of this:

> Is this a dagger, which I see before me,
> The handle toward my hand? Come, let me clutch thee:–
> I have thee not, and yet I see thee still.
> Art thou not, fatal vision, sensible
> To feeling as to sight? or art thou but
> A dagger of the mind, a false creation,
> Proceeding from the heat-oppressed brain? . . .

Mine eyes are made the fools o'th'other senses,
Or else worth all the rest.

(II, i, ll. 33–9, 44–5)

Once again, Macbeth's initial metaphor – of the hand and the eye being dissociated – is given a startling literalness. He can see the dagger, but not touch it. A similar effect is achieved by the appearance at the feast of Banquo's ghost. Once more Macbeth is startled by an apparition which his other senses and his common sense tell him cannot be real. It is Lady Macbeth who makes the connection between this vision and Macbeth's previous one:

This is the very painting of your fear:
This is the air-drawn dagger, which, you said,
Led you to Duncan... Shame itself!
Why do you make such faces? When all's done,
You look but on a stool.

(III, iv, ll. 60–2, 65–7)

At this point in the play Lady Macbeth is still level-headed and commonsensical. She is playing the same rôle here as she does straight after the murder of Duncan, when Macbeth starts back in horror from the hands that would 'pluck out [his] eyes'. As he does so, he contemplates his (literally) bloodstained hands, and asks 'Will all great Neptune's ocean wash this blood Clean from my hand?'. Lady Macbeth answers him bluntly: 'A little water clears us of this deed.' Later on in the play, however, his nightmare becomes hers; in her madness, she too begins to see things that are not there:

Yet here's a spot... What, will these hands ne'er be clean?
... Here's the smell of blood still: all the perfumes of
Arabia will not sweeten this little hand

(V, i, l. 30 ff.)

Macbeth's literal horror at the blood on his hands has become Lady Macbeth's hallucination; once again a powerful effect is achieved by a shifting between the literal and the metaphorical levels of meaning.

As Lady Macbeth and Macbeth slip further into evil, they find it harder and harder to trust the evidence of their own senses. Nor is this cognitive confusion confined to these two characters. The entire world of *Macbeth* is a world of shifting realities, in which all the characters have to struggle – often unsuccessfully – to make sense of their surroundings.

Banquo too, for example, is unable to 'interpret' the witches, to fit them into his rational scheme of things:

What are these,
So wither'd and so wild in their attire,

205

That look not like th'inhabitants o'th'earth
And yet are on't? Live you? or are you aught
That man may question? You seem to understand me,
By each at once her choppy finger laying
Upon her skinny lips: you should be women,
And yet your beards forbid me to interpret
That you are so.

(I, iii, ll. 39–47)

The effect is to make him, also, doubt his senses and his sanity.

Were such things here, as we do speak about,
Or have we eaten on the insane root,
That takes the reason prisoner?

(I, iii, 83–5)

Banquo, it transpires, is subject to errors in his interpretations, in any case. It is he who misreads the presence of the 'temple-haunting martlet' at Dunsinane as being proof of the castle's wholesomeness (I, vi, ll. 4–11); Duncan agrees, but he, too, is fooled by outward appearances: having learnt, by the example of the former Thane of Cawdor, that 'there's no art To find the mind's construction in the face' he proceeds to build once more an absolute and misplaced trust upon the new Thane, Macbeth.

Thus in Macbeth the usual conventions by which men and women derive meaning from the visual signals of their environment are not to be trusted. The eye and mind conspire to produce hallucinations, creatures appear that defy interpretation, and appearances deceive.

Linguistic codes are also thrown into confusion. Throughout the play characters repeatedly come up against the limits of language. Sometimes it happens melodramatically, as when the witches proclaim that they do 'A deed without a name', and Macduff cries out, on his discovery of Duncan's murder:

O horror! horror! horror!
Tongue nor heart cannot conceive, nor name thee!
... Do not bid me speak:
See, and then speak yourselves –

(II, iii, ll. 62–3, 71–2)

Sometimes it happens poignantly, as when Macduff is told of another slaughter, that of his wife and children and is shocked into a silence that Malcolm endeavours to break:

Malcolm What, man! ne'er pull your hat upon your brows:
Give sorrow words; the grief, that does not speak,
Whispers the o'er-fraught heart, and bids it break.

(IV, iii, ll. 208–210)

From the witches' first chorus of 'Fair is foul and foul is fair', we are thrust into a world in which the normal rules of language and meaning can be suspended at any time. 'This supernatural soliciting Cannot be ill, cannot be good' says Macbeth of the witches' prophecy, and 'nothing is but what is not'. Words are beginning to fail him, even at this point, and his failure of vocabulary here foreshadows the linguistic crisis which will overtake him in his later soliloquy.

Looked at in one way, in fact, the entire action of the play is founded upon the slipperiness of language. It is the words of the witches' prophecy, that 'Macbeth... shall be King hereafter', which first set in motion the bloody train of events. At first Macbeth attempts to understand the full meaning of the words of these 'imperfect speakers', but later he simply chooses the interpretation which suits him best. But the task of interpreting the witches' words is a deadly one, and in the end it is his misinterpretation of what they say that heralds his downfall. 'None of woman born Shall harm Macbeth... Macbeth shall never vanquish'd be, until Great Birnam wood to high Dunsinane hill Shall come against him'. Macbeth, of course, interprets this as meaning that no one shall harm him, and that he shall never be vanquished. But the slippery language of the prophecies has meanings which evade him, and he recognizes their true import too late. He puts his trust in one interpretation of their words, and is killed by another. By then, in any case, the disintegration of meaning which had begun on the foul and fair day when he had first met the weird sisters, has reached a climax:

Tomorrow, and tomorrow, and tomorrow,
Creeps in this petty pace from day to day,
To the last syllable of recorded time;
And all our yesterdays have lighted fools
The way to dusty death. Out, out, brief candle!
Life's but a walking shadow; a poor player,
That struts and frets his hour upon the stage,
And then is heard no more: it is a tale
Told by an idiot, full of sound and fury,
Signifying nothing.

(V, v, ll. 19–28)

The speech is cued by the news of Lady Macbeth's death. Her world had already fallen apart; reduced to the nightmares of her sleep-walking, her madness enacts the disintegration and the meaninglessness which Macbeth goes on to describe. For Macbeth, unlike his wife, does not lose his sanity; his mind never becomes 'diseas'd' in that way. The play presents us with two different reactions to the emotional stress which has accompanied the guilt of their evil. Lady Macbeth eventually breaks under the pressure, goes mad and dies.

Macbeth remains sane, and it is the rational tone of this final soliloquy which makes it so terrifyingly powerful. For Macbeth there are no meanings left. He had been trying to make narrative sense out of the prophecies of the witches, but had failed. Not only their prophecies, but life itself is now seen by him in terms of bleakest reductionism: 'a tale Told by an idiot ... Signifying nothing'. And it is at this point that a messenger bursts in with the news which will enable the audience to understand, finally, the full meaning of the witches' prophecy – that from the castle the camouflaged men of Malcolm's army make it look as though the wood itself is moving towards Dunsinane. Even as Macbeth reflects on the meaninglessness of life, the meanings that he had constructed out of the words of the prophecies begin to collapse about him.

'Men-children only'

In *Macbeth*, then, meanings shift and words are redefined. We have already seen how Lady Macbeth used a narrowed-down definition of 'manliness' to persuade Macbeth into murder. Macbeth later uses the same technique in order to recruit the murderers of Banquo. 'We are men, my Liege', says the first Murderer, meaning that they are no better and no worse than most. Macbeth, like his wife before him, fastens onto the word.

> Ay, in the catalogue ye go for men;
> As hounds, and greyhounds, mongrels, spaniels, curs,
> Shoughs, water-rugs, and demi-wolves, are clept
> All by the name of dogs ...
> Now, if you have a station in the file,
> Not i'th' worst rank of manhood, say't.
>
> (III, i, ll. 91–4, 101–02)

Like his wife, Macbeth spurns the general and broad sense of 'manliness' by implying that there is a special and superior sense of the word, that there is such a thing as a 'real man', and the way to prove oneself to be a real man is to commit murder. This concept of 'manliness' – which amounts to no more than courage and physical prowess in the face of danger – is used once more as a weapon in argument in a later scene. When Banquo's ghost appears at the feast, the terrified Macbeth is again addressed contemptuously by his wife; 'Are you a man?', she asks; 'What! quite unmann'd in folly?' Macbeth's reply both accepts and elaborates upon this limited notion of what it is to be a man:

> What man dare, I dare:
> Approach thou like the rugged Russian bear,

The arm'd rhinoceros, or th'Hyrcan tiger;
Take any shape but that, and my firm nerves
Shall never tremble: or, be alive again,
And dare me to the desert with thy sword;
If trembling I inhabit then, protest me
The baby of a girl. Hence, horrible shadow!
Unreal mock'ry, hence! – (*Ghost disappears*)
                    Why, so; – being gone,
I am a man again.

(III, iv, ll. 98–107)

This kind of manliness has never proved a problem for Macbeth; the 'brave Macbeth' who unseamed Macdonwald from the nave to the chops was courageous and strong. But as he now knows to his cost, this kind of manliness is no longer enough.

In the world of *Macbeth* it seems to be taken for granted that manliness means, essentially, the ability to kill. Womanliness, which Lady Macbeth defines in theory even as she rejects it in her heart, is seen to be the nurturing and life-giving principle. Western culture has long assigned these values to the sexes: boy children are given toy guns to play with; girls are given dolls to nurse. But although *Macbeth* to that extent merely reflects and repeats the cultural norms of its society, it takes such a polarization to an extreme. The male values which Macbeth admires are a parody of themselves, and are seen to be so. The extent to which this is the case is pointed up by the single moment in the play when another possible definition of manhood is offered. This happens when Macduff finally responds to the news of the death of his wife and children.

Macduff   All my pretty ones?
  Did you say all? – O Hell-kite! – All?
  What, all my pretty chickens, and their dam,
  At one fell swoop?
Malcolm Dispute it like a man.
Macduff   I shall do so;
  But I must also feel it as a man.

(IV, iii, ll. 216–21)

Malcolm's 'Dispute it like a man' appeals to a concept of tough-minded fortitude not unlike Macbeth's own; it is Macduff's reply which suggests, in one of the few instances of the play, that there might be more to being a man than martial valour. The moment does not last long; within a few lines Macduff's grief has turned to anger and a vow to kill Macbeth, and Malcolm's approving response is 'The tune goes manly'.

There is a particular force to Macduff's bitterness. When he says of Macbeth 'He hath no children', he taps into another line of thought which recurs throughout the play, and which is strangely parallel to notions of 'manliness'. This concerns children. We have seen how in the early parts of the play both Macbeth and Lady Macbeth use images of children and babies in their speeches, Macbeth talks about Pity being 'like a naked new-born babe Striding the blast'; Lady Macbeth speaks of how she would be prepared to murder the child at her breast rather than show the weakness she sees in her husband. In these early speeches there are ironies which do not fully reveal themselves until much later in the play. Lady Macbeth metaphorically rejects that part of her nature which could conceive and nurture children; but her childlessness is a literal element in the play as well as a metaphorical one. The critic L.C. Knights once wrote a famous essay attacking the criticism of A.C. Bradley, ironically entitled 'How many children had Lady Macbeth?' Knights' point was that to even ask this kind of question is wrong-headed and betrays an over-literal approach to the play. Knights believed in reading Shakespeare's plays as if they were extended dramatic poems – an approach which has its problems in any case: but even according to Knights' own criteria the question of Lady Macbeth's children is not such an irrelevant one.

'I have given suck', she tells us, 'and know How tender 'tis to love the babe that milks me.' Macbeth, we are now told by Macduff, 'has no children'. The apparent inconsistency is not in itself either strange or inexplicable: what is suggested is a child or children who died in infancy – a common enough event in Shakespeare's time. But there is a special significance to the fact that Macbeth and his wife are left childless. On a personal level the detail serves to increase the sense of their isolation and lovelessness. And politically, it is one of the main factors in the play. Macbeth was told by the witches that although he will be king, it is Banquo whose 'children shall be Kings'; it is this, above all, that leads him to arrange the attack on Banquo and Fleance. It is not only that he fears Banquo's enmity; he is obsessed by the fact that Banquo will found a dynasty whereas he himself will not:

> They [the witches] hail'd him father to a line of kings:
> Upon my head they plac'd a fruitless crown,
> And put a barren sceptre in my gripe,
> Thence to be wrench'd with an unlineal hand,
> No son of mine succeeding. If't be so,
> For Banquo's issue have I fil'd my mind;
> For them the gracious Duncan have I murther'd;
> Put rancours in the vessel of my peace,
> Only for them; and mine eternal jewel

Given to the common Enemy of man,
To make them kings, the seed of Banquo kings!

(III, i, ll. 59–69)

When it is borne in mind that this seed of Banquo's will eventually give rise to the House of Stuart, and finally to the very King James I of England who is sitting watching the play, this insistence on the bloodline of Banquo as opposed to the barrenness of Macbeth takes on a further political dimension (see p. 105).

Without heirs himself, Macbeth attempts to wipe out the bloodline of all who might rival him. The brutal murder of Lady Macduff and her son takes place onstage, and its importance as an image is emphasized when it is relived in Macduff's mind as Rosse brings the news to him. The last act Macbeth will commit before his own death is to kill another son, young Siward. Even those children who escape Macbeth's onslaught, such as Fleance, Donalbain and Malcolm, are forced out of the country. Malcolm and Donalbain are accused of their father's murder; the same happens to Fleance after his escape. Lenox makes it clear what would happen to any of these three if they were to return:

I do think
That, had he Duncan's sons under his key
(As, and't please Heaven, he shall not), they should find
What 'twere to kill a father; so should Fleance.

(III, vi, ll. 17–20)

The childless Macbeth becomes the murderer of children. And in the end it is children who rise up against him. There is Malcolm, of course, Duncan's son who leads the army to destroy Macbeth. But the figure of the 'babe' recurs in another form, too: when Macbeth goes back to the witches to seek reassurance he is told that no man of woman born will ever have power to kill him, and that he is safe 'until Great Birnam wood to high Dunsinane hill Shall come against him'. Both these prophecies are spoken by apparitions: the first is of 'a bloody child', the second of 'a child crowned, with a tree in his hand'. The words, which lead Macbeth into false confidence come from the mouths of babes, and the bloody child who speaks the first prophecy is itself an image of Macduff, who was untimely ripped from his mother's womb. It is precisely because of the nature of his birth that Macduff is the exception to the prophecy; he is the man not 'of woman born' who will kill Macbeth. The 'naked new-born babe' which Macbeth originally envisaged in his soliloquy comes to life in the figure of the avenging Macduff, and returns to kill Macbeth.

I started by saying that because Macbeth is both hero and villain of the story, the play generates a double perspective on him. The metaphor is an apt one for a play so concerned with images of sight and interpretation. But a corresponding duality of perspective which exists throughout the play relates not just to Macbeth but to a whole series of speeches and actions within the play. It concerns the relationship between metaphor and literalness. On the one hand, deeds and events which belong to the world of literal action take on metaphorical meanings: thus the blood on Macbeth's hands after Duncan's death becomes a dominant metaphor for the guilt of both husband and wife; Lady Macbeth's attempt to rid the image of its associations ('A little water clears us of this deed') is short-lived and before the end of the play she is obsessively washing away the blood she thinks she sees on her hands. In her mind the metaphor has become real once more. And it is in this direction that the relationship usually works. Repeatedly in *Macbeth* we see that things which are introduced seemingly as metaphors turn out to have a literal truth as well. The metaphorical 'naked new-born' babe of Macbeth's soliloquy turns into the apparition of Macduff, and then finally into Macduff himself. The impossibility of Birnam Wood coming to Dunsinane, which Macbeth reads metaphorically as meaning 'never', turns into the literal reality of Malcolm's camouflaged soldiers advancing on the castle; the 'dagger of the mind' which Macbeth sees before him becomes the literal dagger which kills Duncan; the metaphors of bodily dismemberment culminate in the literalness of the severed head of Macbeth paraded about the stage.

Postscript: What lies beyond tragedy?

What do you do as a playwright if you have just written *Hamlet*, *Othello*, *Macbeth* and *King Lear*? Where is there for you to go next? These are problems which faced William Shakespeare in the middle of the first decade of the seventeenth century. Shakespeare's career as a playwright is sometimes regarded as having reached its peak with the 'great tragedies' which have just been discussed. However, it did not end there; and if he never again produced a play with the intense tragic power of a *King Lear* or a *Macbeth*, neither did he simply abandon the great creative vein which he had mined in these tragedies. Shakespeare was both a tireless innovator and also a great theatrical re-inventer, a re-teller of both other people's stories and of his own, and in many of the plays which he wrote towards the end of his career it seems as if he is taking for granted the fact that he has already written his great tragedies, and is addressing himself to the question 'What is there beyond tragedy?'

In *Antony and Cleopatra* (written in 1607, soon after *Macbeth*) Shakespeare begins to broaden his canvas. In its central preoccupation with a relationship rather than an individual, *Antony and Cleopatra* both goes beyond and, paradoxically, simultaneously looks back to earlier plays: it is as if he rewrote both *Romeo and Juliet* and *Julius Caesar* in the light of what he had learned from his great tragic period. Cleopatra is both treacherous and noble. Antony is both hero and buffoon: his death scene is relentlessly, almost farcically, anti-tragic – yet also deeply moving. The backdrop for the play is not a single kingdom, or an occupied island, but the entire Roman Empire – as far as the protagonists are concerned, the whole of known civilization. The story of *Antony and Cleopatra* is also the story of Rome versus Egypt. Antony's tragedy is that he is torn between these two worlds; Cleopatra's is that her world is inevitably going to be destroyed by the world of Rome.

The world of Rome is also a central 'character' in *Coriolanus* (*c.* 1608): seemingly a return to individual-centred tragedy, it turns out to be something very different. Marcus Caius Coriolanus thinks of himself as an autonomous individual – the man of action, standing alone with his integrity against the mealy-mouthed and often corrupt voices of Roman politics. What he cannot see is the extent to which he identifies with and is identified with the very group he despises. There are many varieties of 'Roman-ness' in the play, and Coriolanus's ideal of Rome (which is selective, false and 'noble' in a rigidly militaristic and authoritarian way) is so bound up with his

213

own sense of himself that he is unable to tolerate the gap between his ideals and the chaotic reality of a Rome in which (as in Shakespeare's England) a bad harvest means rioting on the streets as the poor demand food. Shakespeare's vision in *Coriolanus* focuses on an individual, but only to affirm that the tragedy is that of a society.

In his last plays, Shakespeare's rewriting of tragedy comes full circle. *The Winter's Tale* (*c.* 1610) is the most graphic example of this. A play whose first two-and-a-half acts seem like a bleak re-run of *Othello*, with a jealous ruler killing his innocent wife whom he suspects of adultery, turns into a joyful fairy-tale of reconciliation and rebirth: statues come to life, impossible reunions take place between child and parent, husband and wife, friend and friend. The shift in gear from pessimism to optimism is powerful and moving precisely *because* it is improbable: here as elsewhere in the late plays, tragedy is implicit in the psychological motivations which drive people to do what they do. The threat of destruction is always present, and usually very real: the world of these plays always contains the possibility of a collapse into a chaos 'full of sound and fury, Signifying nothing'. And yet the essential spirit is one of regeneration. If the great tragedies show us the ways in which men and women move inexorably to their own and other people's destruction, the late plays affirm that – just possibly – the tragic option is not the only one that need be taken.

Part Four
Reference Section

Short biographies

ALLEYN, EDWARD (1566–1626) Edward Alleyn was one of the two greatest actors of his time, rivalled only by Richard Burbage. Alleyn was the leader of The Lord Admiral's Men, and the creator of many of the great non-Shakespearean rôles of the Elizabethan theatre, such as Tamburlaine and Doctor Faustus. He was a theatre-owner and theatre-manager as well as being an actor; in partnership with his father-in-law Philip Henslowe he owned shares in various London theatres, such as the Rose and the Fortune. Renowned in particular for his skill as a tragic actor, Alleyn's greatest acting triumphs were in the 1590s. His career did not long survive Elizabeth's reign and he appears to have retired in 1604.

ARMIN, ROBERT (1581–1615) Robert Armin claimed to have served his apprenticeship with Queen Elizabeth's favourite clown, Richard Tarlton. He had also served another kind of apprenticeship in his youth, as a goldsmith, and this is reflected in the name of one of the parts written for him by Shakespeare – Touchstone in *As You Like It*. He left Lord Chandos's Men to join The Lord Chamberlain's Men as a sharer in 1599 or 1600. His task was to replace the departed Will Kempe, and his own memoirs refer to him taking over from Kempe in the rôle of Dogberry in *Much Ado About Nothing*. Armin's manner was very different from Kempe's, however, and may have influenced the way in which Shakespeare began to use the clown-figure after 1600. Armin's downbeat, introspective and even melancholy comic style and his fine singing voice were used by Shakespeare as he began to develop the figure of the philosopher-Fool. Feste in *Twelfth Night* and the Fool in *King Lear* are prime examples of this. Armin himself wrote plays, and other works, including a typology of the clown called *Foole upon Foole or Six Sortes of Sottes*.

BURBAGE, RICHARD (*c.* 1567–1619) The son of James Burbage, who originally opened the Theatre in 1576, Richard learnt his trade as an actor with The Admiral's Men, who played mainly at a rival theatre, the Rose. When The Lord Chamberlain's Men were formed in 1594 Burbage joined them as an actor and a shareholder, and on the death of his father he and his brother Cuthbert inherited a major share-holding in the company, owning half of it between them. The Burbages' masterminding of the daring theft of the Theatre and the founding of the Globe suggests something about their personal qualities. By all accounts Richard was also a vigorous and dynamic

216

actor, whose presence must have been a vital influence on the way in which Shakespeare went about writing his plays. At least three of the great tragic parts were written for Burbage: we know that he first played the rôles of Hamlet, Othello and Lear, as well as Richard III. It is extremely likely that he also played Macbeth. Burbage was a skilled painter as well as one of the most celebrated actors of his age.

CHAPMAN, GEORGE (*c.* 1559–1634) George Chapman started his career as a playwright with The Lord Admiral's Men in the mid-1590s, although his most successful plays came later: *Bussy D'Ambois* (1604) and *The Revenge of Bussy D'Ambois* (1613) are tragedies with a strong political flavour. In 1605 he collaborated with Ben Jonson and John Marston on the satirical *Eastward Ho!*, which earned him and Jonson a spell in prison, and he has been suggested as the original of the rival poet figure in Shakespeare's sonnets.

CONDELL, HENRY (? –1627) An actor with The Lord Chamberlain's Men from the company's early days, Henry Condell also became a sharer in the company some time after 1603, and thereafter acquired portions of both the Globe and Blackfriars Theatre, as well as valuable properties outside the theatre. Condell is known to have played the part of the Cardinal in John Webster's *The Duchess of Malfi*, and it is conjectured that he also played Horatio in *Hamlet*, Cassio in *Othello*, Edgar in *King Lear*, and Malcolm in *Macbeth*. With John Heminges, to whom he may have originally been apprenticed, Condell edited and published the First Folio edition of Shakespeare's plays. Like Heminges, he is mentioned by Shakespeare in his will and appears to have been a close friend.

ELIZABETH I (b. 1533. Queen of England 1558–1603) Elizabeth, daughter of Henry VIII and Ann Boleyn, maintained throughout her reign a delicate balance between the various forces which acted upon late sixteenth-century England. Her claim to the throne was established by an Act of the English Parliament, but she was seen as a usurper and a heretic by most of Catholic Europe. During her reign there were numerous attempts to remove her as head of state, by means both of conspiracies and attempted foreign invasion; however, with the help of a well-disciplined navy and an efficient secret service, together with her own shrewd political sense, Elizabeth survived them all and forged the beginnings of a powerful nation state, as well as a considerable personal mythology. This was maintained and propagated by the literary establishment among others, and the Elizabethan court masque was a particularly important form of dramatic propaganda. Elizabeth also took an interest in other forms of drama, and played her part in defending the London theatre against some of its more vehement Puritan opponents: she was the patron of 'Queen Elizabeth's Men', a prestigious acting company formed in 1583 which played at court, in the provinces and in London. Elizabeth, however, was never a generous patron, artistically or politically: her reputation for financial penny-pinching was well-founded, and a necessary part of her attempt to keep the economy under control. Even this, however, did not prevent the national debt from standing at £400,000 at the time of her death. Her last years (the period in which Shakespeare began to emerge as the leading playwright of the age) were characterized by crippling inflation, localized famine, bureaucratic inertia and governmental corruption. Elizabeth's death in 1603 was received with ill-concealed relief by many of her subjects.

ESSEX, ROBERT DEVEREUX, SECOND EARL (1566–1601) The Earl of Essex was one of the elderly Queen Elizabeth's favourites, but their relationship was always a stormy one. Essex was a charismatic figure in Elizabethan political life, and one to whom Shakespeare paid homage in *Henry V*, but he was also ambitious, egocentric and unstable. Several times he found himself in trouble with Elizabeth as a result of his defiance of her, and when he finally mismanaged an important military campaign in Ireland he was censured and deprived of office. With bankruptcy staring him in the face, he was foolish enough to attempt to restore his own political power by force: raising a small army, he marched on the court in February 1601. The support he had expected from the City of London failed to materialize and Essex was arrested and executed. (For the involvement of The Lord Chamberlain's men in Essex's rebellion, see pp. 98 and 101, and under 'Southampton', below.)

FLETCHER, JOHN (1579–1625) Fletcher probably succeeded Shakespeare as The King's Men's leading dramatist after 1613. A prolific writer, he seems to have worked best in partnership with another playwright. In collaboration with Francis Beaumont he produced plays such as *The Knight of the Burning Pestle* (1607) and *Philaster* (*c.* 1610): He wrote several plays with Philip Massinger and he is thought to have collaborated with Shakespeare in the writing of *The Two Noble Kinsmen* (1613) and *Henry VIII* (1613).

GREENE, ROBERT (1558–92) A dramatist, romance-writer and satirist, Greene seems to have lived mainly from money earned by writing – a rare thing in Elizabethan times. He was, perhaps because he needed to be, immensely prolific. Greene is credited with the first recorded reference to Shakespeare as actor and dramatist, in his satirical work

218

A Groatsworth of Wit (1592). It is not a complimentary one: he describes Shakespeare as 'an upstart crow, beautified with our feathers, that with his *tiger's heart wrapped in a player's hide* supposes he is as well able to bombast out a blank verse as the best of you; and ... is in his own conceit the only Shake-scene in the country'. Greene's implied charge of plagiarism has an ironic aftermath: nearly twenty years later his prose romance *Pandosto, or The Triumph of Time* (which Greene had published in 1588) supplied Shakespeare with the main plot of *The Winter's Tale* (1610–11).

HATHAWAY, ANNE (*c.* 1556–1623) Shakespeare's wife has nearly always been referred to by her maiden name. She was the daughter of a well-off farmer from the village of Shottery, a mile or so from Stratford itself, and the family farmhouse where she grew up has become almost a national monument, known as Anne Hathaway's Cottage. Eight years older than her husband, she married him in November 1582; their first child, Susanna, was born in May 1583. Before Shakespeare reached the age of twenty-one he was also the father of two more of Anne's children, the twins Judith and Hamnet; the latter died in 1596. We know very little about Anne Hathaway: this, of course, has not prevented much speculation about her and the details of her married life both with and apart from William Shakespeare.

HEMINGES, JOHN (*c.* 1566–1630) John Heminges acted with Edward Alleyn early in his career, and joined The Lord Chamberlain's Men soon after its formation in 1594. A sharer in both the Globe and later Blackfriars Theatre, he was also a close friend of Shakespeare and was mentioned in his will. It has been suggested that he played Polonius in *Hamlet*, Brabantio in *Othello*, Kent in *King Lear*, and Ross in *Macbeth*, as well as the title rôle in *Julius Caesar*. His fame rests, however, on his involvement in the editing and publishing of the First Folio of Shakespeare's plays in 1623. One of the most respectable members of The Lord Chamberlain's Men, he gave up acting to become the company's financial organizer in 1611; for many years of his life he was a churchwarden in his home parish of St Mary's and he was granted a coat of arms in 1629, just before his death.

HUNSDON, GEORGE CAREY, SECOND LORD (1547–1603) George Carey, Second Lord Hunsdon, was the son of the Lord Chamberlain under whose auspices Shakespeare's theatre company, The Lord Chamberlain's Men, had originally been formed. Upon his father's death in 1596 the new Lord Hunsdon took over as the patron of the company (which became known, for a short period, as Lord Hunsdon's Men); a year later he succeeded to the Lord Chamberlain's office itself. It seems that Hunsdon took no great interest in the acting company which bore his name; indeed, he is known to have supported a petition to ban the opening of a public playhouse in Blackfriars.

JAMES I (b. 1566. King of England 1603–25) When James, the son of Mary Queen of Scots and a direct descendant of Henry VII, was named Elizabeth's successor he was generally welcomed; since 1567 he had been King James VI of Scotland, and one of his own dearest political projects was the attempted constitutional union of the kingdoms of England and Scotland. He was unable to achieve this, and as his reign proceeded the early enthusiasm with which he had been greeted began to wane. In his dealings with his own court he earned a reputation for excessive liberality and favouritism, and his court soon came to be seen as a place of corruption. In his dealings with Parliament James was often tactless, and the years of his reign saw growing tensions between king and Parliament. Not a stupid man, he seems to have suffered largely from a poor sense of timing and a lack of self-restraint: France's King Henri IV dubbed him 'the wisest fool in Christendom'. He suffered from paranoia about his personal safety, which may have had some bearing on the obsessive interest he began to take in witchcraft shortly before his accession to the English throne. On the whole, however, James's reign saw a consolidation of the national stability which Elizabeth had struggled so hard to establish. Under his rule England enjoyed years of comparative peace, forged closer links with other European countries and began to extend her influence into the colonies of the New World. James's influence on the literary and artistic culture of early seventeenth-century England is now beginning to be recognized. Well-read and cultured, he took an active interest in the arts: he was himself a poet, polemicist and translator, but his most important rôle was as a patron and enabler of other men's genius. Not only did he commission the translation of the Bible which bears his name, he also took under his personal patronage the acting company of which Shakespeare was a key member: in 1603 The Lord Chamberlain's Men became The King's Men, and James himself became the most important single member of Shakespeare's audience.

JONSON, BEN (*c.* 1573–1637) Dramatist, actor, poet and essayist, Jonson studied at Westminster School, worked briefly as a bricklayer, spent time soldiering in Flanders, and began his association with the theatre in the mid-1590s. Shakespeare is known to have acted in some of Jonson's earlier plays, and while the two men were rivals on the London stage, Jonson clearly had a high respect for Shakespeare's art. Jonson's influence on later seventeenth-century drama was considerable – much greater than Shakespeare's own – and the plays of his which have lasted best are comedies such as *Volpone* (1606), *The Alchemist* (1610) and *Bartholemew Fair* (1614). In his chequered career, Jonson was imprisoned both for manslaughter and for over-transparent political satire in his plays; he was also later granted a pension by James I for his part in the creation of a series of brilliant court masques. He subsequently quarrelled with the architect, Inigo Jones, his partner in these enterprises, and his career declined. Under Charles I he fell from favour completely. Jonson's inclusion of plays in the lavishly produced collected edition of his works marked an important step in the gradual acceptance of dramatic literature as works of art.

KEMPE, WILLIAM (*c.* 1550–*c.* 1607) Will Kempe had left The Lord Chamberlain's Men by the time Shakespeare began writing his great tragedies, but his influence on the development of the company was great. His speciality was broad comedy – he played Dogberry in *Much Ado About Nothing* – and he was a great exponent of the jigs and dances which traditionally followed the plays. He was the most popular of the clowns of the 1590s, and a sharer in The Lord Chamberlain's men and one of the original Globe syndicate. When the company actually moved to the Globe in 1599, however, Kempe sold up his interest and left. The following year, for a bet, he undertook his famous nine-days' marathon dance to Norwich. He seems to have had a talent for bawdy and impromptu humour, and an impressive rapport with an audience. However, he may also have had a tendency to upstage his colleagues, and to have preferred a cheap laugh to a faithful rendition of the text. Tradition holds that when Hamlet cautions the Player to 'let those that play your clowns speak no more than is set down for them' he is voicing Shakespeare's own irritation at the departed Kempe's tendency to improvise more than was good for him.

KYD, THOMAS (1558–94) Kyd's most famous play, *The Spanish Tragedy* (*c.* 1585) was a great success and performed by most of the theatrical conpanies of Elizabethan London. It adapts to the needs of the English stage many of the tricks and techniques of the Roman dramatist, Seneca, and was influential in establishing the vogue for revenge plays which were popular in late sixteenth- and early seventeenth-century English drama. It has been suggested that Kyd was also the author of the conjectural 'Ur-*Hamlet*', the predecessor and source of Shakespeare's own *Hamlet*. Kyd was an associate of Christopher Marlowe, with whom he shared lodgings towards the end of his life; he was arrested in 1593, and tortured in order to obtain information concerning Marlowe's involvement in heretical and treasonable activities. Kyd died in poverty the following year.

MARLOWE, CHRISTOPHER (1564–93) Marlowe was Shakespeare's almost exact contemporary, and until his death in suspicious circumstances in a Deptford tavern, he was at least Shakespeare's dramatic equal. Like Shakespeare he came from a background of respectable craftsmanship in a small provincial town (his father was a shoemaker in Canterbury), but unlike him Marlowe was university-educated (at Corpus Christi College, Cambridge), and by 1587 was enjoying the acquaintance of some of the most powerful people in the land. He seems at one stage of his life to have been associated with Walsingham's secret police, and in all probability spent a period of time abroad, spying on behalf of the English government. He also, however, had the reputation of being a heretic and even an atheist: certainly, in his plays he explores some of the darker sides of Renaissance man. *Doctor Faustus, Tamburlaine the Great* and *The Jew of Malta* (all written between 1587 and 1593) depict men obsessed by various kinds of power. Shakespeare's own dramatic writings are greatly influenced by Marlowe, and it may be more than just coincidence that Shakespeare begins to grow in confidence and stature as a playwright after Marlowe's death. It is not impossible that the young Shakespeare felt a little overshadowed by his brilliant contemporary while Marlowe was still alive.

NASHE, THOMAS (1567–1601) One of the most aggressive of the Elizabethan satirists, Thomas Nashe was educated at St John's College, Cambridge. He announced his arrival on the literary battlefield of Elizabethan England in 1589 with a preface to *Menaphon*, a romance by his friend Robert Greene. In this preface Nashe wrote witheringly about what he saw as the uneducated taste of the English stage – an attack which he continued in his first pamphlet *The Anatomy of Absurdity* (1589). He was engaged as official satirist and propagandist in defence of the Church of England during the so-called Marprelate Controversy, when he wrote a series of tracts in reply to Puritan attacks on the Church of England. Like Shakespeare, Nashe enjoyed the patronage of the Earl of Southampton to whom he dedicated his most famous work, the prose narrative *The Unfortunate Traveller* (1594).

SHAKESPEARE, EDMUND (1580–1607) Edmund, or Ned, Shakespeare was William's brother. Like William, he made the trip from Stratford to London to become an actor, but he did not make a very successful one. It is not known with which company or companies he acted.

SHAKESPEARE, WILLIAM (1564–1616) William Shakespeare was born on or around 23 April, 1564. He was the son of the Stratford businessman, John Shakespeare and his early education was at the local grammar school. In 1582, when he was eighteen years old, he married Anne Hathaway, and they lived together in Stratford for about two years, but in 1584 or 1585 Shakespeare left Stratford for London. His London career during the years up to 1592 is more or less a mystery, but by 1592 he had a reputation both as an actor and a playwright: the *Henry VI* trilogy comes from this period. During the years 1592–94 the London theatres were closed almost continually because of plague, and Shakespeare turned his hand to narrative poetry and sonnet-writing. When the theatres reopened he joined The Lord Chamberlain's Men as a shareholder, so that he was now sharing in the profits of the company as well as receiving payment for his acting and writing. The latter included comedies such as *A Midsummer Night's Dream* and early tragedies such as *Romeo and Juliet*. Clearly Shakespeare did quite well financially during the next few years, for he was able to buy one of the best houses in Stratford, New Place, in 1597. The Lord Chamberlain's Men's move to the Globe Theatre in 1599 consolidated his fortunes, and their adoption by King James in 1603 improved things even further: The King's Men, as they were now known, gave 177 performances at court between 1603 and 1613. Shakespeare's great tragedies were written between 1601 and 1606, and first performed at the Globe. The romances known as the 'late plays' were all written after The King's Men had expanded to acquire the indoors Blackfriars theatre in 1608. However, it seems probable that by the time *The Tempest* was first staged in 1611, Shakespeare had already moved back to Stratford. His last play was *Henry VIII*, written in collaboration with John Fletcher. It was an ill-starred work: on the afternoon of its first performance in 1613, a cannon fired in the play caused a fire which destroyed the Globe. Shakespeare's last few years were spent in retirement in Stratford, and he died there on 23 April, 1616, aged fifty-two.

SOUTHAMPTON, HENRY WRIOTHESLEY, THIRD EARL (1573–1624) A courtier, a soldier and a politician, Southampton became Shakespeare's patron in about 1593 or 1594, when Shakespeare, turning his hand to non-dramatic literature, dedicated to him *Venus and Adonis* and *The Rape of Lucrece*. There has been speculation, too, that Southampton was the dedicatee of Shakespeare's sonnets, and the subject of several of them, although nothing has been proved on this score. He patronized other writers apart from Shakespeare, among them Thomas Nashe and John Florio. Southampton himself was a devoted follower of the Earl of Essex, and a supporter of his ill-fated rebellion in 1601. He may have been involved in commissioning the famous performance of *Richard II* which implicated The Lord Chamberlain's Men in Essex's rebellion. For his part in the rebellion Southampton was sentenced to death; the sentence was later commuted by Elizabeth to imprisonment in the Tower, and Southampton was pardoned when James came to the throne. During James's reign Southampton took an active interest in the colonizing of the New World. He was a member of the council of the Virginia Company, set up expressly for that purpose, and his involvement with the Virginia project may have influenced Shakespeare in his writing of *The Tempest* (1611).

Further Reading

Texts and textual scholarship

Perhaps the most controversial and influential recent work in this field is represented by the collection of essays edited by Gary Taylor and Michael Warren, entitled *The Division of the Kingdoms: Shakespeare's Two Versions of King Lear* Clarendon Press, Oxford, 1983). Focusing entirely upon *King Lear*, it goes so far as to suggest that the play of that title that we normally read is a muddled amalgam of two separate versions of *King Lear*, both written by Shakespeare and represented by the early published editions of quarto and folio. These two versions differ from each other in several respects – so much so, argue the authors, that it may be completely wrong to think of there ever having been a single 'ideal play' of *King Lear*, and that we should instead think in terms of two separate *King Lears*. This kind of reappraisal of long-accepted ideas about Shakespeare's texts has provided a new impetus in Shakespearian textual scholarship.

One of the fruits of this scholarship is the new Oxford Shakespeare series, which is producing the plays both in separate volumes and in editions (both modern and original spelling) of *The Complete Oxford Shakespeare*. The General Editors of the series are Stanley Wells and Gary Taylor, and they have included in the series an entire volume, entitled *William Shakespeare: A Textual Companion*, which elucidates the ways in which the editors reached their decisions. The principles according to which the Oxford editors have worked have resulted in some radically new versions of texts, and the findings of the new generation of Shakespeare scholars have not always been universally accepted. However, they have certainly provided new stimulus for thought about the plays.

Facsimile versions both of quartos and of the 1623 folio are available and are useful aids to further textual study, *The Norton Facsimile: The First Folio of Shakespeare* (Norton, New York, 1968) is edited by Charlton Hinman, while Michael J.B. Allen and Kenneth Muir have co-edited a collection of *Shakespeare's Plays in Quarto: A Facsimile Edition of Copies Primarily from the Henry E. Huntington Library* (Berkeley, California, 1981).

225

Biography

For many years the best biographical study of Shakespeare was E.K. Chambers' *William Shakespeare: A Study of Facts and Problems* (Clarendon Press, 1930). This has now been replaced as the standard work of biographical reference by Samuel Schoenbaum's *William Shakespeare: A Documentary Life* (Oxford University Press, 1975; revised and reissued in a compact edition as *William Shakespeare: A Compact Documentary Life*, 1977). Scrupulous in its scholarship, Schoenbaum's book makes few claims that are not backed up by hard evidence, and surveys with admirable thoroughness alternative interpretations of the available documents. Schoenbaum has also written a fascinating critical survey of other people's biographies of Shakespeare, entitled *Shakespeare's Lives* (Oxford University Press, 1970), which throws much light on the way in which the Shakespeare legend grew up.

History

Historians divide up the world, and indeed time, in different ways from literary scholars; the 'age of Shakespeare' is not a recognizable entity to historians, and we have to look for information about his world in the context of studies of wider social political and economic issues which concern the England of the sixteenth and seventeenth centuries. Traditionally, at least, historians have often thought in terms of reigning monarchs, and Shakespeare's career spanned the reign of two monarchs: generally speaking, books which concentrate on the reign of Elizabeth are more useful to the Shakespeare student than those focusing upon James and the Stuarts. Some knowledge of the early part of James's reign, however, is very important. James was himself a poet and the extent of his influence on the writers of his time has only been recognized in recent years. It is analysed in detail in Jonathan Goldberg's study *James I and the Politics of Literature: Jonson, Shakespeare, Donne and their Contemporaries* (Johns Hopkins University Press, 1983).

Goldberg is a literary scholar, and his book is aimed at a scholarly audience. Of the various books on the Elizabethan and Jacobean periods which are written by historians and accessible to the non-specialist reader, the following, all comparatively recent, have been particularly useful in the writing of this present study. A thoroughly-researched social and economic history of the England of Elizabeth is to be found in D.M. Palliser's *The Age of Elizabeth: England under the later Tudors, 1547–1603* (Longman, 1983), which is particularly il-luminating on the economic trends of the period. Barry Coward's

The Stuart Age (Longman, 1980) deals with the period 1603 to 1714, but its early chapters provide a useful analysis of political, economic and intellectual movements in the early seventeenth century. S.J. Houston's small book simply entitled *James I* (Longman, 1973) contains both essays on key aspects of James's reign and a section of documents. Keith Wrightson's *English Society 1590–1680* (Hutchinson, 1982) is an eminently readable account of the changes which were taking place in English society in the seventeenth century. It synthesises much of the new wave of thinking about English social history of the period, and also advances some stimulating personal interpretations of the nature and development of English society at this time. The approach taken by Alan G.R. Smith in *The Emergence of a Nation State: The Commonwealth of England 1529–1660* (Longman, 1984) is to relate social and economic issues to the emergence of England as, first, a disparate political unit, and then a major world power.

Some books which are aimed primarily at a more specialist readership of historians should be mentioned. Patrick Collinson's *The Religion of Protestants: The Church in English Society, 1559–1625* (Oxford, 1982) is a major work of reassessment of the religious tendencies of the period. It makes an important contribution to that field of historical research which seeks to determine the relationship between religious theory and social and political reality. In this area, the seminal work is R.H. Tawney's *Religion and the Rise of Capitalism*, (1926, reprinted Pelican Books 1972), which deals with changes taking place over three centuries. Lawrence Stone's *The Family, Sex and Marriage in England, 1500–1800* (Weidenfeld & Nicolson, 1977) has made a great contribution to knowledge of family structures in Shakespeare's age, and has provoked much rethinking of the ways in which family relationships are portrayed in the plays. An excellent documentary source book for the social history of both the theatre and the society of Shakespeare's England is the New Mermaid 'background' book entitled simply (if a little misleadingly) *Elizabethan–Jacobean Drama* (A. & C. Black, 1987) and edited by G. Blakemore Evans. This collection reprints a large range of contemporary Elizabethan and Jacobean texts, culled from both printed and manuscript sources, which relate to the theatre and to everyday life in the period.

Language

There are several general books about the development of the English language which contain sections on Elizabethan English. The most easily available to the English reader is C.L. Barber's *The Story of Language* (Pan Books 1964), an excellent and lively study in general, but one which is disappointingly thin on material about Shakespearean English. Less easy to get hold of, but more instructive, are the relevant chapters in Albert C. Baugh and Thomas Cable's *A History of the English Language* (Prentice-Hall, 1957, reissued 1978).

Two books which take a detailed look at the problems of Shakespeare's plays from a linguist's point of view are *Shakespeare's Language: An Introduction* (Macmillan, 1983) by N.F. Blake and *The Language of Shakespeare* (André Deutsch, 1976) by G.L. Brook. Both deal with issues of Shakespearean grammar and vocabulary: the former is more accessible to the general reader, the latter is more usefully regarded as a reference book. A much more free-wheeling and polemical work than either is Terence Hawkes's *Shakespeare's Talking Animals: Language and drama in society* (Edward Arnold, 1973), which takes as its starting point the problematic relationship between the spoken and the written word in Shakespeare's age, and goes on to offer a series of thought-provoking essays about the language of Shakespeare's plays.

Elizabethan and Jacobean theatre

The standard work of reference on the theatre of the period is now *The Revels History of Drama in English, vol. III* (Methuen, 1975). However, two classic early twentieth-century studies of theatre practice in Elizabethan times are E.K. Chambers' *The Elizabethan Stage* (Oxford, 1923), and T.W. Baldwin's *The Organization and Personnel of the Shakespearean Company* (Princeton University Press, 1927; reissued by Russell and Russell, New York, 1961). Both are still worth reading, Chambers' book for his wide-ranging erudition about the Elizabethan theatre in general, Baldwin's for his (occasionally speculative but always informative) focus on the details of organization in Shakespeare's company of players. More recent works which tackle the same area, but with the benefit of more recent research include Andrew Gurr's, *The Shakespearean Stage* (Cambridge University Press, 1970) and Michael Hattaway, *Elizabethan Popular Theatre: Plays in Performance* (Routledge & Kegan Paul, 1982). Hattaway's book analyses several Elizabethan plays in terms of their relationship with popular dramatic forms; for present purposes the chapter on Shakespeare's early tragedy, *Titus Andronicus*, is particularly relevant. In the same series, Peter Thomson's *Shakespeare's Theatre* (Routledge & Kegan Paul, 1983) examines pragmatically some of the potentials of staging plays in Shakespeare's Globe theatre, as well as giving a readable and fascinating interpretation of the known facts about the Globe Theatre. An earlier work which is also informative about the Globe is *Shakespeare at the Globe* (Macmillan, 1962) by Bernard

Beckermann. A short factual account of the London theatres of the sixteenth and early seventeenth centuries is published by The Bear Gardens Museum, it is edited by C. Edwards and is entitled *A London Theatre Guide, 1576–1642*. With recent reconstruction work in progress the most useful book is Andrew Gurr and John Orell's *Rebuilding Shakespeare's Globe* (Weidenfeld & Nicolson, 1989).

Audiences in Shakespeare's theatre have been much discussed; Alfred Harbage's *Shakespeare's Audience* (Columbia University Press, 1941) offered a picture of a homogeneous audience spanning all classes of society, a picture firmly rejected by Ann Jennalie Cook in her book, *The Privileged Playgoers of Shakespeare's London, 1576–1642* (Princeton University Press, 1982). Andrew Gurr's *Playgoing in Shakespeare's London* (Cambridge University Press, 1987) treads a middle ground between two extremes, and as well as offering a convincing and detailed argument about play-going patterns in Elizabethan and Jacobean London, he reprints a large amount of the relevant contemporary material.

Shakespeare reference books

The student of Shakespeare will occasionally need to find out some statistical details of the vocabulary of the plays. It may be useful, for example, to establish how many times the word 'blood' appears in *Macbeth*, or where and how Shakespeare uses the word 'character'. Rather than working laboriously through a play or the *Complete Works of Shakespeare* doing one's own word-count, the student can turn to a concordance, and find the material already tabulated. Marvin Spevack's *Harvard Concordance to Shakespeare* (Georg Olms Verlag, 1968–80) was compiled from a computer database, and it records, analyses and cross-references Shakespeare's vocabulary and the contexts of word-usage in the plays. It effectively supersedes John Bartlett's *New and Complete Concordance or Verbal Index to the Words, Phrases and Passages in the Dramatic Works of Shakespeare with a Supplementary Concordance to the Poems* (Macmillan, 1894), which had been the standard work since the end of the last century. The Bartlett concordance, however, is still a useful reference work, and may be more easily available, since Spevack's updated concordance has not yet found its way into all libraries.

Shakespeare was notoriously an adapter of other writers' stories and a good deal of work has gone into tracking down the original sources of his plays. Two complementary studies of Shakespeare's source material deserve particular mention. The definitive work is now Geoffrey Bullough's massive eight-volume study entitled *Narrative and Dramatic Sources of Shakespeare* (Routledge & Kegan Paul, 1957–75; vol. VII, *The Major Tragedies* published 1973). Each play is dealt with by means of an introductory essay surveying the field and tracing various influences, direct sources and analogous material. All relevant material is then printed in as full detail as necessary, so that readers can make comparisons for themselves between Shakespeare's sources and his own plays. Bullough's work is indispensable for any serious study of the literary background to the plays, and it prompted many new insights into the plays themselves. Less detailed, but more affordable, is Kenneth Muir's *The Sources of Shakespeare's Plays* (Methuen, 1977) which effectively operates as a digest of information about the plays. Muir surveys a similar range of material to Bullough, but does not attempt, in his single-volume study, to reproduce the documentation.

A useful general collection of essays which provides fairly up-to-date material about recent developments in many areas of Shakespeare criticism and scholarship is *The Cambridge Companion to Shakespeare Studies* (Cambridge University Press, 1986) edited by Stanley Wells. This supersedes Kenneth Muir and S. Schoenbaum's *New Companion to Shakespeare Studies* of 1971 (which in turn replaced the original *Companion to Shakespeare Studies*, 1934), and it contains essays which place Shakespeare in the context of the thought of his age, as well as accounts of twentieth-century approaches, both critical and theatrical.

The two most influential periodicals in the field of Shakespeare studies are *Shakespeare Survey* and *Shakespeare Quarterly*. The former is published by Cambridge University Press and appears annually. Subtitled *An Annual Survey of Shakespearian Study and Production* it contains reviews of British, European and American productions of Shakespeare, as well as reports of recent work in Shakespeare studies and individual monographs on particular topics – often thematically related, volume by volume. *Shakespeare Quarterly* is produced by the Folger Shakespeare Library in Washington DC, and it appears, as its name suggests, four times a year. While it, too, contains articles on recent academic and theatrical development, its monographs tend not to be linked by themes.

Shakespeare: general criticism

General studies of Shakespeare are too numerous to count, and each age, predictably, produces its own. The ones mentioned here are comparatively recent; some of them had a specific influence on the writing of this book, others simply offer a particular approach which readers might find useful.

In the last few years several 'overviews' of Shakespeare's plays have been published, and two in particular are becoming standards. Neither of them deals with any one play at any length, but both offer comments on a wide range of plays. Philip Edwards' *Shakespeare: a Writer's Progress* (Oxford University Press, 1986) looks at the plays in more or less chronological order, in an attempt to chart the development of the writer. Edwards describes the book as a personal view of the plays, but it also embodies many of the main tendencies of liberal Shakespeare criticism of the past few decades. Terry Eagleton, on the other hand, provides a swashbuckling radicalism with his *William Shakespeare* (Basil Blackwell, 1986), a reappraisal of the plays in the context of recent developments in Marxist, feminist, semiotic and post-structuralist criticism. Deliberately provocative, aggressive and readable, it challenges many assumptions of Shakespeare teaching.

Two collections of essays which share with Eagleton's work the desire to disrupt conventional assumptions about the significance of Shakespeare's plays are *Alternative Shakespeares* (Methuen, New Accents, 1985) edited by John Drakakis, and *Political Shakespeare* (Manchester University Press, 1985) edited by Jonathan Dollimore and Allan Sinfield. Both collections draw attention to the political dimensions of Shakespearean drama, both in its own time and as a force in contemporary culture.

Marilyn French's *Shakespeare's Division of Experience* (Jonathan Cape, 1982) uses a particular version of essentialist feminist theory as an analytical tool. Starting from the premise that 'the basic distinction in human social order since the beginning of recorded history has been gender', French looks at the plays as dramatizations of shifting relationships between the two gender principles, the masculine and the feminine. A totally different kind of feminist criticism is exemplified by the historically based *Still Harping on Daughters: Women and Drama in the Age of Shakespeare* (Harvester, 1983) by Lisa Jardine, which deals with attitudes towards women in Shakespeare's age. The standard collection of feminist essays on Shakespeare is called *The Woman's Part: Feminist Criticism of Shakespeare* (University of Chicago Press, 1980), and is edited by Carolyn Lenz, Gayle Green and Carol Thomas Nealy.

A variety of developments has taken place in stage-centred criticism of Shakespeare's plays. The Macmillan series entitled 'Text and Performance' (General Editor, Michael Scott) documents various ways in which individual plays have been interpreted on stage. Ann Pasternak Slater's *Shakespeare the Director* (Harvester, 1982) tries, not always successfully, to integrate a study of Shakespeare's language with a study of his stagecraft. Emrys Jones, in *Scenic Form in Shakespeare* (Clarendon Press, 1971) explores the ways in which an understanding of some of the principles of Shakespeare's dramatic construction enrich our enjoyment of the plays. He looks in particular detail at scenes in *Othello*. Another kind of approach to the study of the plays by way of theatrical practice can be seen in John Barton's

231

Playing Shakespeare (Methuen, 1984), based on his series of master-class programmes on Channel 4.

Shakespeare: tragedy and tragedies

A.C. Bradley's *Shakespearean Tragedy* (Macmillan, 1904) has been, for good or ill, one of the most influential works of criticism ever published. As well as influencing readers, critics, actors and directors of Shakespeare from the time of its publication up to the present day, it has spurred successive generations of scholars and critics into vehement rejection of its judgements and approaches. In the 1930s and 1940s the *Scrutiny* critics, spearheaded by F.R. Leavis, launched a series of all-out attacks on Bradley's readings of Shakespeare. Bradley was accused of having misunderstood the whole nature of Elizabethan drama, and of having read the plays as if they were novels, or worse, a collection of psychological studies. L.C. Knights in particular poured scorn on Bradley's literalist approach to the plays in his derisively-titled essay 'How many children had Lady Macbeth?'. The title of another of Knights's essays on Shakespearean tragedy, 'Hamlet – the Prince or the poem?', implies what was the essential approach of many of these critics, whose tendency to read a play as if it were an extended poem turned out to be as limiting as Bradley's quasi-novelistic approach. In any case, Bradley survived the onslaught, and his book still heads the best-seller list in Shakespearean criticism. While Bradley's achievement should not be understated, it is nonetheless odd that his book should speak so loudly to late twentieth-century readers, since it is very much a work of its time, infused with the philosophical idealism of a Europe which existed before the Great War.

The relationship between Shakespeare and earlier dramatists can be seen in Muriel Bradbrook's *Themes and Conventions of Elizabethan Tragedy* (Cambridge University Press, 1935). David Bevington's monumental work *From 'Mankind' to Marlowe* (Harvard University Press, 1962) stops short of Shakespeare's great tragedies but charts with impressive thoroughness the continuing traditions which linked the early drama of medieval England with that of Shakespeare's great contemporary, while Alan C. Dessen's *Shakespeare and the Late Moral Plays* (University of Nebraska Press, 1986) argues for the continuing vitality of the morality tradition during Shakespeare's own working lifetime.

As well as chapters in several of the books mentioned above, further books, chapters and articles exist which provide information about or interpretations of individual tragedies. What follows is deliberately short and selective.

Hamlet

Michael Hattaway's volume on *Hamlet* in the 'Critics' Debate' series (Macmillan, 1987) provides a thoughtful introduction to many of the major critical issues surrounding the text. A detailed work which discusses *Hamlet*, scene by scene, in the context of Elizabethan attitudes towards revenge, is Eleanor Prosser's *Hamlet and Revenge* (Stanford University Press, 1967). The concept of displacement of rôles, which I touch upon in my section on the play, is explored in greater depth in an article by Susan Baker, 'Hamlet's Bloody Thoughts and the Illusion of Inwardness', in the journal *Comparative Drama* (Vol. 21, No. 4, Winter 1987–88). John Jump's *Shakespeare: 'Hamlet'. A Casebook* (Macmillan 1968) contains essays by Ernest Jones, T.S. Eliot, Jan Kott and others.

Othello

Eldred Jones, *Othello's Countrymen* (Oxford University Press, 1965) is a full-length study of the figure of the Moor in Elizabethan and Jacobean drama. G.K. Hunter also has chapters on 'Elizabethans and Foreigners' and 'Othello and Colour Prejudice' in his collection of essays entitled *Dramatic Identities and Cultural Tradition* (Liverpool University Press, 1978). Also worth reading is the chapter on *Othello* in A.C. Bradley's *Shakespearean Tragedy* (Macmillan, 1904) and the subsequent argument with Bradleyan criticism which F.R. Leavis elaborated in his essay 'Diabolic Intellect and the Noble Hero' in *The Common Pursuit* (Chatto and Windus, 1952). William Empson has a fascinating section on the use of the word 'honest' in *Othello* in his book *The Structure of Complex Words* (Chatto and Windus, 1951). A detailed scene-by-scene analysis of the play is provided by Gāmini and Fenella Salgādo in their volume on *Othello* in the Penguin Critical Studies series (Penguin Books, 1985), and John Wain collects together some memorable essays on the play in *Shakespeare: 'Othello'. A Casebook* (Macmillan, 1971).

King Lear

Ann Thompson's *King Lear* volume in the 'Critics' Debate' series offers an introduction to and overview of a variety of critical approaches to the text. Less up-to-date, but usefully eclectic is the collection of criticism edited by Frank Kermode – *Shakespeare: King Lear. A Casebook* (Macmillan, 1969). Some of the main points of the argument about *King Lear* and the Union debate may be found in Glynn Wickham's article 'From Tragedy to Tragi-Comedy: King

Lear as Prologue', in *Shakespeare Studies*, 26 (1973), which argues
that the play was written in support of James and his policies. Marie
Axton, in *The Queen's Two Bodies* (Royal Historical Society, 1977)
has a chapter on 'The Problem of Union: King James I and
"King Lear"' which disagrees, arguing that Shakespeare was not
swayed by Stuart propaganda and that there is no case for con-
cluding that he supported James. Annabel Patterson, in her wide-
ranging book *Censorship and Interpretation* (University of Wisconsin
Press, 1984), has a section on *King Lear* in which she argues that the
play is deliberately ambiguous. In the collection of essays entitled
The Division of the Kingdoms, edited by Gary Taylor and Michael
Warren (Clarendon Press, 1983), some fascinating suggestions are
made as to the way in which textual differences between the folio
and quarto editions of *King Lear* may relate to the play's political
significance.

Macbeth

A large part of Wilbur Sanders's book *The Dramatist and the Received
Idea* (Cambridge University Press, 1968) deals with *Macbeth*, and
some interesting comparisons are drawn between the dramatic
techniques of Shakespeare and Marlowe. John Wain's *Shakespeare:
Macbeth. A Casebook* (Macmillan 1968) contains, like most of the
Macmillan Casebooks, a useful collection of mid-twentieth-century
criticism, as well as short extracts from earlier commentators. L.C.
Knights's famous essay 'How Many Children Had Lady Macbeth?
is not so much an interpretation of *Macbeth* as a study in critical
methodology, but it is an immensely influential piece of criticism
and well worth reading; it is to be found in Knights' *Explorations*
(Chatto and Windus, 1946). Leonard Tennenhouse's *Power on Display* (Methuen 1986) contains a short but stimulating section on
political authority and festivity in *Macbeth* in a chapter entitled 'The
Theatre of Punishment'.

*An engraving of London published in 1572. The approximate positions of the
major playhouses built between 1567 and 1629 are given with the dates of
construction, together with inns used as occasional theatres.*

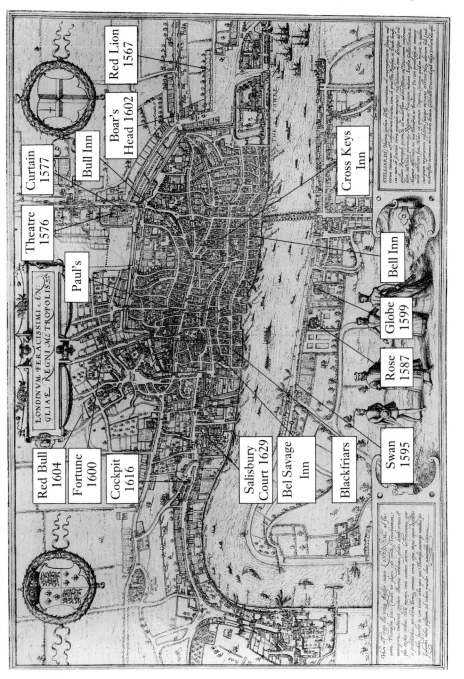

Red Lion 1567

Boar's Head 1602

Bull Inn

Curtain 1577

Theatre 1576

Paul's

Cross Keys Inn

Bell Inn

Globe 1599

Rose 1587

Red Bull 1604

Fortune 1600

Cockpit 1616

Salisbury Court 1629

Bel Savage Inn

Blackfriars

Swan 1595

Appendix: The theatres of Shakespeare's London

THEATRE	DATES	PRINCIPAL OWNER
The Theatre (near Holywell Lane)	1576–98	James Burbage Richard Burbage
The Curtain (near Holywell Lane, opposite the Theatre)	1577– c. 1627	Henry Laneman
The Rose (Rose Alley, Liberty of the Clink, Bankside)	c. 1587– c. 1605	Philip Henslowe
The Swan (Paris Garden, Bankside)	1595– c. 1637)	Francis Langley Hugh Browker
The Globe (Maiden Lane Bankside)	1599–1613 Rebuilt 1614	Richard Burbage *et al.*

COMPANIES, PLAYWRIGHTS AND AUDIENCE

Most of the major companies used 'the Theatre' at one time or another, and it must have seen performances of many of the best Elizabethan plays of the early period. Probably all of Shakespeare's plays before 1598 were performed here.

Again, used by most major companies, especially before 1587. Lord Chamberlain's Company seem to have made it their base in 1598, before the opening of the Globe. It was also famous for displays of jigs and combats, and its audience had the reputation of being unruly.

The Lord Admiral's Men, with Edward Alleyn as their leading actor, dominated the London stage during the early years of the Rose's existence. Marlowe's works were staged here, as were plays by Chapman, Dekker, Greene, Kyd and others. Other companies also used the Rose occasionally (Shakespeare's *Titus Andronicus* was performed here in 1594). It surfaced for a noteworthy period in 1989.

Earl of Pembroke's Company, until 1597, when the satirical play *The Isle of Dogs* incurred the censor's wrath. The Swan thereafter fared poorly as a playhouse, staging a mixture of entertainments including both plays and prize-fights.

Took over from the Rose as the most important London playhouse in the early years of the seventeenth century. Home of Shakespeare's company, The Lord Chamberlain's Men, called The King's Men after 1603. Among the plays performed here were Shakespeare's works from 1599 to 1608 (including the great tragedies), revivals of some earlier plays and probably most of the post-1608 plays as well. In addition, plays by Jonson, Dekker, Marston and Tourneur are known to have been staged here.

Appendix (cont'd)

THEATRE	DATES	PRINCIPAL OWNER
The Fortune (near Cripplegate, Finsbury)	1600–21	Philip Henslowe Edward Alleyn
The Hope (Hopton Street, East of Bankside)	1614–56	Philip Henslowe Edward Alleyn
Blackfriars (1) (The Blackfriars' Monastery)	1576–84	Richard Farrant
Blackfriars (2) (The Blackfriars' Monastery)	1596–1655	James Burbage Richard Burbage

Henslowe and Alleyn's attempt to challenge the increasing supremacy of the Globe was based here. Many revivals of old favourites from the Rose were staged here, since Henslowe and Alleyn owned many of these scripts. These included plays by Marlowe, Jonson, Dekker and Kyd. New writers who were commissioned by the Fortune included Middleton, Rowley and Heywood, and the theatre had a reputation for spectacular heroic plays and sentimental romances. It attracted an audience with a high proportion of artisans and apprentices, more boisterous than at the Globe, and it had a reputation for being the haunt of thieves and prostitutes. Prince Henry's Men (formerly The Admiral's Men) were the main company playing here.

Strictly outside the relevant period, but interesting in that it was designed to serve both as a theatre and as a bear-baiting arena. Jonson's *Bartholemew Fair* was one of the first plays staged here.

The 'First Blackfriars', located in the Old Buttery of the dissolved monastery was used – not quite legally – by Farrant as a theatre for performances by the Children of the Chapel Royal and of Windsor Chapel until 1580. In 1583–84 it was used by the Children of Paul's and the Chapel. Blackfriars was a comfortable suburb, and although the inhabitants complained of rowdy play-goers, audiences here were comparatively well-to-do.

The 'Second Blackfriars', another hall in the monastery, was first adapted for use by James Burbage, but he was unable to get a licence for a public theatre here. From 1600 to 1608 it was leased to the Children of the Chapel. In 1608 the Children of the Chapel were forced to leave, following a political scandal surrounding Chapman's play *The Tragedy of Biron*. The King's Men assumed possession of Blackfriars, and this indoor theatre became their second home. Many of Shakespeare's later plays were first performed here to an audience who could afford admission prices several times higher than at the Globe.

Index